t

New
W·R·I·T·E·R

Techniques
for
Writing Well
with a
Computer

Joan P. Mitchell

PUBLISHED BY

Microsoft Press
A Division of Microsoft Corporation
16011 NE 36th Way, Box 97017, Redmond, Washington 98073-9717

Library of Congress Cataloging in Publication Data

Mitchell, Joan P., date
The new writer.
Bibliography: p.
Includes index.
1. Authorship—Data processing. 2. Word processing.
I. Title.
PN171.D37M58   1987   808′.042′0285   87-7895
1-55615-029-6

Printed and bound in the United States of America.

1 2 3 4 5 6 7 8 9 MLML 8 9 0 9 8 7

Distributed to the book trade in the
United States by Harper & Row.

Distributed to the book trade in
Canada by General Publishing Company, Ltd.

Distributed to the book trade outside the
United States and Canada by Penguin Books Ltd.

Penguin Books Ltd., Harmondsworth, Middlesex, England
Penguin Books Australia Ltd., Ringwood, Victoria, Australia
Penguin Books N.Z. Ltd., 182-190 Wairau Road, Auckland 10, New Zealand

British Cataloging in Publication Data available

John Sullivan

22·12·88

To Maura and Thomas

Contents

Preface

I have written *The New Writer* as a practical guide to show how computers can improve your writing at every stage of the process, from thinking of ideas to revising to printing and publishing the final document. The book is based on the premise that computers can make you a more creative and productive writer and your documents more polished and professional looking. Computers can even help you enjoy writing (though perhaps "enjoy" isn't the most accurate word; good writing still remains an exacting, if rewarding, task). To take advantage of these benefits, however, you must use your computer as a new tool and not merely as a fancy typewriter with a TV screen. That may mean giving up old methods and tools (like your favorite yellow pad) and learning new techniques. And experimenting. And changing.

I have taught hundreds of people to do just that—experiment and change—in computer writing classes at the University of California, Santa Barbara. What I have learned from teaching others and from my own computer writing experiences, as well as what fellow writers have told me, forms the heart of this book. I have tried to be as practical as possible; I suggest guidelines and give tips that from experience I know really do work. I show you how to build on your strengths as a writer, how to correct weaknesses and solve problems, and how to adapt my advice to suit your writing style and the particular types of documents you write. I also show you how to avoid common pitfalls of computer writing. By the time you have finished reading *The New Writer,* you should join the writers—from poets and technical writers to students and journalists—who praise the computer as a writing tool.

This book is not my work alone, however. Many people have influenced its contents. I want to thank just a few:

The people who started me using computers: Carol Price, who encouraged me to take my first text-editing class; Markus Sandy, who answered my questions when I bought my own computer; Joseph Martin, whose work in computer writing at Cornell University's Writing Workshop inspired me to teach my first computer writing class.

Jeffrey Marcus, manager of the Microcomputer Laboratory, University of California, Santa Barbara, who first urged me to write this book.

Other personnel at the Microcomputer Laboratory who gave me advice and technical help, especially Bill Koseluk, Chris Gieger, and Brad Hitchcock. Also Steve Zeitlin, who has the most complete set of fonts for the Macintosh of anyone I know.

Susan Startt, Microsoft's Education Accounts Executive for the Northwest, who brought my work in computer writing to the attention of the editors at Microsoft Press.

University colleagues like Porter Abbott, chair of the Department of English, who has actively supported instructors' efforts to teach computer writing; Mark Ferrer and Stephen Marcus, who have shared their expertise in computer instruction; Muriel Zimmerman, whose advice is always worth listening to and who read and critiqued chapters of this book; Sheridan Blau, Donald Pearce, and Anne Pidgeon, who deeply influenced my writing and teaching; Marvin Marcus, who gave professional advice and support to my various computer projects; Stanley Nicholson, who acted as consultant on instructional materials and development.

Maura Mitchell, whose creative suggestions made important contributions to this book.

Valerie Kalupa, the artist who drew the parrot in Chapter 8.

The various writers who told me how they use computers in their writing.

My many students, who taught me how to teach computer writing, and especially James Brett and Alice Slaughter, who critiqued an early version of *The New Writer.*

I haven't touched a typewriter in 4½ years, but I started out anticomputer, as part of my *1984* consciousness. Then I got an assignment—a 3000-word article, at $1 a word—due in two weeks, and on a subject I didn't know much about. In desperation I went to a friend who had a computer. "I'm sunk," I told him. "I can't even do the research in two weeks!" He just dialed a social science database and put in two key words, and suddenly twenty-six pages of abstracts started spilling out of the computer. I had all the information I needed. Next he showed me how to enter and erase text. And with that much training I finished a 3000-word draft in 5½ hours of actual typing!

Normally I'd do seven or eight rewrites on a typewriter, but when I looked at my second computer draft, I saw it was finished. Ever since, I've written on a computer. And I write better. I'm much freer.

I've always had a physical dislike of typing—such a bore and bother and very restrictive. I wouldn't want to change what I had written because I didn't want to retype. I had "paper anxiety." When your words are typed on paper, you're committed to them; they have a kind of weight they don't have on the screen. There's a tremendous impulse when you type on paper to do it right the first time; there's no room for the flashes of insight that you might get later. The typewriter directs your writing.

But when words are on the computer screen, they're in a kind of sixth dimension: They exist and they don't exist. I think this mimics the way we think. It's easier—physically and emotionally—to change computer writing. Now my prose comes out much more simply and directly; I'm more inventive. And I'm less defensive about what I'm doing; editors find me easier to get along with because I'm more willing to make changes.

Gary Karasik
Journalist

CHAPTER ONE

A New Tool
for the Writer

Computers and the writing process
Computer tools
Traditional tools

This book is for people who have a computer and write: business people writing letters, memos, and reports; volunteers writing for nonprofit organizations; would-be authors about to submit their first manuscript; professional writers and editors; scientists and engineers producing technical documents; students writing academic papers or dissertations; researchers submitting articles to scholarly journals. Whatever you write, the computer can help. Even though I am an enthusiast about writing on the computer, don't take my word for it. Listen to what others have to say:

- The fact that I don't have to worry about making mistakes improves my typing skills.
- I can let my ideas fly as fast as my fingers can type.
- The computer has given me the ability to experiment with my writing.
- My handwriting is very messy, but now I can *see* my ideas.
- The computer makes me want to write, even when I'm not in an especially creative mood.
- When I sit at the computer, my thoughts flow out; I lose track of time.
- The computer lessens my inhibitions because I know I can write and write and just erase what I don't like.
- Writing on a computer gives you a sense of power and security not possible on a typewriter.
- I am so much more confident about my writing, and I'm not afraid to edit and revise.
- Computers take care of all the trivial things that can make writing monotonous.
- On a typewriter, correcting mistakes can become a messy and ugly job. However, on the computer, all one has to do is push the backspace, and zap, the errors are ripped away.
- The computer makes it easier to see my mistakes. The need for a transition glares at me from the terminal, and there's no way to avoid fixing it.
- I can focus my attention on being creative and writing down my ideas instead of worrying about how difficult it is to change sentences or paragraphs.
- The psychological boost from seeing my papers with a professional look makes a big difference!
- Appearance means a lot in a memo or letter or report. I feel professional about my work.
- I am able to communicate my ideas clearly through graphs and pictures.
- Writing on the computer has helped me to think and write in a highly organized manner.
- I have learned that writing can be fun, thanks to the computer!
- Computers require discipline and encourage creativity, the very qualities needed by a good writer.

These people are responding to the enormous potential of the computer to help writers at every stage of their work. The computer is far more than a fancy typewriter with a TV screen; it is a completely new writing tool that helps you write in more effective ways. Rather than merely keying in and revising a document before printing it, you can think and plan on the computer, communicate your ideas visually as well as verbally, and design professional-looking documents of all kinds. You can also learn a great deal about yourself in the process. When you sit in front of a computer terminal, you are face to face not only with a machine but with yourself, as a writer and as a person. The computer does only what you tell it to do. If you don't know what you want to do, or if you don't know what the computer is capable of doing, then you won't be able to exploit its potential.

This book sets out to accomplish several goals:

■ Help you analyze yourself as a writer
■ Explain to you the steps in the writing process
■ Show you how to exploit the special capabilities of the computer at every step in this process

Let's look at each of these goals.

Analyzing Yourself as a Writer

Writing is a highly personal and individual act, and no two people go about it in exactly the same way. What works for one person won't work for another. Often, however, people straitjacket themselves; they think there is only one correct way to write, and they struggle to conform, even though the results are poor again and again. Or they define themselves as poor writers and give up trying to improve. Or they think they know how to write and steadfastly resist change. To be a good writer, you have to move beyond such misconceptions and do some self-analysis. What kind of person are you? What are your work habits? What do you like or dislike about your writing? What comes easily to you? What problems do you have?

This book shows how to analyze yourself as a writer, how to critique the work you produce, and how to benefit from self-criticism. It also shows you how to experiment on the computer with writing techniques and helps you approach writing from a new point of view. You are given many guidelines and tips, but the emphasis is always on your needs as an individual writer. You are urged to discover the techniques that work best for you and to use them. You can also modify the techniques the book suggests or even make up your own. The goal is to tailor computer writing to your needs and purposes and to help you become your own best writing critic.

THE WRITING PROCESS

Prewriting
Brainstorming
Dialoguing
Visualizing
Analyzing

Planning and Organizing
Defining subject, audience, and purpose
Formulating a thesis
Deciding on writing strategy
Outlining

Creating a Rough Draft
Writing step by step
Freewheeling
Coping with writer's block
Building paragraphs
Writing introductions
Writing conclusions

Revising
Revising content, logic, and structure
Revising sentences and words
Proofreading

Getting Reader Response
Accepting criticism
Understanding criticism

Revising Again
Correcting and editing
Rethinking ideas

Preparing for Publication
Using typography
Designing layout
Providing graphics

Formatting academic papers
Formatting manuscripts for submission
  to publishers
Formatting business and technical documents
Managing long documents

Practicing the Writing Process

If people have misconceptions about themselves as writers, they also have misconceptions about the nature of writing itself. For example, you may think the ability to write is a special talent granted only to a few, and since you lack talent, you will never be able to write. Or perhaps you believe that good writing depends on inspiration, and if you are uninspired, you won't be able to do a good job. Or you see writing as an onerous task to be finished as quickly as possible, preferably late at night, with numerous cups of coffee to keep you going as you grind out a rough draft and type a finished version — all in one sitting.

On the contrary, the basic premise of this book is that writing is a skill — actually a series of skills — that can be learned like any other skills. You may not win a literary award, but you can become a competent writer (even an excellent one) if you are willing to practice these skills and learn some new ones. Furthermore, although some writing does seem to come from "inspiration," doing the necessary groundwork and following the steps in the writing process are more reliable in the long run. Experienced writers usually do not accomplish a writing task in a rush or at one sitting; rather, they proceed carefully through a series of steps, with each step involving different skills, strategies, and responses. This book takes you step by step through that process.

Breaking down the sometimes overwhelming task of writing into a series of manageable, understandable steps is a way to master the process at each stage along the way. You can learn which writing strategies work for you and which nonproductive work habits need to be changed. You can also experiment with ways to modify the steps to suit a particular writing project or to bring out the strengths of your own writing style.

Using the Computer as a New Writing Tool

Most important, you can learn to take advantage of the computer at each step of the writing process. A computer can do much more than help you move text around, make quick and easy deletions or additions, or check the spelling of your document. Because the computer is a new writing tool, it lets you become a new kind of writer: freer, more experimental, more open to change, more imaginative. You can make the electronic letters shimmering on the computer screen reflect the quicksilver changes of your thoughts. No longer is it so difficult to put ideas into words, and the words themselves are no longer engraved in stone, as they seemed to be with pencil or typewriter. You can change them easily until they say what you mean.

You can also become a more powerful writer. The computer lets you shape and manipulate text exactly as you want in order to accomplish your goals. Editing and revising are only part of the story; computers let you see your ideas on a neat screen or printout, and this visual clarity makes it easier to achieve logical clarity and good organization. Computers also keep track of information, organize material, format your text, generate special parts of your document (footnotes, bibliographies, contents pages, indexes), and even check grammar and style as well as spelling. With the drudgery of many writing tasks gone, you can concentrate on ideas. And you learn that visual communication—effective document design and use of computer typography and graphics—can be as important as verbal communication.

But to use the computer as an effective writing tool, you have to know how to exploit all its features, and that is the main purpose of this book: to show you how to use the special capabilities of the computer at every step of the writing process. By the end of the book you will find that the computer

- Increases your efficiency so that you can spend more time on creating and much less on the menial tasks of handwriting or typing words
- Allows you to be more flexible about the writing process
- Encourages you to be more creative, inventive, and experimental
- Develops your ability to generate more and better ideas
- Helps you to organize your ideas and to see their logical progression
- Encourages you not only to correct and polish your prose but also to rethink your ideas
- Enables you to design and produce professional-looking documents—to become your own publisher, in fact
- Gives you a sense of mastery, not only over a machine, but over the written word and the graphic picture as well
- Gives you a sense of enjoyment and satisfaction as you write and perhaps even a sense of playing with words and ideas as you "play" with your computer
- Increases your pride and confidence in yourself as a writer

Computer Tools for the Writer

This book is for anyone writing on a computer. You don't have to be a computer hacker; in fact, you can be learning how to do word processing as you read through this book. (If you're an expert, you will still find plenty to challenge you.) Furthermore, you don't have to use any particular computer or word-processing program.

This book assumes that all word-processing programs have standard features—the ability to add, delete, copy and move text, indent paragraphs, set margins and line spacing, and provide bold and underlined text. Such standard programs should also have search and replace functions, tabulation, and automatic pagination. But a truly powerful program can have much more:

Electronic notebook or scrapbook for storing text or graphic images

Full justification of both margins

Sophisticated formatting of individual paragraphs

Automatic hyphenation

Running heads

Glossary

Various highlighting or style options: italic, double underlining, superscript, subscript, small capitals, strikethrough, shadowing, and outlining (plus the standard bold and single underlining)

Various fonts (styles of type) and font sizes

Measurements in inches, centimeters, or points

Split screen capability

Multiple windows on the screen at one time

"Hidden" text

Boxed text; lines and rules

Automatic footnoting

Ability to embed graphics

Support for letter-quality or near-letter-quality printing

Multiple-column printing

Outlining

Spell checking

Contents and index generators

Style sheets

Mail merge system

Separate formatting for different document divisions

Different page-numbering styles

Page preview function

Of course, you don't need all these features to write effectively on the computer, but they do help; you should invest in the most sophisticated word-processing program you can afford. You might also want to invest in other programs and accessories useful to the writer. Some of these, discussed in the following paragraphs, can greatly enhance the power of a relatively simple word-processing program.

Typing Tutorials. These are programs that teach you touch typing. You can learn the traditional system, named QWERTY after the first six letters on the standard keyboard, or you can reconfigure your computer keyboard with special software and learn

Dvorak (a system that assigns different letters to the keys). QWERTY was designed in the 1870s to slow down typists, because the typewriters of the time couldn't handle fast typing. Dvorak, however, enables you to type much faster and much more efficiently. (To be fair, Dvorak is seldom used; computer typing is so easy that even two-fingered hunt-and-peckers can type efficiently on a QWERTY computer keyboard.)

Idea Processors and Outliners. These programs help you generate and organize ideas. Some are free-form, allowing you to use the computer screen as a notebook for electronic doodling and brainstorming; others are more structured and allow you to develop outlines and branching tree charts. If outlining is part of your word-processing program, you may be able to look at the same document in two different modes: outline and text.

Spell Checkers. Some of these "electronic dictionaries" come as stand-alone programs; others can be installed within your word-processing program. Spell checkers for microcomputers typically have dictionaries of between 40,000 and 80,000 words against which they check the words in your document. Words that don't match words in the dictionary are flagged, and you can correct them or leave them as they are—a necessary option, because the program won't know that proper names, like "Albert Einstein," are correct. Sometimes the program offers a selection of alternatives for a misspelled word, but often you must rely on a standard dictionary. Good spell checkers allow you to add to or change their main dictionary and also to create your own specialized dictionary on disk. Some spell checkers also have a thesaurus which lists synonyms and antonyms for a word you specify. Increasingly, software companies are developing specialized dictionaries for specific professions, like medicine and law.

Thesauruses. Stand-alone thesaurus programs also exist, but if they have a very large selection of synonyms and antonyms, they will probably require a hard disk because they use so much memory. These run along with your word-processing program, so you can look up an alternative word or expression while you work on your document.

Glossaries. Some spell checkers and word-processing programs also come with glossaries. Glossaries allow you to assign an abbreviation to a frequently used term or phrase or even to a fairly long passage of text. This text is then stored in a special file; when you type its abbreviation and use the glossary command, the full text appears in the document. Glossaries increase your efficiency and ensure accuracy in spelling and consistency in wording.

Macro Programs. More powerful than glossaries, macro programs allow you to enter not only text but also long command sequences by typing a single key or a short key sequence. Your typing speed goes up and routine drudgery goes down, leaving you more time for thinking and writing.

Word Counters. Usually you install a word counter as an accessory within your word-processing program. As its name indicates, a word counter counts the words in your document, a handy feature when your writing project has a word limit (and most writing projects do). Spell checkers often have built-in word counters, and today many word-processing programs are including them as a standard feature.

Style Checkers. These programs, which tend to require a large amount of memory, analyze the text of your document and flag possible writing problems or errors: commonly misused words and phrases, vague expressions, clichés, "to be" verbs, nominalizations (use of nouns instead of verbs), sexist language, some punctuation errors, and so on. Not every flagged word or phrase is wrong or ineffective; you must decide whether or not to make changes. Some style checkers can also count words, calculate the average length of sentences, and give you a general idea of the readability of your prose. They can also help you check the document's organization.

Templates and Forms. If you do a lot of routine writing (business letters, for example, or standardized legal instruments), electronic templates are for you. These are form documents on disk. You fill in the blanks or modify the wording slightly to suit the specific situation.

Mail Merge Programs. This kind of software is essential for mass mailings. You create the main text of the document and then merge it with individual addresses and names (or other information) as you print copy after copy.

Electronic Notepads. An electronic notepad can be a handy accessory if your word-processing program doesn't come with one. You can call up the notepad as you work on your document and jot down ideas, questions, and problems to be researched. Often you can copy text from the notepad to your main document, and vice versa.

Graphics Programs. You may be interested in three types of graphics software: (1) free-form drawing and paint programs, which enable you to do freehand illustrations and to use various types of textures and patterns to achieve paintlike effects; (2) more structured drawing, design, and drafting programs, which are particularly good for drawing geometric shapes, designs, and diagrams or for creating scaled plans; and (3) graphing and charting programs, which enable you to give visual form to numeric data. All three types allow a limited amount of text generation. The graphics produced can often be inserted in the text you have created in your word-processing program.

Clip Art Portfolios. A clip art portfolio consists of a disk containing predrawn pictures based on standard themes—the seasons, sports, domestic animals, common symbols, borders. The pictures can be transferred to your graphics program, modified, and then used to illustrate your document. (The name comes from big books of commercial artwork that newspapers use, primarily in their ads; the pictures are literally clipped out with scissors.)

Fonts. For some computers you can buy disks of extra fonts, or typefaces — various standard styles and sizes for body text, display fonts for headlines, novelty fonts for decorative purposes, or fonts for foreign languages and scientific notation. Some programs allow you to design your own fonts.

Page Layout (Desktop Publishing) Programs. One of the most profound effects computers will have on writing is allowing authors to become their own publishers. Programs that are alternately called "page layout" or "desktop publishing" allow you to arrange text and graphics in any variety of ways for newsletters, brochures, advertisements, manuals — whatever you need to produce. (Usually the main text and graphics are generated in other programs.)

Database Programs. A database program relies on the computer's ability to keep track of enormous quantities of facts and figures. Databases store, retrieve, sort, match, and combine this information in any number of ways and use the results to generate reports. Writers generally don't need complicated databases, but a simple program can replace the bother of 3-by-5-inch index cards with a powerful electronic filing system. A database is especially useful for a long or complex writing project; you can use one to keep track of research and lab notes, reading lists, abstracts of articles, and bibliographic entries.

Modems. A modem is a device that connects a computer to a telephone line and from there to various computer networks. Combined with appropriate software, modems allow you to access databases and programs on other computers and also to transmit your work, via the telephone line, to these computers. Work generated in a particular program on a particular machine can be translated to another machine's program via a modem. Databases you can access with a modem range from the general, such as CompuServe, to the highly specialized, such as LEXIS (which deals with law), ERIC (education), and Sociological Abstract (sociology); usually there is a subscriber's fee. Modems allow you to do research in your office; send finished documents to a distant editor, publisher, or another office in your company; have conferences with other people on the same network; and leave messages on electronic bulletin boards.

Computer programs come in all varieties and sizes, and new ones keep flooding the market, so how do you choose the right ones for you? Start by getting a broad overview of the subject. Read a book that gives guidelines for buying software; check the bibliography at the back of this book as well as the bookshelves of your local bookstore or library for helpful titles. Then talk to people who use the programs you are interested in. Ask for a demonstration. Sit down and use the programs yourself. Also read software reviews in computer magazines. (Computer writers should subscribe to at least one such magazine to keep abreast of new developments; if you don't, then go to your local library regularly.) Computer dealers can give you information, too, but remember, they stock only a limited number of programs and will push the ones they carry. Often you can go by the reputation of the software house; if you use and like one program a house has developed, you may very well like its others, too.

Traditional Tools for the Writer

No matter how high-tech a writer you become, you still need to keep traditional writing references on your bookshelf and consult them frequently.

Dictionaries. First on the shelf should be a large, up-to-date dictionary. Don't be satisfied with a paperback edition or the dictionary that your great-uncle Horace took to college in 1920. Language changes. You want a dictionary that defines modern terms such as "laser," "DNA," "gene splicing," and "silicon chip"; gives synonyms and antonyms; and tells you something about the connotations of words and their grammatical acceptability. You may also want to invest in specialized dictionaries: dictionaries of slang, economic terms, medical terms, signs and symbols, acronyms, biography, or the like.

Thesauruses. A thesaurus supplements a dictionary. Although it usually doesn't give definitions, it provides lists of synonyms, antonyms, and related or equivalent words.

Writer's Handbooks. Handbooks are indispensable reference tools for a writer. In concise form they give the standard rules of grammar, punctuation, spelling, and capitalization. They give the correct form for footnotes and bibliographies, set down guidelines for word choice, and analyze the construction of well-written sentences and paragraphs. Handbooks also provide a glossary of usage (a list of commonly misused words and expressions) and a glossary of grammatical terms. Choose the one you like best. If you are a serious writer, however, buy more than one; each handbook has different strengths and weaknesses. Again, make sure the book is up-to-date—standards of what is right and wrong do change.

Style Guides. Sometimes also called a "style sheet" or "style manual," a style guide is a set of instructions or guidelines designed to help writers prepare particular types of documents (term papers, journal articles, dissertations, reports, manuals, books) for publication or distribution in particular situations. Style guides deal primarily with details of format (the layout and appearance of the document) and mechanics (grammar, punctuation, spelling, capitalization, use of abbreviations, word division). Usually they are issued by publishers, professional or scholarly societies, university libraries, newspapers or magazines, companies, or writing instructors.

The bibliography at the end of this book gives the titles of specific books that will help you in your writing. More and more of these reference tools are being put on disk, but right now the electronic versions are not nearly as comprehensive as their printed counterparts, and some people still prefer to look up information in a book rather than on a screen. Whatever your preference, however, the main point is to use these tools frequently. They are necessary supplements to this book and the powerful writing capabilities of your computer.

Using This Book

The book is divided into chapters that discuss the main steps in the writing process. Chapters 2 through 7 deal in turn with prewriting, planning and organizing, creating a rough draft, revising, getting reader response, and revising again. At each point you will see how to use the potential of the computer to sharpen the writing skills and strategies needed for that particular stage. You will also learn how to adapt the computer to your own working style and specific writing needs. Read through these chapters as you work on the different stages of your writing project or as you learn a word-processing program.

The last two chapters deal with putting your document into final form and getting it ready for distribution or publication. In Chapter 8 you will learn how to communicate with visual aids (computer graphics, typography, and page layout). Chapter 9 shows you how to format various types of professional documents; consult the sections relevant to your particular writing project.

As an added bonus, a special section at the end of each chapter—"Let's Solve It!"—provides practical solutions to common writing problems like procrastination and writer's block. Another special section, "Computer Writing Tips," gives you tricks of the trade for handling your computer efficiently and successfully. Both sections try to solve the problems you are likely to run into at specific stages of the writing process. Finally, the bibliography at the end lists useful publications and books for the computer writer; you may want to consult it even before you start writing.

Let's Solve It!

For the computer writer, some writing problems involve coping with the computer rather than matters of diction and style. Let's solve the computer problems first.

Problem: Computer Writing Jitters. You don't know how to use a computer, you feel intimidated by the machine, or you are just plain scared. All the other people know what they're doing: They are self-confident experts, you are lost.

Solution. Remember that you are not alone; many if not most beginning computer writers feel the same way: "The first day in the computer lab I felt so lost, as if I were the only one who didn't know how to work this beast." "Even now, after I've got past the initial panic of learning to use the computer, I still get very nervous when I sit down to write." "Everyone else is rushing into the future, while I'm left behind." But in two or three weeks these same people were far more confident: "I found that after you tackle the basics, computers are not untouchable." Soon they were giving advice to people less experienced than themselves and praising the computer for the improvements it was making in their writing.

If you are an uncertain computer novice, follow these steps:

- Spend time practicing on the computer. Allow yourself to make mistakes without blaming yourself or giving up. Experimenting and making mistakes is an important part of learning how to use the computer.

- Get some short, easy-to-follow directions and keep them handy on the desk. Sometimes the manufacturer provides a brief reference list or command sheet, or you can make up your own. Worry only about the basics at first, and remember that the list of basics is short — starting the machine; opening a new document; typing in text; adding, deleting, or moving text; saving your work; printing; and quitting. The fancy stuff can come later.

- Ask people to help you. Computer users are usually friendly and willing to show you what to do. Don't be intimidated by their expertise; often they are delighted to put it to work, even when your problem is trivial. If your helper goes too fast, ask her or him to repeat the demonstration more slowly — or better still, to write down a brief list of steps to follow. You can add these directions, in your own words, to your reference list or command sheet.

- As you practice on the computer, work on a real document (not too long, though) that will be given to someone else. Having a motive for writing makes learning the computer go faster.

Problem: Computer Catastrophes. You are writing productively when something goes wrong. You lose hours of work and suddenly your confidence drains away; you blame yourself or hate the computer or both. Your frustration and anger spill over onto your writing project.

Solution. Realize that mistakes and disasters are part of the computer writing process: Learn to cope with them. Over my desk I have a quotation that is serious and funny at the same time: "There are moments when everything goes well; don't be frightened, it won't last." When the inevitable error message appears, try to look at it objectively and do some troubleshooting:

☐ What went wrong?
☐ How can I fix it?
☐ Why did it happen?
☐ How can I prevent it from happening again?
☐ What can I learn from this experience?

If you learn from the disaster, it really isn't a disaster. Marvin Minsky, founder of MIT's Artificial Intelligence Laboratory, thinks that learning what is wrong may be just as important as learning what is right. He calls such knowledge "knowledge about bugs." And if that is too theoretical for your situation, take heart from what another computer writer has to say: "All a person can do is take a deep breath, hold back the tears, unclench the hands from the keyboard, and start over again. Believe me, you'll never make that mistake again!"

This book tells you how to avoid common computer mistakes; as time goes on, you will find yourself making fewer and fewer of them.

Problem: Fancy Typewriter Syndrome. A state-of-the-art machine sits on your desk and a high-powered word-processing program flashes from its screen—and you still use it like an old-fashioned typewriter. Perhaps you simply don't want to change your writing habits. ("But I *always* write my rough drafts on yellow paper!") Or perhaps you don't know how to exploit the computer fully. (Researchers estimate that people utilize only 40 percent of their word-processing programs.)

Solution. Read this book and be willing to experiment. Be prepared to give up some cherished prejudices, to try new ways of writing, and to explore the marvelous writing tool that can make you a new, and better, writer.

Computer Writing Tips

Before you start writing, take time to learn the basic principles of computer care.

- Get acquainted with your computer. Learn how to use it correctly and how to maintain it. Read the introductory section of the user's manual. Talk to others who use the same machine. If possible, find a mentor, someone who is willing and able to give you good advice when things go wrong.

- Keep your work area clean. No matter how sturdy your computer is, it is still a complex, delicate piece of machinery. Protect it from dust and extremes of temperature (no direct sunlight) and humidity. If you use a mouse, keep the table or desktop dusted and oil-free.

- Don't smoke, eat, or drink while you write on the computer. Smoke can damage magnetic tape, food crumbs can clog the keyboard, and spilled liquids can damage electronic circuitry. If you are tempted to break these rules, think of how much money you have invested in your computer. Is the cup of coffee worth it?

- Treat your computer and data disks gently. Don't pound the keyboard or jam disks into the disk drives. Computers, like fine cars, perform better when they are handled with care.

I've always approached computers as a helpful tool, but it took me two years to get around to writing on one. Then I deliberately took a writing course involving computers and immediately realized the benefits.

The brainstorming process, for example, is much faster and more coherent, because clearly defined text appears on the screen rather than an illegible mess on a notepad. Right from the start you can organize your thoughts by manipulating the text on the screen. Your work literally evolves before your eyes, as brainstorming becomes an outline and an outline becomes a paper. This evolutionary process makes writing easier.

In fact, what I've found with computers is less of a distinction between the various stages of writing; one blurs into the other. When you handwrite or type, there are breaks in the process, and you almost stumble over these breaks. But with computers your writing flows because you move ideas around quickly and easily.

Two other things I like about computers. First, we're always constrained by time, whether we're students or professionals, and computers are time-savers. And because they save time, I'm not inhibited about making changes right up to the last minute. Now I write a better paper in a shorter period of time; it's more developed and more refined.

Second, computers reduce the amount of drudgery. As quickly as possible, I like to reach the stage where I have a complete paper ready to be finely honed. But in the past, typing out the final product took 25 percent of my time. I'd be finished with all the creative and intellectual aspects and left with only droning, mindless activity. With computers, though, typing is part of the creative process. I'm watching my piece of writing grow in front of me.

John Concklin
University Student

Thinking
on the Keyboard

Brainstorming
Dialoguing
Visualizing
Analyzing

Before you start to write on the computer, take some time to analyze yourself as a writer. What do you really think about the whole notion of writing? About your writing abilities? As an exercise in self-analysis, open a new document—that is, create a new file on your disk—and write honest answers to the "Writer's Questionnaire."

Now read your answers and write a description of yourself as a writer. You might complete the following sentence: "I am the kind of writer who..." What picture begins to emerge? Perhaps you are a highly motivated, self-confident writer who always produces creative and insightful work, who is always organized and on time. But you are more likely to be bothered by one or more problems common to most writers.

For example, you may put off writing until the last minute and then rush through your project. You don't have time for all the changes you know you should make, and the final result is never your best work.

On the other hand, you may start thinking about a writing project early enough and gather a lot of information, but when you sit down to write, you have trouble getting started. Hours slip by with little or nothing to show for your efforts.

Or perhaps you start writing and then lose confidence halfway through. You run up against a writing block. And the pressure of a deadline only makes things worse.

Perhaps you find the whole idea of writing overwhelming. You don't know where to start, and when you do plunge in, you're not sure where to go next. You tend to lose track of the main idea. Everything seems disorganized and chaotic.

WRITER'S QUESTIONNAIRE

- ☐ What is your immediate reaction when you have to do some writing?
- ☐ What kinds of writing do you like to do? Why?
- ☐ What kinds of writing do you dislike? Why?
- ☐ What do you find difficult about writing? Make a detailed list.
- ☐ What is the worst thing anyone could say about your writing?
- ☐ What rewards do you get from writing? List them all, big and small.
- ☐ What is the best thing someone could say about your writing?
- ☐ Which one of your completed writing projects are you most proud of? Why?
- ☐ Do you procrastinate? In what ways? Why do you think you put off writing? How do you cope with procrastination?
- ☐ Do you ever get writer's block? When? How do you cope with writer's block?
- ☐ Describe how you handle a writing assignment from start to finish.

Another kind of problem is planning your writing carefully enough but then running out of things to say. If the project must be a certain number of words or pages, you resort in desperation to padding and repetition.

Or perhaps your writing is inhibited and your creativity stifled because you worry too much about the rules. Or you may resent writing because it takes time away from other projects. Or you don't know how to hold your readers' attention. In short, you find it painfully difficult to translate your good ideas into words.

Your self-portrait as a writer undoubtedly differs in details from these sketches. But the point is that writing is inherently difficult; even the great writers have complained about it. In 1844 Nathaniel Hawthorne wrote in his journal that "when we see how little we can express, it is a wonder that any man ever takes up a pen a second time." Ernest Hemingway said in an interview that "what you ultimately remember about anything you've written is how difficult it was to write it." And Flannery O'Connor flatly stated in one of her letters that "all writing is painful and if it is not painful, then it is not worth doing." If you get discouraged about writing, you are in good company.

Understanding the writing process and learning how the computer facilitates it, however, can ease the burden of expressing yourself in words and can solve many of the problems you identified in your self-analysis. It can also increase the rewards of good writing—the sense of accomplishment, the pride in your work, the confidence you have about your ability to express ideas and feelings effectively, the recognition you get from others, the satisfaction of meeting a goal.

Save your questionnaire (perhaps print it out), and sometime in the future, when you are proficient in computer writing, answer the questions again. You will be pleasantly surprised by how positive your answers are.

The Writing Process and the Computer

In Chapter 1 the basic steps in the writing process were listed:

Prewriting
Planning and organizing
Creating a rough draft
Revising
Getting reader response
Revising again
Preparing for publication

In theory, a writer goes through each of these steps in this order. In practice, however, writers differ, and different writing projects have different requirements and constraints. Thus you may not always follow the steps in their listed order. You may move back and forth between some steps, or you may work on two or three steps simultaneously. The amount of time you spend on each step may vary, too. In writing a routine business letter, you may do almost no prewriting, revise only a little, and follow a set format. A serious research paper or complex report, however, may require extensive work at each step of the process. So be prepared to modify the suggestions in this book to suit your personal writing style and to meet the requirements of a specific writing project.

Prewriting

Prewriting (sometimes called "brainstorming") can be defined as any writing you do *before* you start your rough draft. According to one researcher, Donald Murray, professional writers spend 84 percent of their time prewriting, 2 percent composing a rough draft, and 14 percent revising. Inexperienced writers, in contrast, spend most of their time composing and little time prewriting. And because they neglect prewriting—the brainwork of a document—their writing tends to be shallow rather than well thought-out, general rather than detailed and concrete, skimpy rather than fully developed.

True, some people literally discover their ideas as they compose rough drafts; their rationale for such an approach is, How do I know what I think or want to say before I see what I have written? And their rough drafts are a special kind: tentative and free-wheeling explorations that undergo many transformations and heavy editing. (See Chapter 4, pp. 71–73, for a discussion of this type of writing.) The majority of us, however, need to brainstorm and think through a writing project before we start a rough draft. Moreover, we need to put our flights of creativity down in words. Ideas that float freely through our minds tend to get lost or diluted if we don't capture them in print. Do what a high school teacher of mine called "thinking with a pencil"—except now you will be thinking with a keyboard.

Why do prewriting? Because it is one of the most versatile and useful techniques a writer can learn. First, it can help you get started. It can overcome writer's block and cure procrastination. Prewriting makes writing psychologically easier, in that you are not making an ambitious commitment to produce a rough draft in one session. And prewriting generates more material for your writing project—new ideas, more examples, and sharper details. It encourages you to look at your subject from different points of view and helps you discover hidden angles. It can also make you more productive: Instead of staring blankly into space, wondering what you can find to say, you actually get something down in black and white. Finally, prewriting can start what all writers long for — the seemingly spontaneous rush of ideas that flow into words, sentences, even whole paragraphs, so that your text (or at least part of it) seems to write itself.

Some people feel wedded to pencil and paper for brainstorming and rough drafts. I was convinced I could never give up my yellow pad and pencil. But the computer has given me a powerful alternative, and now I do all my writing on screen. Like many other writers, I find that I can be more creative and productive when I start from scratch on the computer. Another writer puts it this way:

> With the computer to experiment on, prewriting can actually be fun! I am free to write whatever comes to my mind; my ideas get written down instead of staying locked up inside my head. Then I have something to look at, to play with, and to organize. Once I start writing the actual draft, I feel less frustrated, because all my ideas are already written on the screen.

Eventually you may decide that you work best by combining pencil, pad, and computer, but for now completely set aside your old ways and experiment with a new tool. Be open-minded. Try the various techniques discussed below. These have been divided into four broad categories: brainstorming, dialoguing, visualizing, and analyzing. After you experiment with them, analyze yourself as a writer and determine what helps you the most.

Techniques

To save time and to keep up with your thoughts, don't try to write in complete sentences; words and phrases will do. Don't interrupt your flow of ideas to revise or edit; that comes later. And don't be overly critical; too much self-criticism can stifle creativity. Finally, if the prewriting exercise suddenly lets loose a rush of ideas and words, write it all down. Don't let a method or a set of directions stop this flow.

When you finish your prewriting, save it on disk and give it a distinctive name. You will use this file again when you plan your document and start on the rough draft. For a long or complex writing project, there will undoubtedly be several sessions of prewriting, and the prewriting you did at one session will provide a springboard for the next session.

Brainstorming

These prewriting techniques involve writing down, often very quickly, what you know or feel about a topic.

Free Association. Write continuously for five or ten minutes; literally don't lift your fingers from the keyboard. Don't stop for grammar, word choices, spelling, punctuation, or mistakes. Don't delete. If you can't think of a word, leave a space. If your mind goes blank, keep writing "I can't think of anything" until a relevant word or idea occurs. If words appearing on the screen distract you, dim the screen. Free association (also known as free writing or free flow) can be totally random—you write down whatever pops into your mind. Or it can be focused—you concentrate on a particular topic. Figure 2-1 shows an example of free association on the computer.

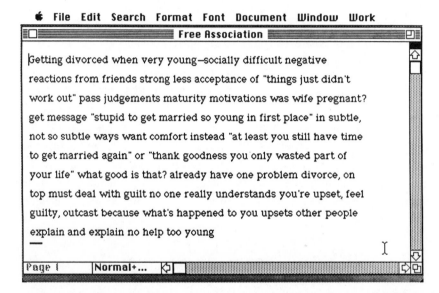

FIGURE 2-1.   *Free association*

After five or ten minutes of free association, select particularly interesting statements and highlight them, using bold or capital letters or underlining. At the end of this free-association exercise, copy one of these statements and expand on it (in regular type) by doing more free association or by trying one of the methods discussed below. Do the same with each highlighted phrase.

Advantages. Free association is particularly good for breaking up writer's block. It can start the flow of ideas and intuitive responses, tapping your subconscious mind and bringing emotions and memories to the surface. Try this technique for personal narratives, human interest articles, and creative writing of all kinds. It also works well as a warm-up exercise before you tackle analytic or expository projects, such as a research report.

Listing. First, *briefly* list what you think or know about your topic. Such a list might consist of your own ideas, feelings, insights, observations, and experiences. Or it might summarize facts, figures, ideas, theories, and arguments you have discovered through research and study. When you finish the list, number the individual items in an order that is meaningful to you (as in Figure 2-2), and rearrange them in that order on the screen. Then expand each item by inserting supplementary material.

Finally, list all the questions about your topic that you still need to answer, the problems you need to think through, the facts and evidence you still need to gather. Look not only at the gaps in your knowledge but also at what your intended audience will need or want to know. This second list will guide your future research and thinking; the answers to the questions will form the basis of your second session of prewriting.

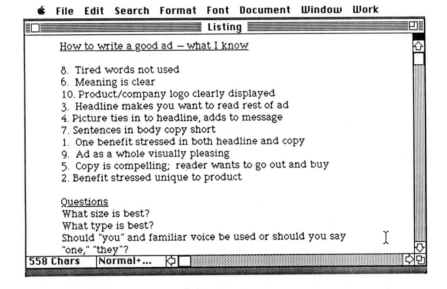

FIGURE 2-2. *Listing*

Advantages. Listing is more structured than free association, drawing on your strengths—what you actually know or think—and providing guidelines for future exploration and research. It is particularly useful for beginning factual documents, solving problems, and setting agendas for research projects, although it can also generate imaginative and creative material.

Reporter's Notebook. In italics list the traditional questions reporters always ask: who? what? when? where? how? why? (Press Enter after each one so that they form a vertical column.) Answer each one in turn, writing in regular type directly under the question, as in Figure 2-3. Be as detailed, accurate, and clear as possible.

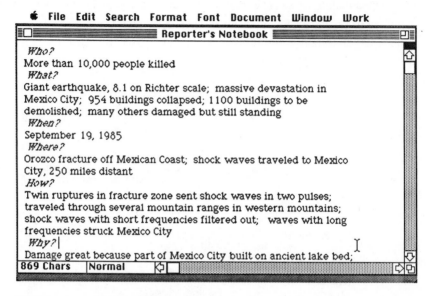

FIGURE 2-3. *Reporter's notebook*

Advantages. This prewriting technique is particularly effective for informative writing that involves people and events. It ensures that the basic facts and information are provided. Thoughtful answers to the question "why?" can result in illuminating analysis. The reporter's notebook can also be adapted to other types of writing— short stories, for example.

Dialoguing

Dialoguing techniques involve intellectual conversations of one kind or another: with your computer, with your future readers, with other writers on the subject.

Talking with the Computer. We tend to personify computers and half-seriously treat them as thinking creatures. A prewriting dialogue takes advantage of this tendency. Imagine that your machine is a sympathetic listener and a perceptive respondent, and tell it about your assignment. Write your comments in one style or typeface (bold, italics, underlining, or capital letters) and the computer's in another, as in Figure 2-4.

(If your machine offers a variety of fonts, use two different fonts.) In this imaginary conversation, vent your feelings, positive and negative, and then write down the encouragement the computer gives you. Describe all the difficulties you see ahead of you, and let the computer, in its part of the dialogue, propose some solutions. Jot down your main ideas and imagine the computer evaluating them. Honestly analyze your writing weaknesses and let the computer propose some guidelines or solutions. Your imagination and insight can take flight here.

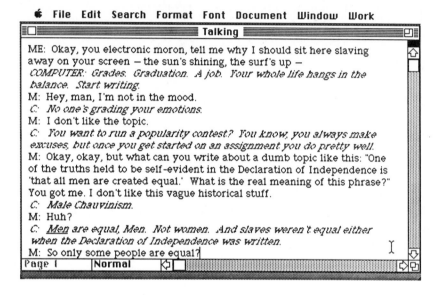

FIGURE 2-4. *Talking with the computer*

Advantages. Talking with the computer is good for getting started when procrastination, negative feelings about an assignment, and self-doubts make getting down to the actual job of writing difficult. Just expressing such feelings often dissipates them, especially when you write with a bit of humor and creativity. In addition, the internal dialogues we have often yield forthright and perceptive ideas. Some writers actually talk out their papers in their mind before they commit words to screen or paper; for such people, this dialogue method of prewriting can be particularly valuable.

Provocative Questions for the Reader. Write down five or six questions about your topic that you think your reader would like answered. Use bold or some other distinctive style. Under each question jot down as much material as you can for an answer, using regular type. Number these questions in their most logical order, as in Figure 2-5, and then arrange the questions and their answers in numeric order on the screen.

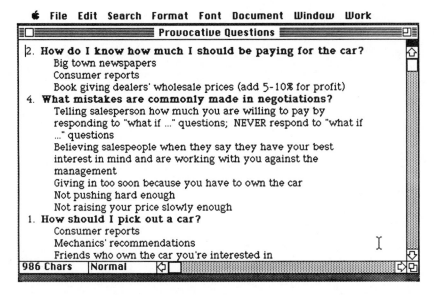

FIGURE 2-5. *Provocative questions for the reader*

Advantages. This method of prewriting is especially helpful for putting you in your readers' place and for seeing the topic from that point of view. It ensures that you write directly to your readers. It also helps with organization. You can use the original provocative questions (with some changes) as headings in a long document or as topic sentences in a short one. Provocative questions are especially helpful for reader-oriented documents—how-to articles and manuals, some business letters and reports, informative brochures, and the like.

Devil's Advocate. A devil's advocate is someone who argues the opposing side to point out possible weaknesses in the issue under discussion. Take a stand on a controversial subject you feel strongly about. Across the top of the screen, in one or possibly two sentences, write a brief but strong assertion of your view; choose a different font and a large type size so that the statement stands out. Next, in regular type and size but in a contrasting style option like bold, list all the possible arguments against your position. Start a new paragraph for each argument. (On some computers you press the Return key; on others, you press Enter. This book uses Enter.) Now insert your counterarguments (using regular type) immediately below each opposing argument, as in Figure 2-6. Make these counterarguments as detailed and convincing as possible. Try to refute the opposition; if you cannot refute it entirely, at least show that your stand is preferable in most cases.

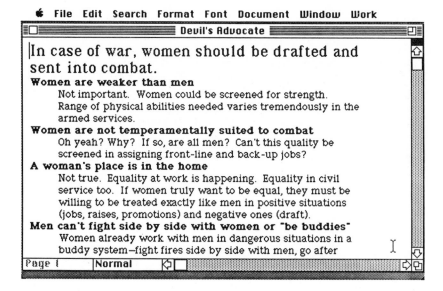

FIGURE 2-6. *Devil's advocate*

Advantages. Playing devil's advocate helps hone your arguments and anticipate others' objections. The give and take of argument/counterargument should arouse your combative nature—a good thing when you write on controversial subjects—and generate convincing arguments for your point of view. The devil's advocate approach results in more persuasive documents, whether they be letters to the editor, sales pitches, or public relations statements.

Critical Comments. Read books and articles on your topic, or listen to what the experts have to say on radio or television or in a lecture; in either case, take notes. In your notes on a writer's or speaker's statements, be sure to identify the person and include all bibliographical material (book, journal, or newspaper title, publisher, year, page numbers, and the like) as well as similar information for broadcasts (network, program title, date, and so on). Select a specific assertion, opinion, idea, theory, criticism, or argument, and jot down all your responses to it. What ideas does it stimulate? What questions does it raise? Do you agree or disagree? Be expansive. Continue the process with a second assertion or opinion.

If you are fortunate enough to own a laptop computer, you can take it with you to the library or lecture hall and take notes there; otherwise, use paper and pencil. But once you are back to your regular computer, put your notes on screen. Use a special style option or typeface to distinguish your responses from the ideas or assertions, as in Figure 2-7. Think of this prewriting as a dialogue: You are responding directly to the authors or speakers and telling them what you think of their ideas.

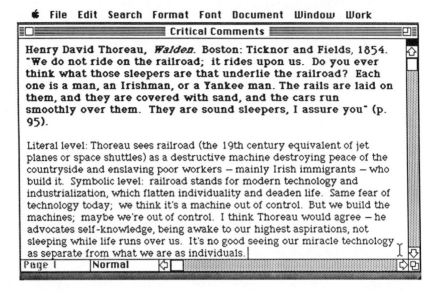

FIGURE 2-7. *Critical comments*

Advantages. This method of prewriting forces you to react to, rather than passively accept, what others think and say. It challenges you and stimulates your own thinking. Critical comments are especially useful for writing projects involving analysis, interpretation, criticism, or refutation. Use them for critical reviews, research articles, and argumentative pieces.

Visualizing

Prewriting doesn't have to start with words; the following techniques involve visualizing or drawing your ideas. If you have a computer graphics program, try using it. The novelty of doing prewriting with computer graphics may stimulate your imagination and make you more creative. Computer graphics are fun. They involve "playing around," and from playing around on the computer it is a quick and easy jump to playing with words and ideas, which is a vital part of fresh, imaginative writing. If you don't have a graphics program, or if you find it easier to draw by hand, simply use old-fashioned paper and pencil.

Clustering. Open a graphics program. In the center of the screen, draw a bubble and write the key term of your subject. What ideas or associations does this term generate? Write them in smaller bubbles. Then draw connecting lines between them to mark the flow of your ideas, as shown in Figure 2-8. A minor bubble can become the center of its own network of associations.

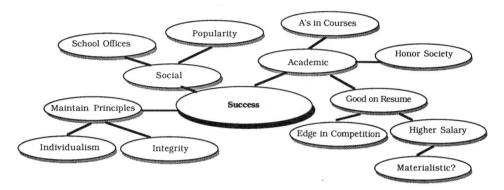

FIGURE 2-8. *Clustering*

Advantages. Clustering comes naturally to people who are strongly visual and like to doodle. It graphically portrays how our associations cluster around key terms or topics, and it depicts the flow of thought or feeling from one topic to another. Seeing how minor points have their own clusters of associations will help you generate small details.

Diagraming. Some writers, especially technical writers, like to start with diagrams, graphs, charts, or other illustrations and then write their text. (See Figure 2-9.)

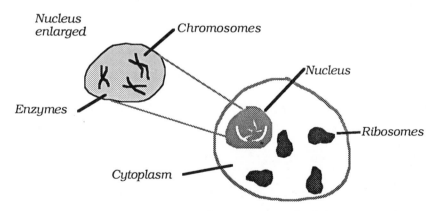

Talk about how cell is divided into 2 parts—nucleus & cytoplasm. Nucleus—contains chromosomes, transcriptional enzymes; discuss role in protein synthesis. Cytoplasm—cytoplasmic ribosomes; explain how they interpret information from chromosomes & translate it into sequence of amino acids.

FIGURE 2-9. *Diagraming*

Advantages. Highly visual people think as much in pictures as they do in words; whereas starting a writing project may daunt them, drawing a diagram does not. Once the graphic is done, even if it is only a rough sketch, the text follows much more easily. The writer now has something concrete and objective to describe. Although this method should appeal especially to technical writers, creative writers, too, may want to draw their flights of fancy before putting them into words.

Tree Charts. Tree charts (such as family trees and organizational charts) are much more organized and formal than clusters; think of them as graphic outlines. They use structured branching to show how a topic can be divided into subordinate ideas or parts. To create a tree chart, start with the broadest aspect of your document: the main idea, the problem to be solved, the entity to be described or analyzed. Break down this broad category into several components, then each of these components into its subordinate parts, as in Figure 2-10. Continue subdividing, or branching, until you have thoroughly analyzed your topic.

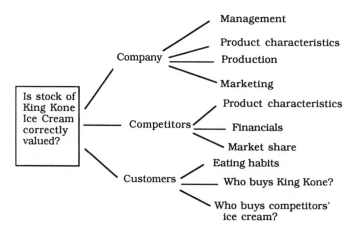

FIGURE 2-10. *Tree chart*

Advantages. Tree charts are especially useful for analyzing and dividing—that is, breaking down a topic into its component parts—and showing, in a highly visual way, the logical relationships among the parts. They also generate details needed to support generalities. Use tree charts for those writing projects that involve analytic thinking and organized problem solving.

Analyzing

Prewriting techniques for analyzing involve verbal ways of breaking a topic into component parts; they also involve making preliminary planning and strategy decisions.

Writing Strategies. Type the names of different writing strategies on your screen: "Definition," "Examples," "Causes," "Effects," "Analogies," "Classifications," "Process," "Comparisons/Contrasts," "Problems," "Solutions." Underline or capitalize these headings, then explore your topic by considering it in terms of the appropriate strategies. Answer such questions as these:

- ☐ What needs to be defined?
- ☐ What examples can be given?
- ☐ What can be contrasted or compared?
- ☐ What analogies can be made?
- ☐ What are the causes? The effects?
- ☐ How can the process be broken down into steps or stages?
- ☐ What are the components or types or categories? Divide and classify.
- ☐ What is the problem? The solution?

Of course, not all strategies apply to every topic. One example of this approach is presented in Figure 2-11.

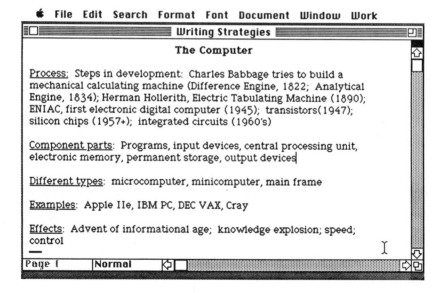

FIGURE 2-11. *Writing strategies*

Advantages. This method of prewriting generates ideas and illustrative material and forces you to think about strategy — the decisions you make about how to put ideas and examples into words most effectively. Chapter 3 discusses in more detail various writing strategies for developing and expressing ideas.

Comparison/Contrast Table. When your writing involves substantial comparison and contrast, make a table like the one in Figure 2-12. Set up three columns, labeling the first "Categories" and the last two with the topics to be compared or contrasted (or both). In the first column, jot down a broad category that can be the basis of a comparison or contrast. In the second column, fill in appropriate material for topic A; in the third column, do the same for topic B. Continue adding broad categories and relevant ideas in the appropriate columns. Finally, organize the table by numbering the categories in a logical order. Note that sometimes you will have little or nothing to say about one topic in a given category.

COMPARE/CONTRAST CATEGORIES	COMPUTER WRITING	TRADITIONAL WRITING
Efficiency	Less time typing; more time composing. Attention span longer.	Slow typist; spend hours typing long project; many mistakes. Frustrated.
Creativity	Much freedom, can experiment, change. Not inhibited, can try new styles.	Once something is typed, don't change; have to get things right the first time.
Editing	Spend a lot of time on this. Get to be a perfectionist; every little mistake must be corrected.	Change some things, esp. on rough draft, but once things are typed it's lots of liquid paper or leave it alone.
Appearance	Looks professional; can design typography of papers; aesthetics important.	Can't type well; final copy blotched; what's the point of trying?

FIGURE 2-12. *Comparison/contrast table*

This comparison/contrast table was generated by a graphics program. You may not have a suitable graphics program or may not want to bother with one, but this method of prewriting is very useful, so don't hesitate to use pencil and paper. There is, after all, nothing inherently sinful about returning to old tools occasionally! If you have a super word processor, generate your comparison/contrast table by specifying that the various items are to be printed side by side in three columns. Although the items will appear in a vertical sequence on screen, simple commands ensure that they will print next to each other on paper.

Advantages. The comparison/contrast table not only generates more material but also forces you to look at the two subjects point by point and provides a general organizational scheme. Thus you can organize vertically, first, by writing all about topic A, using material in the second column of your table, and by writing about topic B, using material in the third column. Or you can organize horizontally, by category. In that case you alternate between topics A and B, using material in the same category from both the second and third columns.

Audience Profile. Before you start to write, ask yourself, If I publish (or distribute) this document, who will read it? Write a profile of your potential audience by answering questions like the following:

- ☐ How big is my audience?
- ☐ Why are they interested in my subject?
- ☐ What are their attitudes, beliefs, prejudices?
- ☐ Are their attitudes, beliefs, and so on similar to or different from mine?
- ☐ What is my audience's socioeconomic, political, and cultural status?
- ☐ Will their status affect how they respond to my document?
- ☐ What do they know about my subject?
- ☐ Are they above me in authority, on the same level, or below me?

Visualize your audience as specifically as possible; Figure 2-13 provides a good example. Even if you think you are writing only for yourself or for one other person (like a writing instructor), imagine an ideal audience for your work and write for those people.

Advantages. This method of prewriting, which should be used in conjunction with all the others, ensures that you write to real people and not to a blank wall. Having a clearly defined audience in mind is crucial if your writing is to be anything more than an academic exercise. Knowing your audience and writing to real people is especially important in business and professional writing.

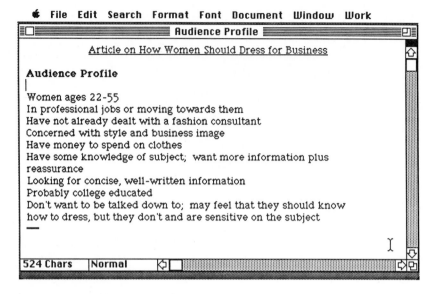

FIGURE 2-13. *Audience profile*

Statement of Purpose. Write a succinct statement defining your purpose. You might start by saying, "In this document I want to . . ." As you go on to describe exactly what it is you want to do, answer such questions as these:

- ☐ What exactly do I want to convey to readers?
- ☐ Why do I want to tell them this?
- ☐ How am I going to get my message across?
- ☐ What impression do I want to leave?
- ☐ Just who are these readers? (See the audience profile method.)
- ☐ What is going to be the general tone and approach of this document?

Try to be detailed and specific in your answers, as exemplified in Figure 2-14; often, fuzzy writing is the result of undefined purpose. If you are confused and unsure, so will be your reader.

Advantages. You should use the statement of purpose with all the other methods of prewriting. Its main benefits are that it clarifies your thinking and gives you an over-all conception of your writing project. A statement of purpose also helps you formulate your thesis or main idea (although in most cases, it cannot substitute for a thesis in the actual document).

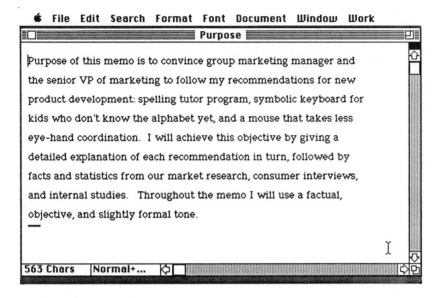

FIGURE 2-14. *Statement of purpose*

Many writers, however, are not ready to define either their audience or their purpose until after they have done prewriting, thinking, and research. Or they write sketchy profiles of their audience and briefly state their purpose as part of prewriting and then greatly enlarge and refine these statements later in the writing process, when they discover exactly what they want to say. For this reason, the relationship between subject, audience, and purpose and the differences between a statement of purpose and a thesis are examined more closely in Chapter 3, "Planning and Organizing on the Computer."

Special Computer Programs for Prewriting

The ingenuity of programmers is rapidly coming to the aid of computer writers. Idea processors is the generic name for programs that help you do prewriting. They come in two varieties: free-form and structured. Free-form idea processors take advantage of computer graphics and turn the screen into a notepad for brainstorming and clustering. For example, in one program you jot down ideas on the screen as you brainstorm. (Light bulbs appear for each of your bright ideas!) Later you can indicate logical relationships with lines and greatly expand each idea in a separate window. Eventually, you can link these windows together in an organized sequence.

A structured idea processor lets you create outlines with main headings and a series of indented subordinate headings. (Chapter 3, pp. 52–58, discusses outlining in detail.) You can sort and move this material around or collapse (hide) the subordinate headings. Sometimes you can attach a short word-processing document to a particular headline. Graphic versions of structured idea processors let you incorporate diagrams and pictures as part of the outline or to convert the outline to a tree chart.

Other computer programs also help you be creative. For example, with free-form databases—the electronic equivalent of index cards or notepaper—you can jot down notes. These databases are ideal for research notes, interview notes, results of experiments, comments on other people's ideas and theories, summaries of articles and books, and so on. They can also be used for plot scenarios and character biographies for creative writing projects (TV scripts, short stories, novels). By flagging key words, you can sort, match, combine, and retrieve exactly the information you need.

Project management software that creates flowcharts for ongoing jobs can also be adapted for brainstorming. Experiment with this kind of software when your writing project consists of describing a process—giving directions for doing something or showing how something works. Prewriting then involves creating a flowchart that outlines the sequence of steps in the process.

Once you try computer prewriting techniques, you will see firsthand that they can generate a great deal of material, much of it interesting and worth further development. Try combining different techniques: diagraming with the reporter's notebook, for example, or listing with statement of purpose and critical comments, or talking with the computer, audience profile, and provocative questions—the possibilities are endless.

Notice, too, that some methods of prewriting are more suited to a particular writing project than are others: Free association may do an excellent job of warming you up but may not be very useful for a research paper; a dialogue with the computer may generate material for a humorous essay, but the devil's advocate approach may work better for a controversial article. Take into account the nature of the subject, your audience, and your purpose in writing.

Don't be afraid to try your own variations. No two writers are alike, nor are their writing methods. Know your writing style, or writing personality as it were, and suit your prewriting to that. Be prepared to prewrite in several sessions if your project is long or complex. You may start with unstructured writing like free association or clustering to warm you up, then proceed to more structured techniques, and finish by planning strategy, analyzing your audience, and formulating a statement of purpose. Each time you sit down at the computer, reread what you did before, and use the best material to get you started again.

Finally, just because you are becoming a computer writer, don't throw away your old tools. Keep a notebook or some scratch paper handy when you are away from the computer. Good ideas will pop into your head when you least expect them; be prepared to jot them down before they disappear.

Remember that no matter what kind of prewriting you do, most of it will be fairly loose and disorganized. At some point in the writing process you have to decide which idea to write down first, which second, which third. Some writers solve this problem by writing meticulously detailed outlines that act as blueprints for their work. Others start on rambling rough drafts that, after repeated revisions and rearrangement, are finally transformed into polished and organized documents. Between these extremes are other alternatives for transforming prewriting into workable rough drafts. The process of that transformation is the subject of the next two chapters.

If you haven't saved your prewriting, do so now, giving it a distinctive name. You will need it for the discussion in the next chapter.

Let's Solve It!

Prewriting may not solve all your problems of getting started. Here's how to conquer procrastination and lack of confidence.

Problem: Procrastination and Inefficiency. You keep putting off writing, and when you finally do get down to work, little gets done. Because writing eats up so much of your time and you have so little to show for it, you come to dislike writing and procrastinate even more.

Solution. Of the many techniques for coping with procrastination, one of the most useful is setting quotas—a number of words or a number of hours or a combination of both. Be realistic in setting quotas, though: There is no sense in being overly ambitious and then feeling guilty when you fail. But do reward yourself when the writing session is over and you have met your quota; do something you enjoy.

Problem: Lack of Confidence in Your Abilities as a Writer. Even before you start to write, you are discouraged because you think your writing won't measure up to other people's or because you are sure you won't have enough interesting or important things to say. You don't even want to begin.

Solution. Write about what you know; everyone is an expert of sorts on some subject. If you are interested in the topic, your enthusiasm will be communicated to the reader. If you are assigned to write on a particular subject, learn as much about it as you can. And do twice as much prewriting as you think you will need; then you can choose the best material to put in your document.

Problem: Too Much Self-Criticism. No matter what you write, it isn't good enough. You delete almost everything you have written. Or you take so much time to write one perfect sentence that you become frustrated.

Solution. Don't try to combine creating and editing; these are two separate processes that should be done at two different times. When you first start writing, simply let your ideas flow without criticizing their content or form; turn off that critical inner voice that says they are not good enough. Later, when you have something substantial down in words, be critical—edit, revise, change, and rewrite to your heart's content.

Problem: Fear of Criticism from Others. Worrying about what your peers, instructor, supervisor, or editor might say about your writing makes it difficult to expose your inner thoughts and feelings on paper.

Solution. Writing is a highly personal act, and we feel that somehow our self-worth, along with our writing, is being judged. One way to cope with outside criticism is to meet it head-on before you write. Jot down every objection a critic might make, and then answer those objections. A therapeutic form of prewriting, this method can also develop stronger arguments and more effective strategies for your writing.

Computer Writing Tips

Professional writers know that a writing routine and a good working environment increase creativity and productivity. Take some advice from them.

- Set a special time for writing. Most writers agree that scheduling a time for writing every day—preferably the same time—cuts down on procrastination and prevents writer's block. And when you write, don't do anything else but write: no reading, researching, looking up words, daydreaming, or talking to others.
- Establish a special place for writing where you are likely to have a minimum of distractions. If you are lucky, this means your own room with your own computer, but for many it may mean a shared room, a busy office, or even a crowded computer lab. Partitions at individual workstations can block out visual distractions. If noise is a problem, however, try creating "white noise" by listening to bland and soothing music over earphones.
- Fatigue can impair your ability to think and write. Be sure you are comfortable as you work at the computer. Sit up straight, with your feet squarely on the floor. Move the keyboard so that it is directly in front of you; your arms should be bent at right angles, with the forearms parallel to the floor. The screen should be an easy-to-read distance from your eyes. Turn the brightness up or down to suit your needs. From time to time look away

from the screen, possibly closing your eyes for a while. Periodically get up and move around. People who work at computer terminals are subject to various kinds of stress and strain if they don't take preventive measures.

■ Physical messiness is another kind of distraction. With a computer on your desk, work space may be crowded, so organize your writing materials neatly. A stenographer's stand that holds notes and rough drafts upright, placed next to the terminal, is helpful.

I got a computer because I was on a deadline with a book and knew I couldn't otherwise finish it on time. I wrote that book—about Robert Burton, author of *The Anatomy of Melancholy* (1621)—from beginning to end on the computer. The computer did all the things we expect in revising and editing, but I mainly used it as a super typewriter. Most people start out this way; only afterward do they begin to see other possibilities for their scholarship.

Now I use the computer to keep track of my research. A year ago I bought a laptop for taking notes in the library. It's very light, very small, and easily fits into my briefcase.

Last summer, doing research on Baroque art in the Biblioteca Hertziania in Rome, I found out just how wonderful a laptop computer can be. I took notes as I read in the library: bibliographic information, summaries of the main arguments, general comments, notes on whatever interested me. I flagged four to six key words: authors' names, key words in titles, main concepts, artists' names, and so on. I also entered the embedded codes needed in my database program for my desktop computer in the United States.

When I got back to our apartment on the "piccolo Aventino," I hooked up the laptop to a tiny thermal printer and printed out my notes. Then I hooked it up to a portable cassette recorder and transferred the day's work to tape. By the end of our Roman stay, I had managed to get my whole summer's research onto four tapes.

Eventually, I transferred these notes to my desktop computer's database. Now I can search all the entries, looking for specific concepts or authors or any other key terms and ideas I originally flagged. And if I want to use a quotation from a book or article, I can call it up from the database and put it in the document I'm writing. As far as I'm concerned, laptops are a much safer and more efficient way of doing research. I have all my data stored in three different forms now—on paper, on tape, and on floppy disks—so I'm much less likely to lose anything. And the data is much more accessible.

Michael O'Connell
Renaissance Scholar

Planning and Organizing on the Computer

Defining subject, audience, and purpose
Formulating a thesis
Deciding on writing strategy
Outlining

The planning and organizing stage in the writing process involves some writing, but primarily it involves thinking—analytic thinking—and decision making. Once you have finished prewriting, you are ready to start analyzing your audience and purpose, formulating a thesis, deciding on a writing strategy, and organizing your material. This chapter presents these activities as separate steps, but in real life some of them may happen simultaneously or be so interconnected that you don't consciously perform them as separate steps. For example, you may have analyzed your audience or purpose during the prewriting stage or even before. And some writers, a minority, do their analytic thinking and decision making as they write their rough drafts. (See the section on freewheeling rough drafts in Chapter 4.) Most people, though, especially beginning writers and those who have trouble writing, need to go through the planning and organizing stage before they start their rough drafts.

How much time you spend on this stage depends on several elements: the importance of the writing project, its length and complexity, and your previous experience with this kind of writing. Thus, for a brief, routine letter or report, something you have done many times before, you will spend relatively little time planning. However, if the project is lengthy and complex (an academic paper or dissertation or a highly technical report), or if it is controversial, or if it will lead to important decisions and results— and you have had little experience with this type of writing—then planning and organizing should be a long and thoughtful part of the writing process. It could mean the difference between success and failure. Part of becoming a good writer involves learning how to allocate your time wisely.

The computer is an ideal tool for planning. Unlike the rigidly fixed print of a typewriter or the relatively permanent writing of pencil and pen, computer writing is fluid and changeable. It allows you to experiment and be tentative. You can try first one thing, then another, and the rapidly moving cursor will keep up with your changes. The computer's capability to move text easily results in better organization; no longer will you tend to stick to one organizational plan simply because you have written it down and it is too much trouble to change. The ability to add text means you can start with the bare bones of a plan or outline, then insert more material and make it grow as you see your way more clearly or get new ideas. And all the while the computer's delete function gets rid of unwanted material and keeps your work legible and neat.

The trick in computer writing, however, is to look at your work in two phases: electronic, a work space that is fluid and ever-changing; and paper, a forecast of the relatively more permanent and finished product. Learn how to move back and forth creatively between these two phases. Most people see things on paper that they miss on the screen, and vice versa. So before you start on the steps discussed below, print out your prewriting. Go through it carefully, underlining or highlighting the areas that look particularly important or helpful. Keep this prewriting near you as you work on the computer.

Alternatively, if your word-processing program has the capability, you might want to divide your screen into two or more sections, or windows; then you can scroll through your prewriting in one window, for example, as you plan your rough draft in another. But even if you do this, you will probably find it helpful to keep printouts of your prewriting close at hand.

Defining Subject, Audience, and Purpose

Writing never takes place in a vacuum; you are always writing about a specific topic, to a specific person (or persons), for a specific reason. Even your most personal writing, a private diary for example, has a purpose and an audience—yourself. How you define your subject, audience, and purpose largely controls the rest of your writing strategy or planning. If this definition does not exist, your writing is apt to be vague, unfocused prose, whose purpose is as unclear to you as it is to the reader.

You may have written an audience profile and statement of purpose and carefully delimited your subject during the prewriting stage. If so, now is the time to call up these materials on the screen and refine them. But it is also possible that you weren't ready to analyze such elements until after you had completed substantial amounts of prewriting and thinking and possibly even research. In that case, before attempting to formulate a thesis or to outline your document, you first need to ask yourself some questions: What are you writing about? Who is your audience? Why do you want to reach this audience? You may argue that this kind of analysis can be done in your head rather than on the computer, and for short, simple, or routine types of writing, you may be right. But writing your analysis down facilitates the process, because you will analyze more perceptively if you must articulate your ideas in specific words.

Open a new document, or add to your original prewriting. Start by typing "Definition of Subject," "Audience Profile," and "Statement of Purpose" in bold in a vertical list. (Here and elsewhere, substitute capital letters or underlining for bold if your computer doesn't show bold on the screen.) Then position the cursor after each one in turn, and jot down your analysis using regular type. As you write, you may find yourself moving from one category to the other, because these three—subject, audience, and purpose—are so closely interrelated.

Analyze your subject by answering basic questions: Is the topic important (the threat of nuclear war) or relatively trivial (the annual company picnic) or somewhere in between? Is it complex (the structure of deoxyribonucleic acid) or simple (the design of plastic paper clips)? Is it general and abstract (natural law) or specific and detailed (how to win in small claims court)? How will the nature of your subject affect how you write about it? You also need to look at scope: Is your subject sharply focused and definite or vague and amorphous? Is it narrow enough; can you discuss it adequately in the space you have available? Conversely, is it substantial enough to warrant a full-length treatment? Finally, look at your relationship with your subject: Are you relatively detached from it or deeply involved?

Now consider your intended audience. Are you writing to yourself, to one other person, to a small group, to a huge crowd? What are their interests and beliefs? Are they above you in age, expertise, or authority; on the same level; or below you? What do they want or need to know about your subject? Why would they want to hear what *you* have to say on it? What do you think their response will be? (Students writing an assignment for a single instructor should imagine the ideal audience for their work if it were to be published.)

Finally, and perhaps most important, what is your purpose? Why do you want to address *this* audience about *this* topic? Are you trying to persuade, inform, amuse, or teach them? Refute their arguments? Urge them to take some course of action? Hand down an unwelcome decision? Are you merely thinking out loud and allowing readers to "overhear" your musings? Or are you trying to present the facts objectively? Perhaps you are angrily denouncing an injustice. What do you want their response to be? The possibilities are endless, but the important thing is that you try to articulate clearly to yourself precisely what it is you are trying to do. If your purpose is not clear to you, it certainly will not be clear to your readers. (Before I started writing this book, I spent a lot of time thinking about my subject, audience, and purpose. Some of my early ideas appear in Figure 3-1.)

Remember that writing is also a process of discovery. Thus you may learn about your subject, audience, and purpose as you write, and only after your rough draft is finished may the complexities of your subject, the needs of your audience, and your own intentions become completely clear. Even so, in this planning and organizing stage of the writing process you still need tentative answers. How you define your subject, audience, and purpose will influence, if not control, how you formulate your thesis and present your material.

Formulating a Thesis

A thesis is the central idea of a document. It is not merely the subject of your writing but also your stand on that subject, what you assert about that subject and set out to prove. "Cats" could be the *subject* of an essay, but the statement that "Cats, although often temperamental and exasperating, are ultimately the most rewarding pets" would be its *thesis*. Frequently, a thesis has an argumentative edge to it; it invites agreement

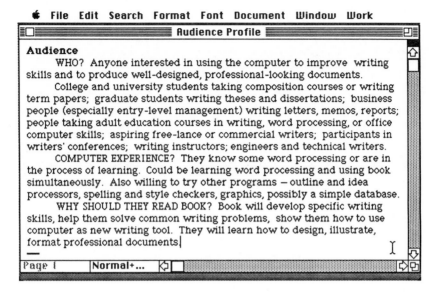

FIGURE 3-1. *Audience profile*

or disagreement. Dog lovers, for example, would dispute your assertion about cats or at least wait to be persuaded.

Usually you explicitly tell your readers what your central idea is; that is, you write a thesis statement. The length of this statement depends on the complexity of the idea and the nature of the document. A short sentence will do for a simple letter, two or three sentences for a longer essay or article. In a substantial research paper or report, however, you may write a paragraph stating your thesis, and in a long and complex book, several paragraphs or even a short chapter might be needed.

The more complete thesis statement can have several parts. You write the core assertion, then add a sentence or two that *limits* that assertion in a significant way. Thus your core assertion claims that rent control is necessary to protect tenants from soaring rents, but your limiting statement narrows your focus to multi-unit apartments in the unincorporated areas of the county. Or you add a *clarifying* statement, explaining or defining particular concepts or terms in the core assertion. In the thesis statement "Deregulation has eliminated most discount airlines," you may want to define exactly what you mean by "deregulation."

Thesis statements always make a declarative assertion. Thus, questions are not thesis statements. But questions can be a good rhetorical device for leading into the thesis statement. For example, your whole document could be an answer to a question posed at the beginning. In that case, your thesis would be *implicitly* rather than *explicitly* stated—the reader must infer your thesis from everything you say rather than find it spelled out in a sentence or two. Although there is nothing wrong with implied theses, especially in the hands of skilled writers, there is the real danger that without an explicit thesis statement readers won't get what you are trying to say or will misunderstand you. Even worse, your writing may lack an explicit thesis statement because you don't know what you want to say.

What are the qualities of a good thesis statement? First, it should be as specific and concrete as possible. Avoid vague generalities, obvious statements, and truisms of the "love-means-many-things-to-many-people" variety. It should also take a definite stand: "A consumption tax is the best way to raise revenues and lower the deficit." Don't waffle; avoid variations of "Some people may think this, but others don't."

In addition, a good thesis statement is limited yet comprehensive. Don't promise to cover more than you actually do, but be broad enough to include everything you want to say. Because of this requirement, that it be both limited and comprehensive, a thesis statement in the planning stage can only be provisional. Until you have finished writing, you won't know if it is too broad or too narrow. Finally, the thesis statement must be interesting. Be provocative; invite readers to continue. If they are bored by the central idea of your document, the rest of your writing is futile.

Before you start writing you may know exactly what your thesis is, or you may discover it as you go along. In either case you still have to put this idea into words; the form these words take, the actual thesis statement, depends on your subject, audience, and purpose. To help you formulate a thesis, reread the material you wrote about subject, audience, and purpose. Then condense it into a single statement and

THESIS STATEMENT VERSUS STATEMENT OF PURPOSE

Note the difference between a thesis statement and a formal statement of purpose in a document. The latter, often used in technical reports and in some articles for professional journals, explicitly defines your purpose, usually in a sentence or two beginning with a formulaic phrase: "It is the purpose of this article to . . ." or "In this paper I propose to . . ." You may be writing a document in which a formal statement of purpose, rather than a thesis statement, is customary. But if you use a statement of purpose in documents where thesis statements are customary, you run the risk of sounding overly formal and stilted.

write it down. If you are a personal writer, use "I" and descriptive verbs: Fill in the blanks in the statement "I want to _____ so that I can _____"; for example, "I want to describe the sufferings of the urban poor so vividly that I will rouse people in this community from their apathy and persuade them to contribute money to the Hunger Fund." If you are a more detached writer, write a more formal statement of purpose: "The purpose of this paper (or memo or letter or report) is to _____ in order to _____." "The purpose of this memo is to review Mary Donlan's performance so I can recommend her for a merit increase." Statements like these are merely reminders to you of what you want to do; they guide you as you compose thesis statements, but they are not thesis statements yet.

Writing the actual thesis statement warrants opening a new document. (Later you will use this document to write your outline or to start a freewheeling rough draft or both.) Across the top of the document, write a statement, in one to three sentences, of what you want to assert or prove about your chosen topic. Put it in bold, or use a larger size of type, to emphasize its importance. Remember that this is only a provisional thesis statement. In the process of writing you may discover new ideas, expand your original purpose, narrow your focus, or change your mind. So after you have finished your first draft, come back and revise your thesis statement at least once.

Avoiding Strategy Traps

After composing a thesis statement, many beginning writers immediately want to start writing a rough draft. Any planning strategies they may formulate are simplistic and inadequate. Have you ever fallen into one of these strategy traps?

Writer-based Strategy. Linda Flower, a composition researcher and textbook writer, defines this strategy as talking to oneself rather than communicating with the reader.[1] The resulting document focuses on you; it meets your personal needs. You might, for example, write what you remember about a particular subject, so that the structure of the finished document depends on the order in which you recall the various points. Or you might write the story of how you discovered an idea, identified a problem, or arrived at a recommendation. In this case your document has a narrative structure; it tells the story of your thinking processes. Or perhaps you assemble all the information you have on a subject and then write a comprehensive survey; in this case the structure of the document has to be designed to present everything you know.

---

[1]Linda Flower, *Problem-Solving Strategies for Writing*, 2nd ed. (San Diego: Harcourt Brace Jovanovich, 1985) 162–65 and *passim*. Flower draws a useful contrast between what she calls "writer-based prose" and "reader-based prose."

In all these examples, the writing strategy consists of recalling and presenting material in the easiest, most efficient, and most complete way for the writer. But readers may not want or need all the information you know about a subject; they may want your recommendations but not the whole story of how you arrived at them. Furthermore, your recall of a subject may not emphasize the points that concern them most. Although it may help you recall or discover what you know, a writer-based strategy frequently does not meet the needs of your readers.

Bottom-up Strategy. The term "bottom-up" comes from computer programming and has negative connotations. Bottom-up programmers hastily start coding programs before they have properly designed them; they become immersed in details before deciding on overall structure. The analogy with writing is obvious. When you opt for a bottom-up strategy, you start with details and hope that somehow an overall plan or design will emerge. Sometimes it does; more often it doesn't. You keep moving from detail to detail, incorporating each one into your writing but not clearly showing its place in the overall design. At the end, the reader (as well as you, the author) is surrounded by individual facts and ideas, but there is little or no sense that a carefully thought-out plan has determined how those facts are arranged, emphasized, and connected. Starting with details and working from the bottom up may help you in the prewriting stage, when you are marshaling information, but it is often inadequate as a planning strategy.

Three-Point, Five-Paragraph Strategy. In using this strategy, you compose a thesis statement so that it contains three points and then mechanically organize your material to fit into five paragraphs: Paragraph 1 provides a panoramic introduction and concludes with a three-item list; paragraph 2 discusses the first point in the list; paragraph 3, the second point; and paragraph 4, the last point. Paragraph 5 summarizes what has just been said.

Usually the result lacks a sense of discovery and development, because the list gives away everything you have to say. And repetition abounds: You have summarized your ideas in both the first and last paragraphs and have repeated them in the middle three paragraphs. So although this strategy might be good as a learning model, it is usually inadequate for complex or sophisticated documents.

There are other inadequate writing strategies; these three merely happen to be common. If you rely on any of them, or if you don't follow a writing strategy at all, it is time to break your old habits. The following sections will help you make smart strategic decisions about how to develop and present your material.

Choosing a Method of Development

Writing strategy, to a large extent, depends on your subject, intended audience, and purpose. Review your prewriting and analysis so far and then ask yourself: Am I going to narrate an event? Describe an object or scene? Explain a process? Compare or contrast two items? Classify a large number of items? Trace causes? Explain effects? Define a concept or term? Argue for a particular point of view? These are rhetorical methods of development, and although you may briefly use many of them in the course of a single document, very likely you will rely primarily on one. This method should not only suit your subject and purpose but also meet the needs of your readers. There is no point in narrating how you conducted a review of accounting procedures when your readers want only a list of the problems you found.

Typical methods of development include the following:

- *Narration*—recounting events in a chronological order; telling a story
- *Description*—giving details (about a tangible object, scene, or person) that appeal to the five senses and describe motion
- *Exemplification*—providing one or more examples (facts, incidents, people, details, concrete reasons, quotations) that illustrate or support the point being made
- *Process*—explaining, in chronological order, the steps or stages in how something is made or done, how something works, or how some result is achieved
- *Comparison/contrast*—pointing out similarities between items or topics, pointing out differences, or doing both
- *Analogy*—metaphorically comparing two different items or topics in order to make the abstract or complex or unfamiliar topic understandable
- *Analysis*—breaking down a large topic or concept or item into its component parts and showing the relationship among those parts
- *Classification*—placing items (or component parts) in appropriate categories; grouping, categorizing, dividing, typing, classifying
- *Enumeration*—listing a series of subpoints or items in a broader category; often numbered
- *Causation*—determining the causes of a particular phenomenon or event
- *Effects*—explaining the effects of a particular phenomenon or event or predicting future effects; may describe a cause/effect sequence in which A causes B, which results in C, which in turn causes D
- *Definition*—stating the meaning of a term or concept or giving the distinctive characteristics of an item
- *Argumentation/persuasion*—logically proving that a particular stand on an issue is correct or that a particular solution to a problem is better; refuting opposing arguments; persuading others to agree or to take specific action

If you want to classify these methods, you will see that they fall into four broad categories of writing: narration, description, exposition, and argumentation/persuasion. Note that exposition includes exemplification, process, comparison/contrast, analysis/classification/enumeration, cause/effect, and definition.

These methods of development can be combined. Thus exemplification can and should be used with all the others; narration could be used in an introductory anecdote; a process is often a type of cause/effect sequence; comparison/contrast is a special type of analysis/classification; causes may be classified as main and subsidiary, effects as short term and long term, and sometimes causes and effects are combined; definition and argumentation/persuasion traditionally draw on other methods of development to make their points; and so on. Nonetheless, you can usually determine that your subject and your purpose call for one of these methods as the primary means of rhetorical development.

Organizing Your Prewriting

As part of this stage of the planning process, it is helpful to get a broad overview of what you are going to write and to organize your prewriting accordingly. If you are a free spirit, you may not mind leaving your prewriting in chaos, or at least in the disorder that freewheeling creativity originally put it in. But for important writing projects, you will find that arranging your prewriting in some sort of basic order improves your ability to see the writing as a coherent whole and to think about it logically. You can use one of three useful methods: (1) group prewriting material under basic divisions; (2) follow a method of development as a guide; or (3) decide on a basic plan of organization. With any of these you can easily organize your prewriting electronically, by moving material around and (if helpful) using a simple numbering system, or you can simply pencil in notes on your original printout.

Basic Divisions

Any document can be divided into a beginning, a middle, and an end—or introduction, body, and conclusion—but at this point, you want to look more closely at the body of your projected work. In the broadest terms possible, what is its structure going to be? Try to see the basic parts, the largest divisions possible. If you step back far enough from any piece of writing, you will see that it has few truly major divisions: four or five, perhaps, for very long pieces, but only two or three for short to moderately long pieces. Here are typical examples of basic divisions:

> Past, present, and future
> Old and new

> Problem and solution
> Advantages and disadvantages
> Pro and con
> Assertion and support
> Evidence and conclusions

Write down the main divisions in bold, and move the appropriate items in your prewriting under the correct heading or simply insert numbers, putting "1" next to all items that belong in the first division, "2" next to items belonging in the second division, and so forth. If your word processor has a sort function, use it to sort and group together the numbered items. At this point you may see what sections and subsections should come under the main divisions.

Methods of Development

The method of development you choose can also suggest basic divisions for your writing. Thus narrative can be broken down into exposition, complications, climax, and results; comparison/contrast can be divided into topic A and topic B; cause and effect can be simply those two categories or subdivided into main and subsidiary causes or into short-term and long-term effects; analysis, classification, and enumeration, by definition, involve dividing into parts. Again, organize your prewriting by moving items or by numbering and sorting them.

Plan of Organization

Alternatively, you may want to decide on an overall plan of organization: How are you going to get from the beginning of your document to the end? How are you going to decide what to put first, what second, what third? An overall plan of organization will help you make outlining decisions later on. You can choose from five basic organizational plans:

1. *Going from the general to the specific.* Start with a broad generalization and then give supporting material in the form of concrete examples and specific details.
2. *Going from the specific to the general.* Start with specific evidence—one or more concrete examples or a series of details—and then draw some general conclusions.
3. *Arranging material chronologically.* Proceed sequentially, putting down what happened first, what happened next, and so on.
4. *Arranging material spatially.* Describe an object or scene from a fixed viewing point in space. Or the viewing point moves as you take a panoramic look across or above, below, or behind the object or scene.

5. *Arranging material climactically, in order of importance.* Start with the least important item and progress to the most important, or start with the weakest or smallest or worst and progress to the strongest or largest or best. Alternatively, you can use an anticlimactic order; that is, you put the most important item first, proceed to the next most important item, and so on down the list. Repeating the most important item at the end may be good strategy in using an anticlimactic order.

Be sure your plan of organization is readily discernible without being mechanical or too obvious. A clear, logical plan makes it easier for you to organize your material and eventually write your document; it also makes it easier for readers to follow your train of thought. As previously noted, you will want to rearrange your prewriting so that it follows this plan. Move or number items to indicate the order of the various elements.

You may be able to use variations and combinations of the methods. Experiment. Find out what suits your personal style and the writing project. And if the project is especially important, complex, or long, print out another copy of your prewriting in its organized form. You can also insert a page break after each major division if you want to divide your prewriting physically.

Writing an Outline

The next step in planning is writing an outline. How you outline and when you do it often depend on the kind of writer you are and the nature of your writing project. For a short document, a scratch outline will suffice; for long or complex documents, a carefully planned, formal outline that has been revised several times may be necessary. Some writers construct elaborate outlines *before* they start their rough drafts; others, because they do not discover what they really want to say until they have done some writing, construct their outlines *after* they have finished a freewheeling rough draft. And many writers move back and forth between outline and draft, changing and elaborating their outline as they develop ideas in their draft and then using the revised outline to reorganize their draft. Choose the system that works best for you—but experiment before you make up your mind.

If you outline before the rough draft, keep your organized prewriting handy for ready reference, because outlining and prewriting are interactive processes.

Computer Outliners

Truly sophisticated word-processing programs have outlining capabilities. In general, these allow you to indent quickly and to number and letter headings automatically. Five special features are particularly helpful for computer writers.

Two-Way Viewing. You can view your document in two modes: outline and text. Both of these modes can be on screen at once (in two different windows). Changes you make in the text are reflected in your outline, and vice versa. This feature is especially helpful in encouraging you to move between your draft and your outline as you write.

Hidden Text. You can embed text in your outline—comments and notes to yourself—that need not be printed in the finished outline. Being able to prepare an annotated outline will help you revise the outline and give you more guidance when you create your rough draft.

WHY YOU SHOULDN'T SKIP OUTLINING

You may hate outlining and try to avoid it at all costs. Or you may claim that you don't really need to outline because it stifles your creativity. And besides, short documents don't warrant outlines anyway.

The experts think otherwise. For example, author Dwight MacDonald once said in a lecture that the most important thing he learned early in his writing career was to put all material on the same subject in the same place. It's a difficult lesson to learn—and some writers never do.

An editor who has read hundreds of disorganized manuscripts during the last fifteen years flatly states, "Outlining is just plain hard work that is absolutely necessary."

Most publishers demand a detailed outline before they will consider publishing a book.

What can happen to a document if you don't outline? Obviously it can end up being physically disorganized with paragraphs out of sequence. But there are other problems as well:

- Your argument becomes hard to follow.
- Your reader doesn't know where you are going next.
- *You* don't know where you are going next.
- You don't emphasize the main points clearly enough.
- You wander off the subject.
- You spend too much time on one topic, not enough on another.
- You leave important items out.
- You repeat yourself and get wordy.
- Your document is so hard to follow that your reader misunderstands it or loses interest or, worst of all, tosses it away.

There are alternatives to traditional outlining, but sooner or later you must make informed decisions about what comes first in your document, what comes second, what comes third, and so on.

Collapsing Text. You can "collapse," or hide, all the text under a particular heading. This feature is particularly useful for giving you a broad overview of the document's organization; you can collapse all the subheadings and look only at the main ones. When you need to work on the details, you merely expand the collapsed subtext.

Movable Headings. When you move a heading, you can automatically bring all its associated subtext with it. This feature encourages you to experiment with your outline's organization until you have achieved the best order for presenting your ideas.

Sorting. You can automatically sort information, alphabetically or numerically, and you can do this for the whole outline or for individual portions. Thus you can use the outline to organize large amounts of data. Alternatively, you can simply sort all the headings on one level.

In addition, stand-alone outlining programs sometimes have graphic capabilities, and you can move interactively between an outline and a tree chart. These kinds of outliners also allow you to incorporate graphics — the illustrations and diagrams you create — into your outline. This feature is invaluable for people (such as technical writers) who need to plan carefully the integration of text, graphics, and layout before they start a rough draft.

Even with a simple word processor, computer outlining is still far superior to pencil or typewriter. Simple commands let you indent text swiftly and easily to the right or "outdent" it to the left; cut and move functions let you rearrange headings to improve organization; insert and delete functions let you develop and change the content. Finally, being able to open several windows at the same time lets you move interactively between your prewriting and outline; you can save yourself work by copying or moving text from one window to another. And even if your program doesn't have multiple windows, you can still copy from one file (document) to another.

Scratch Outline

There are various types of outlines. A scratch outline, for instance, consists of the bare minimum: a thesis statement, three to five main points, and a conclusion statement — nothing more. To write a scratch outline on the computer (and you need only a simple word processor for this one), type your thesis statement in bold. Move to the next line and indent. Now write down three to five main points you want to make, numbering them in order. Write in complete sentences and press Enter after each one. Like the thesis statement, these should make definite assertions. Finally, starting at the left-hand margin, write a one-sentence conclusion statement in bold; make it a logical and worthwhile conclusion that can be drawn or deduced from the material immediately above it, as in Figure 3-2. Do not merely repeat what you have said.

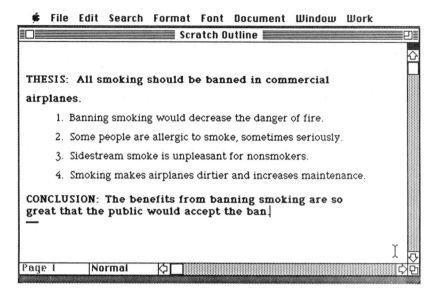

FIGURE 3-2. *A scratch outline*

Scratch outlines are ideal for short, simple documents, but they are inadequate as planning tools for longer, more complex work.

Formal Outline

Most writers are familiar with the formal outline — the highly organized and schematic presentation of the thesis, main points, subpoints, supporting details, and conclusion. These outlines come in two types: item and sentence. In *item outlines* you merely list the topics to be covered in a single word or in short phrases; try to make these stylistically parallel. This kind of outline is like a table of contents: You indicate which subjects are to be covered but don't describe what you are going to say about each one. In *sentence outlines*, as the name indicates, you write in complete sentences and not only indicate the topic but also briefly describe what you will say about it.

There are advantages and disadvantages to both. Item outlines are quicker to write and less restrictive; they guide rather than dictate. However, they may tempt you to rely on vague headings (like "Introduction," "Definition," "Arguments"), and they may hide the fact that you have nothing specific to say. Sentence outlines, on the other hand, force you to make specific assertions, but they also can be restrictive. Once you have written an outline in complete sentences, you may find that you have nothing left to say. Choose the type of outline that suits your topic and your writing style best, then be guided by your planning decisions as you arrange ideas in their correct order and indicate the logical subordination of subpoints to main points.

Formal outlines use a conventional system of visual signals to show the relationship of ideas. Indention, for example, graphically depicts the subordination of one idea to another. Start your outline by writing the thesis statement at the left-hand margin; then indent and list supporting points and subsidiary details. Keep indenting farther and farther to the right as you move from broad generalizations to semispecifics to specifics to fine details. Ideas on the same level (shown by their amount of indention) should have the same relative importance. Emphasize this similarity by stating the ideas in a parallel way.

Indention is reinforced by a conventional system of numbering and lettering, which also indicates the logical sequence of your ideas. One system works like this:

> Main ideas are given capital Roman numerals: I II III IV.
> Subordinate ideas have capital letters: A B C D.
> The next level of subordination has Arabic numbers: 1 2 3 4.
> Next come lowercase letters: a b c d.
> Minor points have lowercase Roman numerals: i ii iii iv.

Ideas with the same kind of number or letter should have the same amount of indention and the same relative importance. If you have a powerful outlining program, it will number and indent automatically, but the logical decisions are still up to you. Your finished outline might look like Figure 3-3.

Use the basic capabilities of the computer—to add, change, delete, and move—to let your outline grow and develop as you think it through. An effective way to start is by writing down the thesis and all the main headings or categories. These categories should reflect the various planning and strategy decisions you have made. Next, start adding subsidiary material. If you don't have automatic numbering, however, don't add numbers or letters yet. Move back and forth between your prewriting and the outline. (Keep a printed copy of the prewriting near you, or open it in a second window on the screen.) Select relevant material to insert under the various headings of your outline—or perhaps the prewriting will suggest new headings. But don't think that merely because you have written something down you have to find a place for it.

Move items around as you decide on the most effective and logical order; consult your planning decisions. Change subordination and the level of indention as the logical relationship between ideas becomes clearer. From time to time, collapse the subtext and look only at the main headings, if you have an outliner that will do that. Add new ideas or details as they occur to you; delete extraneous or dead-end material. Be

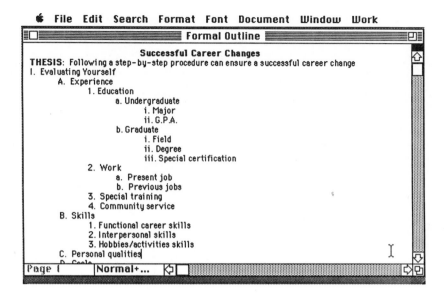

FIGURE 3-3. *A formal outline*

sure that all categories in the outline are fully developed; if they aren't, go back and do some research and prewriting. At this point you may want to embed comments to yourself in hidden text, if your outliner can do this, reminding yourself of what needs to be done to flesh out a particular category. When the outline begins to get fixed, add numbers and letters (if this hasn't been done automatically).

For important or complex documents, don't expect your first outline to be final; plan to revise and refine it. Later on, when you start working on a rough draft, you may want to make further changes to reflect new directions in your writing. With the computer you can easily move back and forth between text and outline.

Hybrid Outline

You can transform a scratch outline into a quasi-formal outline, what I call a "hybrid." When you finish a scratch outline, position the cursor after each main idea, press Enter, and indent. Then briefly describe subsidiary ideas or merely list topics to be covered in order, for example, to substantiate, illustrate, clarify, or prove the main idea. This kind of outline—more detailed than a scratch outline, but lacking the graphic system of progressive indentions and numbering of a formal one—may help you move from a broad overview of your subject to more specific details. And if you are a certain kind of writer, there may be psychological benefits from working in this way. It is relatively easy to create a scratch outline and then expand it. You do not have to commit yourself to working out all the complexities of ordering and logical subordination that a formal outline demands; rather, you are simply doing more advanced prewriting. The hybrid outline has obvious limitations, however, and probably should be reserved for relatively short and simple documents.

Designing from the Top Down

There are alternative ways of organizing material before you write that can be adapted from computer programming. For example, good computer programmers use a technique called *top-down design* (or *stepwise refinement* or *modular programming*) to divide long, complicated programs into individual segments or modules. They start with an overall view of the whole problem, then break it down into its major parts or steps (level 1). When they have finished developing the components of each step at this level, they move to the next lower level (level 2) and work on the steps there. Then they move to the next lower level (level 3), and so on down the line. Finally the whole program has been broken down into a series of steps or modules on different levels: the lower the level, the smaller the details. Programmers thus work from the top of the program, from the broad problem or concept, to the bottom, to the specific details. They establish logical relationships and plan overall design before tackling individual steps; they move from the abstract to the particular.[2] Application of a top-down approach to a writing project might look like Figure 3-4.

This kind of design is the perfect antidote to bottom-up trouble in writing and could be an excellent alternative to traditional outlining. The hierarchical tree charts you created in your prewriting can be developed into top-down models for your rough draft. Or you might want to adapt the Warnier-Orr diagram used in computer programming for top-down design. (See Figure 3-5.)

Diagraming your ideas has several advantages over outlining. Outlines, despite indention and numbering, tend to emphasize the chronological order in which different categories or ideas are to be treated. The Warnier-Orr diagram, on the other hand, turns the traditional outline on its side and graphically emphasizes the different levels of ideas. All your major ideas are vertically grouped together in column ii; subordinate ideas are grouped in column iii, and the supporting details in column iv. When you make

---

[2]Based on Nell Dale and David Orshalik, *Introduction to PASCAL and Structured Design* (Lexington, MA: D. C. Heath and Co., 1983) 66–71.

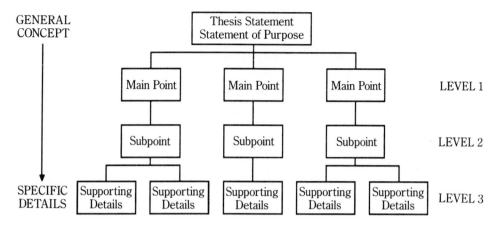

FIGURE 3-4.   *Top-down design in writing*

decisions about logic, about levels of importance, about basic content, you concentrate on the material arranged in vertical columns.

However, this diagram also tracks the chronological order or progression of your ideas; you simply move horizontally from item I to items A and B to items 1 and 2. In addition, the horizontal levels graphically display the development of your ideas; as you move from left to right, the material should become more and more detailed, concrete,

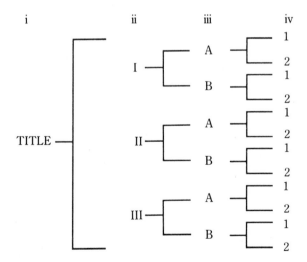

FIGURE 3-5.   *The Warnier-Orr diagram adapted for outlining*

and specific. Thus you can see the overall shape of your future document and at the same time pay equal attention to logic, organization, and development.[3]

You may be able to adapt your outlining program so it produces the equivalent of the Warnier-Orr diagram, or you may have to use a graphics program. Note that this kind of diagraming can be used in the prewriting stage as well as in the planning stage: The details you generate while brainstorming are placed in the column farthest to the right; when you start to plan, however, you start at the left and then work your way to the right. As you fill in the various columns and rows, you may find gaps in your knowledge or logic, a sign that you need to do more thinking, research, or prewriting. Always remember that the writing process is not linear but recursive; you may go back to earlier steps before continuing with the present one.

When you finish with the planning and organizing stage, you will have created several documents for a single project. Save and label them clearly. One good way is to use the project's name and code or number, plus the step in the writing process, as, for example, "Mkt. Rpt. Audience," "Mkt. Rpt. Strategy," "Mkt. Rpt. Outline. 1."

Let's Solve It!

Professional attitudes and good work habits contribute as much to successful writing as does a good prose style.

Problem: A Tunnel View of Audience and Purpose. You define your purpose narrowly: You have to complete a writing assignment someone else has imposed on you. And you don't think about an audience at all, or you simply envision a single reader — the person who made the assignment. There may even be confusion or possibly resentment about this reader: "I don't know what she expects!" "I have to write exactly what he wants!"

Solution. Writers, naturally enough, start out being egocentric. Merely expressing your own ideas or feelings in a personal writing style is hard enough. Ultimately, though, you must go beyond self-expression to communicating with others. As you write, try to see the difference between writing from your point of view and writing for an outside audience, between merely expressing your thoughts and influencing other people. Look at your work from two angles: yours and the readers'. You may know what you want to say, but your readers will not — unless you make the effort to put yourself in their shoes. Imagine an ideal audience and write to them.

---

[3]Diagram and concepts from Henry R. Harrington and Richard E. Walton, "The Warnier-Orr Diagram for Designing Essays," *Journal of Technical Writing and Communication*, Vol. 14.3 (1984): 196.

Problem: Slapdash Planning. You plunge into the rough draft after doing little or no planning. You go from paragraph to paragraph or point to point without formulating an overall writing strategy or plan of attack. You say this is the way you always write, but the result lacks clear structure and coherence. Readers complain that you wander about among the trees without ever giving them a view of the forest.

Solution. True, you may be a writer who has to write a freewheeling rough draft before you know what you want to say or where you are going. Your needs are discussed in Chapter 4. But more likely, you are an inexperienced writer who doesn't realize the value of planning before you write. Perhaps you are rushed and looking for shortcuts, or just plain lazy and wanting to avoid hard decisions. The solution is to pay attention to the various steps in the writing process and allocate your time accordingly. Set a series of small deadlines: for prewriting, for planning, for completing the rough draft, and so on. Be realistic, though: It is just as bad to spend too much time on a particular stage of the writing process as it is to spend too little. But if you allow enough time for the planning stage outlined in this chapter, writing the rough draft will go faster. And the results will be better.

Problem: Self-limiting Outlines. You compose outlines in complete sentences and find, when you come to write the rough draft, that you have nothing more to say. Writing seems to consist of merely adding transitional phrases to the outline. The resulting document is shallow, undeveloped, and general rather than specific.

Solution. Gather much more information than you think you will need on your topic. Investigate it in depth and don't be satisfied with superficialities; look for concrete examples and detailed evidence to support your ideas. Do much more prewriting. If you have twice as much material as you think you will need, you will be able to choose only the best. Finally, write item outlines rather than sentence ones, or try tree charts or the Warnier-Orr diagram. Use these planning aids to guide, rather than predetermine, the content of your writing.

Problem: Empty Outlines. You write item outlines, but each item is a broad abstraction or vague generality, and there are few subdivisions. The resulting document is, once again, shallow, undeveloped, and general.

Solution. Again, part of the solution is more investigation and more prewriting. In addition, make items in the outline concrete and specific: They should convey precise information. Do much more subdividing; consciously move in your outlining from broad generalities to semispecifics to concrete details. A tree chart or the Warnier-Orr diagram instead of the traditional outline may help you.

There are other outlining problems—disorganization, incorrect subordination, irrelevant or missing material—but these faults are usually easy to spot if enough effort has been put into planning. Self-limiting outlines and empty outlines, however, tend to be hidden problems; writers are often unaware of them.

Computer Writing Tips

Once you start writing on the computer, you want to safeguard your material. This is what the professionals do.

- Save your work frequently; every twenty minutes should be the rule. Then, if there is a power outage or the system crashes or you make a mistake, you will have lost comparatively little.
- Whether you save your files on a hard disk or a floppy disk, make a backup of your work on a floppy disk or tape. (If you make major changes in the original, remember to redo the backup.) Store this disk in a safe place and keep it write-protected when you are not actually using it. ("Write-protecting" a disk means that the information on the disk can't be changed or accidentally erased.)
- If you have trouble with a disk drive, immediately go to another machine with your work, if at all possible. Use an unimportant disk to troubleshoot on the drive that is acting up.
- Always print out your work at the end of a writing session. This is partly an insurance policy; if something should happen to your files or your disk, you still have the printed copy. But more important, the effect of printed words on paper is subtly different from electronic words on a screen. Get in the habit of reading your words on paper and making changes and corrections in pencil, as well as editing on screen.
- Keep a printout of completed work near you as you write or revise on the computer. Use this printed copy as a guide for the new work.

I've been using a word processor for only two months. I'm using it because the office manager came to me a while back and asked, "How'd you like a nice new electronic typewriter instead of this old clunker?" Well, I had seen a cheap Brand X dedicated word-processing system at a local stationery store for only $499—printer, monitor, keyboard, the works. So I said, "How much is the typewriter?" "About $500," she replied. That afternoon, I had the Brand X in my office. A real word processor, by golly. I was entering the computer age.

The first thing I found out is that you pay for simplicity. The Brand X is not simple. The Macintosh is simple. My friends have Macintoshes. They love them. I do not love the Brand X.

The second thing I found out is that, yes, I could compose simple letters and copy blocks quite easily and then print them out neatly.

The third thing I found out is that the printer won't do envelopes or mailing labels. And filling in forms? Forget it. Where's my typewriter?

After about a month of struggling, stumbling, cursing, and resisting the temptation to take the word processor to the dumpster, I made some progress. I learned how to make a data disk and to set up directories. I learned how to make templates. I learned how to move chunks of text around. (I'm still a little hazy when it comes to changing margins, though.)

But early on, I realized what a boon this machine is to copywriters. You can edit and reedit until you finally get your copy as right and tight as it can possibly be. You stare at that green screen and the best copy you ever wrote comes out. Because now you don't have to scribble and retype and cut and paste and use whiteout and correcting tape. *You don't have to be afraid to rewrite.*

Learning to use a word processor can only make you a better writer. If I can learn, anybody can learn. Even on a Brand X.

Bill Henry
Advertising Copywriter

Creating a Rough Draft on Screen

Writing step by step
Freewheeling
Coping with writer's block

When faced with writing a rough draft, how do you react?

For some writers, the rough draft is the whole writing process. They skip over the preliminary steps and immediately plunge into their draft as soon as they hit upon a topic. Completion of the draft signals the end of the writing project: They make a few revisions, type the final copy, and call it quits. For others, the rough draft looms as an enormous obstacle; they do everything to avoid starting on it—even to the point of spending huge chunks of time on research, prewriting, and planning. And still others find the rough draft a slow, painful, frustrating experience; they are never satisfied with what they write and cannot go on until they have perfected an individual sentence or paragraph. Their finger is always on the Delete key.

Some people, however, have no trouble writing reams and reams of rough draft: Words and ideas flow out in an uncontrolled, chaotic, and often repetitive stream. When these writers are finished, they have a lot of words—and some of them very good—but not a unified, coherent piece of writing. Their opposite numbers dutifully plod through a rough draft, methodically following their outline, item by item, but when they finish, they feel disappointed: Their work lacks creativity; there is no sense of discovery or spontaneity. Then there are the people paralyzed by writer's block; part way through their work they freeze and can't get going again.

Do you see yourself in any of these descriptions? Granted, they are extreme, but they are based on real people and they describe some of the real pitfalls and frustrations involved in writing a rough draft. The purpose of this chapter is to show you how to avoid these pitfalls by using the computer. You will find out how to transform the material developed in Chapters 2 and 3 into a good first draft; how to impose order and direction on your writing while also maintaining a sense of discovery and creativity—in short, how to make this step in the writing process a productive rather than a painful experience.

Analyzing Yourself as a Writer

Writers can be roughly categorized as either linear or recursive. Each group takes a different approach to writing rough drafts. Linear writers start at the beginning and proceed, step by step, until the end is reached. They write one sentence after the other; they complete one paragraph before going on to the next. They always write an introduction before starting the body of the essay or report. Everything is done in sequence. Such writers are likely to plan their work in detail before they start a draft and to follow an outline as they write.

Recursive writers, on the other hand, skip around as they write. They may start in the middle and work toward the end or toward the beginning. They may break off in the middle of a sentence or paragraph in order to work on some other part of the document. They like to shift words and sentences, or even whole paragraphs, around. Frequently they go back and add or change material. They, too, may do a lot of planning and outlining beforehand, but they are more likely than linear writers to discover their ideas and organizational scheme as they write.

Neither of these methods is better than the other. What is important is that you know what works best for you. Finding that out means doing some self-analysis as a writer, like completing the "Writer's Questionnaire" in Chapter 2 and experimenting with different writing techniques, such as those described below. These are grouped in two main sections: "Writing Step by Step" and "Freewheeling." The names should tell you that the first set of techniques will appeal more to linear writers and the second set to recursive writers. In fact, though, whichever you are, you will find suggestions to help you in both sections. These two sections are followed by a third, "Combining and Experimenting," which briefly offers advice for both kinds of writers.

Preparing to Write

Before you try the different techniques, however, prepare yourself for writing. Plan your time. For short, routine work, the rough draft may take only twenty or thirty minutes, but longer projects may require several sessions over a period of time. (Dissertations and books require months or even years of work.) For longer projects, write in the same place at the same time during every writing session. Try to write when you are at your peak efficiency and energy levels; some people are at their best in the morning, others in the afternoon or evening. Try to arrange your work and social schedules so that you will not be interrupted. Your productivity will go up if you establish a routine for writing.

As you write your rough draft, do only writing. Do not clean your computer, rearrange files on your disk, edit past work, look up material (not even the spelling of words), talk to other people, eat, or do anything else that distracts you from the task at hand, which is writing a rough draft.

Get out the printed copies of your prewriting and outline (if you did one) and keep them close at hand. Also call up these documents on the screen. The multiple-window feature on your word processor allows you to scroll through your prewriting and use your outline as a guide when you write the rough draft. You can also copy material from both documents and move it into your rough draft. And if you need to modify your outline or your thesis in light of new developments in your rough draft, you can easily do that as well.

If you have an outliner with two-way viewing, make a copy of your outline; you may want to review the original at some later point in the writing process. Then open one of the copies and set it up so that you can look at your document in two modes: text and outline.

Whether you are using a simple word-processing program or a powerful outliner/word-processing/graphics combination, be prepared to adapt the following suggestions to the capabilities of your particular computer and software, your personal writing style, and the requirements of the particular writing project.

Writing Step by Step

The following methods of writing facilitate the orderly development of a rough draft; you progress logically from point to point or develop your document section by section. Using the computer rather than pen and paper makes this process easier and more creative and, at the same time, more organized and efficient.

The Bold Thesis

Call up a new document and write your provisional thesis statement in bold across the top of the document. Use the split-screen capability of your word processor to keep this statement in view as you write your rough draft. It should remind you of exactly what it is that you are trying to convey to your readers. If your ideas change as you write the rough draft, revise the thesis statement to reflect that change. You may also want to include a brief statement of purpose next to your thesis statement. Writers sometimes flounder about trying to write a rough draft because they lose sight of their basic purpose. Having it visually before you will act as a powerful guide to your writing.

Your outline will guide you, too, but don't follow it slavishly. Make writing an interactive process, moving between outline and draft on the screen and adding, modifying, and deleting as your document grows and begins to take shape. (An outline program with two-way viewing will do this automatically, but be sure you periodically compare your growing text to the organized structure of the outline.)

The Disappearing Outline

Make a copy of your outline and open it as a new document. Position the cursor after each item or sentence and add more material; make it grow. If it is an item outline, change words or phrases into complete sentences; if it is a sentence outline, expand

and polish the sentences. Go into more detail. Explain and clarify the supporting material. Bring in examples and details. Perhaps you will get new ideas or can explore your original ones in more depth. As you keep adding and refining, start to close up indentions and delete the outline numbers; paragraphs will begin to emerge. The outline is slowly disappearing, and a rough draft is taking its place. (If you want to check your growing draft against the original outline, remember that you have a second copy of the outline on your disk.)

Section by Section

This approach is especially helpful for people who use top-down design. Start by writing your thesis and purpose in bold at the top of a new document, then write a list of headings, also in bold, for various sections of your projected work. Your organized prewriting, outline, or Warnier-Orr diagram should suggest appropriate headings. Make each one brief but descriptive. Now position the cursor under the heading you feel most confident about and start writing. (Each section will probably be at least two paragraphs long.) When you have finished all that you have to say about that section for the present, move on to the next one. Use the split screen to keep your thesis and purpose always in view so that your writing doesn't become disjointed. When you have written something under each heading, your rough draft is completed.

If the writing project is a report of some kind, you will want to keep the headings, although they may have to be revised. (See Chapter 8 for a discussion of headings.) For other types of writing, you might change the headings into transitional sentences or topic sentences, or you can simply delete them. (See Chapter 5 for a discussion of topic sentences and transitions.)

Scratch Outline to Topic Sentences

This is a variation of the preceding technique. Copy your scratch outline into a new document. Position the cursor at the top and write an introduction that leads into the thesis statement. Then move the cursor to the first point in the outline and transform it into a *topic sentence* that will govern the next paragraph. Now write a paragraph that explains, clarifies, supports, or illustrates the topic sentence. Continue to change the points in the outline into topic sentences and to write supporting paragraphs until the rough draft is completed. If the document is long enough, you might want to transform the points into *block topic sentences* that govern a group of related paragraphs. (Chapter 5 discusses topic sentences and block topic sentences in detail.)

Strategy Guide

In the planning stage you may have decided on a method of development that determines the organization of your work and hence makes writing a rough draft a fairly straightforward task.

- If you have chosen a *process*—how something is made, how something operates, or how some result is obtained—start with the first step or procedure and then discuss each of the succeeding steps in turn. You are never at a loss for what to say next; you merely discuss the next step.
- If you have chosen *comparison/contrast,* you can choose one of two basic methods. In the first, divide your thesis into two statements, one about topic A and the other about topic B. Position the cursor under the first statement and write about topic A; do the same for topic B, and from time to time refer back to topic A. The two sections of the document should be roughly parallel in content and structure. Later you will insert a pivotal sentence or paragraph where you turn from topic A to topic B.

   In the second method, make a list of categories, and under each category, compare the two topics, contrast them, or do both. Moving back and forth between topics can become mechanical, however, if you are not careful. In fact, most comparisons and contrasts use a combination of the two methods described above.
- If you have chosen *classification,* write the thesis statement in bold and then make a list (also in bold) of the categories or types (or kinds or groups) in your classification scheme. Position the cursor after each item and write one or more paragraphs about it. Later you can delete the category names and make sure there are smooth and logical transitions, or bridges, between paragraphs.

All these techniques for writing rough drafts depend heavily on the planning decisions you made earlier. With the exception of the bold thesis, which is more or less the traditional way of writing a rough draft, all consist of ways to break the overwhelming task of writing a long document into a series of smaller, more easily written subtasks. Thus you are not making the enormous psychological commitment of writing a complete draft. Rather, you have the much easier task of writing one or two paragraphs or a short section or two. Because adding, deleting, and moving are so easy on a computer, you can eventually shape these sections into a unified whole. But that comes later, in the revision stage of the writing process.

Linear Perfection

The small number of successful linear writers have their own special way of writing a rough draft. They labor over each sentence until it is perfect, and only then do they go to the next one. Their rough drafts take an extremely long time but need little revision, because they have already made so many painstaking corrections and improvements. I don't recommend this perfectionist approach unless it truly works for you. The vast majority of writers who try to create, revise, and perfect all at the same time usually short-circuit the writing process for themselves and often end up with writer's block. And even if you are a successful linear perfectionist—a rare breed in my experience!—I still urge you to experiment with other approaches. You might surprise yourself by finding an easier, more satisfying method of writing.

Freewheeling

Perhaps the orderly, step-by-step development of a rough draft stifles the free flow of your ideas; you need a less structured method. The computer can be a liberating tool for writers like you, because it encourages the use of experimental approaches such as the following.

Converting Prewriting

Certain types of prewriting can easily be converted on screen to a rough draft. If, for example, you used the devil's advocate technique to generate material for an argumentative piece, you may have found yourself getting deeply involved in the dialogue, with your refutation of opponents' arguments getting longer and more detailed and your writing voice more emphatic. Call up this prewriting and expand it. Turn opponents' arguments into rhetorical statements—for example, "Opponents may claim that _____, but this is nonsense." Strengthen your refutation; provide supporting evidence; arrange material in the best order. What started out as prewriting is soon converted into a rough draft.

Provocative questions can also be turned into a rough draft. Arrange the questions in the best order, adding new questions if necessary. Transform the notes under each question into fully developed answers. Use material in the questions for transitional statements or topic sentences, or turn the questions into journalistic headings.

If you are a highly visual writer and create graphics before you start on the text, copy the graphics into a word-processing document on screen and start your rough draft by explaining what these graphics depict, describing the concepts behind them, and analyzing their significance. The illustrations, diagrams, graphs, or charts on the screen will provide material for your text. And once you have this much written, the rest will follow logically.

Starting in the Middle

There is no reason you absolutely must start at the beginning. Plunge into the middle of things and start at the point where you have the most to say or feel most strongly. Write as much as you can, then skip to some other part of the document and write about that. Move around within the document as you get new ideas. You may want to label the various parts; write a brief description in bold and place it in brackets. Or write a longer comment, a note to yourself, about what you are trying to do at this particular point and how it fits into the total scheme of the paper. As the draft progresses, move individual sections of text around until you find the right order for them; also provide smooth and logical transitions or bridge passages. Your notes will guide you. Eventually, of course, you will delete these notes; writing them in bold merely makes them easy to spot.

In sophisticated word-processing programs, comments like these can be embedded in "hidden text." (This feature is briefly discussed in Chapter 3, p. 53.) You can make this text visible while you are writing and invisible when you print a copy of your draft. Or you can do the reverse, making the embedded text invisible while you write but visible when the document is printed. Some writers like to open their document in two different windows and make their embedded comments visible in one but invisible in the other. In any option you choose, hidden text allows you to annotate your draft. Thus you can clearly see your thoughts about your text, as well as the text itself.

Your purpose, and even your thesis, may be clear to you before you start this freewheeling draft; if so, write them in bold at the top of your document and use the split screen to keep them in view. On the other hand, you may not be able to see your thesis clearly at first; for you, writing is a means of discovering and clarifying ideas. In that case, don't compose the introduction and thesis statement until after you have finished the rough draft.

Writing Out Loud

For many people, writing is difficult because it seems so different from talking. They can easily express their ideas when they are conversing with someone, but when they start to write, they suddenly become stiff, inarticulate, hesitant—the writing equivalent of tongue-tied. The trick here is to write as if you were talking, to write out loud. Vividly imagine yourself communicating face to face with your intended audience. Think carefully of the arguments, the evidence, the examples that would move them. Now tell them all this material. Imagine your tone of voice, your words, your gestures as you talk to them. Mentally listen to your speech—and write it down. Simply transcribe the speech in your head to the screen on the computer. If you are distracted by the appearance of words, dim the screen and concentrate on listening to your mental speech. Some writers actually talk out loud as they compose on the computer. (This is what I do, but only in the privacy of my office!) Others talk into a tape recorder and later transcribe their words from tape to computer.

Outlining After the Fact

If you are the type of writer for whom words simply pour out in a copious but disorganized stream, let the computer help you. With a computer you can type as fast as your words flow; nothing needs to get lost. And no matter how rough the first draft, the computer enables you to revise and reorganize it. But before you start to revise, make an outline—an ex post facto, or "after the fact," outline. Open a second window and write the outline there as you scroll through the draft in the first window, or print out the draft and work from the paper copy. In either case, outline exactly what is in the draft, in the precise order as it appears; don't reorganize, add, or delete yet.

When you are finished, print a copy of the outline and study it carefully. It should reveal, in concise and graphic form, all the disorganization, repetition, imbalance, logical gaps, and missing material of the draft. Now revise the outline carefully, making it as taut and logical and complete as possible. If necessary, reformulate your thesis or conclusion or both. Then, using the revised outline as a guide, thoroughly rewrite the rough draft. Reorganize blocks of text, delete repetitious or irrelevant material, and fill in gaps with additional ideas and evidence.

If you use an outliner with two-way viewing, the procedure is somewhat different. First, make a copy of your rough draft before changing its outline; you may want to compare the changes with the original version. Also print out copies of both the draft and the outline; you need to be able to review the full sweep of your work in printed form. Then critique the outline carefully, as described above. As you revise on screen, your text will reflect changes made in your outline, but don't be fooled by the neatness of your work. The computer may automatically number and indent for you, but that doesn't mean your outline is logical, balanced, or well developed. Only you can provide those qualities.

Combining and Experimenting

The techniques discussed above are only some of the ways to write a rough draft. Experiment with them, devising your own variations or combining techniques. For example, you might start with a freewheeling rough draft, but halfway through you stop, consider where you are going, and formulate an outline for the remaining material. From here on you write the traditional, fairly well-organized rough draft. This is my method. Of course, at the end you have to go back to the freewheeling first half and thoroughly revise it from top to bottom.

Whatever method you use, consider the draft as something fluid and changing. Don't hesitate to experiment as you write it. If you aren't sure of the exact word you want to use or the precise idea you are trying to articulate, try several alternatives and leave them in the text. With the computer you can easily delete unwanted material later. (Putting alternatives in bold will make them highly visible when you start editing, or you can use hidden text.) If you can't think of something, type in a string of bold question marks and get on to the material you do know. Fill in blank areas later. And don't get bogged down in petty details of spelling, punctuation, and grammar, what writing instructors call "mechanics." Spell-checking programs will help you take care of the former; the latter you can flag by typing an asterisk or other symbol next to them. Later, when you are revising, use the search function to find and correct all the flagged problems.

The sheer task of typing the rough draft can also inhibit creativity and thought. Let the computer help you here, too. If you want to repeat a phrase, sentence, or paragraph, copy it with the computer rather than retyping it. Some word processors have special files called glossaries that are particularly helpful if you must do long stretches of routine writing (what is colorfully known as "boiler plate"). You can store these passages in glossaries and assign them distinctive abbreviations. When you write, merely type the appropriate abbreviation plus the glossary command (usually a few keystrokes) and the full passage will appear. You can then modify it to suit the circumstances. Glossaries also eliminate typing long technical terms or names of books or authors over and over again; instead, you type only a short abbreviation and a command.

Remember: Your main task is to write, to let your ideas flow from your mind to your fingertips. Exploit the power of the computer so that you don't get bogged down by routine drudgery.

Locating the Thesis Statement

Whether a freewheeling or step-by-step writer, sooner or later you have to decide where to put your thesis statement. When you write an outline, it is conventional to put the thesis statement at the very beginning. When you write a rough draft, however, you may decide to locate it at the beginning of your document, at the end, or in the middle. Each of these locations has advantages.

The beginning of your document receives the most attention. Putting the thesis there tells your readers immediately where you are going and also keeps you on track as you write. A thesis statement at the beginning projects an air of authority; you announce what you are going to prove, illustrate, or explain. Such a location suggests that you will start with a general statement and move to specific support or proof.

Putting the thesis statement at the end, however, can be effective, too. The end is a memorable position; what is said here makes a final impression on readers. Such a location implies that you will start with particulars and end with general conclusions; your writing strategy will involve discovery or revelation.

Theoretically, the thesis statement can also be located in the middle of a piece of writing, but there is a strong likelihood it will get lost there. The exception is the document that makes a dramatic change in direction halfway through—a comparison/contrast piece, for example, in which you finish with topic A and turn to topic B, or a problem/solution piece, in which you define the problem, then turn to a solution. In these cases, you may decide to split your thesis statement, putting part of it at the beginning and the rest at the pivotal point where you make the change.

Finally, using a journalistic technique, you can make your title your thesis statement: "Commercial TV: A Wasteland in Need of Creativity."

If you are a step-by-step, linear writer, all the planning and strategy decisions you made before starting on your rough draft may dictate precisely where your thesis statement goes. If you are the freewheeling, recursive type, you may not know what your thesis is, let alone where it goes, until after you have finished your rough draft. But no matter what your writing method, the final placement of the thesis statement deserves careful consideration. This is the point where you give readers your message; this is why you are writing to them. Emphasize your main idea, show it off to advantage, by locating it where it gets the most attention and works most effectively with your overall writing strategy.

Coping with Writer's Block

But what if you can't write? Almost every writer, from rank amateur to prizewinning professional, encounters a momentary block now and then, and a few writers face agonizing paralysis. The experience is frustrating, even frightening, but it's not fatal. You can overcome writer's block if you know how to go about it, and the computer will help.

Momentary Blocks

Often writers have trouble getting started at the beginning of a writing session. To prevent this, professionals recommend breaking off in the middle of a sentence or paragraph when you finish your writing session, so that when you start again you have something definite to finish saying. By the time you complete the old idea, you will be warmed up and ready to start on new material. Another technique is writing an agenda for the next day: When you finish one session, write a short list of topics you want to cover or issues you want to explore next. Keep the list at the top of the screen when you start writing again and let it guide you. Delete the list when you are finished.

Some writers find that their minds keep working even after they have finished a writing session; problems that seemed hard to solve on the screen suddenly become clear. The telling phrase, the clinching argument, the graphic example suddenly occurs to them when they are away from their computer. If you are a savvy writer, you will keep a notebook or a sheet of paper handy for jotting down these sudden inspirations. Otherwise, you are likely to forget them under the pressure of other activities. When you write again, these notes will help you get started and overcome any momentary block you might have.

Also try correcting or even rewriting the last paragraph you wrote before tackling new material. Strictly limit the amount of time you spend on this kind of revision to ten or fifteen minutes. Or try some warm-up writing: free association, a dialogue with the computer, a journal entry, a bit of creative writing (that song or poem you always wanted to write but never dared). Again, strictly limit the time spent on these techniques; if misused, they can become a form of procrastination.

If you get stuck because you can't put your ideas into words, ask yourself, What am I trying to say here? Answer your question as simply and directly as possible, using one sentence or two at the most. Say the answer out loud if that helps. Now type this answer on your screen. It may not be elegantly phrased, but you can change that later. At this point all you want is a clear and specific statement. Elaborate this statement and give some examples. Articulating clearly what it is you are trying to say will probably break up the temporary block.

A variation of this technique is writing a note to yourself. Stop struggling futilely with your text and type "What I really want to say here is . . ." Now describe what you would say if only you didn't have such a block. If you feel more comfortable having a personal audience, write this note as a letter: "Dear X, What I would like to tell you is . . ." Describe your ideas; tell the person what you would like to make clear; explain why it is important. If you think the person will have any objections, meet those objections head-on. Keep writing this letter for as long as you have something to say. This technique works well because, pyschologically, you are not committing yourself to the difficult task of writing a paper or report or article. Rather, you are doing a much easier job, writing a letter—a letter, moreover, that merely explains what you would do if only you could. You will soon find yourself writing more and more as the fiction of the letter fades into the background and you go back to writing the original document. The computer will enable you to make the necessary changes easily to integrate this patch of writing into your formal text.

Free writing can also help you over a momentary block. Stop worrying about writing a well-constructed, coherent exposition of the point in question and start brainstorming. Position the cursor at the trouble spot and write whatever comes into your head. Focus on the point in question, yes, but let your thoughts run freely. Don't stop to criticize, evaluate, organize, or even write in complete sentences. More formal writing will start to flow eventually, and your block will be over. Later you can come back and revise the free writing, deleting the dross and saving the gold.

Persistent Blocks

Unfortunately, not all writing blocks are momentary. Some linger so long that they seriously impair people's ability to write. But even the worst blocks can be overcome if you identify your real problem and actively try to solve it.

Start by doing some self-diagnosis. Write down everything about writing that you find hard. Be completely honest with yourself—and extremely detailed: Jot down the little items as well as the big. Then classify these under broad headings. A finished list might look like this:

- Priorities
    Can always think of "better things to do"
    Writing too time-consuming
        Job endless; my writing is never good enough
        I get stuck, and project takes longer than I planned

- Negative Feelings
    I worry about how writing will be judged: Will it be accepted?
    Feel intimidated by other people's work; I have to compete
    I can't live up to my own perfectionism

- Negative Behaviors
    Can't get started
    I lose confidence, throw work away and begin again and again

■ Outside Constraints or Conditions
　Deadlines and word limits
　Poor writing environment
　　Noisy
　　Interruptions
　I'm under pressure from higher-ups

Everyone has different difficulties; your job is to identify your own. Once you have done that, you can systematically try to do something about them. Change what you can and learn to cope with what you can't. You may not be able to change the deadline for a writing project, but you can learn how to meet deadlines in a less stressful way. If lack of privacy and noise are your problems, you may be able to change your environment to make it more conducive to writing.

Over the years, as I have written books and articles myself, and as I have talked to other writers and would-be writers, I have found that problems causing writer's block tend to fall into typical patterns. But these patterns can be changed. See if you find yourself in one of the descriptions below—and see if the advice I give doesn't break up your block.

Some people dread writing because the sheer magnitude of the project, the effort that it will require, and the deadline that has to be met loom as huge obstacles. They don't know where to start and consequently feel paralyzed. Writing, however, is a process composed of many steps. Writers who at first feel overwhelmed by a writing project generally do well when they concentrate on one of these steps at a time. Each step is a relatively small task, and small tasks can be accomplished. Don't look at everything you have to do and think it all has to be done at once; break it into steps and take one at a time. Establishing a schedule for the project and setting deadlines also help.

Other people get writer's block because they remain wedded to nonproductive writing methods. That is why it is so important to analyze your present methods and to experiment with new ones. Find out what works best for you. For example, you might be convinced you have to write an introduction and thesis statement before going on, even though you always get stuck at this point. To overcome this difficulty, plunge into the middle of things right away and compose an introduction later. Or you might be the kind of writer who scoffs at writing outlines and always opts for freewheeling rough drafts even though you soon get bogged down because you don't know what topic to deal with next. In this case, planning and outlining techniques will probably overcome your block. Experiment.

Another kind of writing block occurs because of a lack of self-confidence. You are afraid your work will be torn apart, so your psyche conveniently sets up a writer's block to protect you from the pain of criticism: If you don't write anything, it can't be criticized. What helps here is becoming more confident about your ability to write. This book should get rid of any notion you have that writing depends on inspiration or that only specially gifted people can write. Writing is a skill and, like other skills, can be learned. Think of a skill—in sports, for example, or in computing—that you have learned. How did you learn it? Try to make an analogy with writing; if you have learned one skill, you can learn another. You may never become a prizewinning author, but you can learn to be a competent one. Keep reminding yourself of this fact.

Following the steps in this book—especially defining your purpose, envisioning an audience, and prewriting about your topic—should prove to you that you have a lot to say and a definite purpose in saying it. This knowledge will give you confidence. Planning carefully means that you won't be at a loss for what to say next; simply consult your outline or Warnier-Orr diagram and write about the next topic. This, too, will give you confidence. And because you are writing on a computer, you don't have to be afraid about writing something weak or silly or wrong. Changing or deleting is so easy that you can afford to make mistakes. You need not feel inhibited.

But don't let the ease of deleting lure you into yet another kind of block: You get partway through a writing project and suddenly decide your work is no good. Your enthusiasm evaporates. So you reach for the Delete key again and again. Whole paragraphs, even pages, get written and then deleted; you do the electronic equivalent of crumpling up sheet after sheet of scratch paper. Nothing gets finished. Perhaps this block should be called "failure of nerve" or "loss of artistic vision"—you lose faith in the validity of your writing project. The best advice is to keep going. Remember that all projects have enthusiasm curves and it is normal to hit bottom at some point. Finish the document, even though you are convinced it is no good, and then let it sit for a few hours or even days. When you come back, you will be pleasantly surprised by all its good qualities. Encouragement from a mentor is often helpful at this point, but the main thing is, don't give up! Complete the project before you judge it.

Don't try to be perfect and then feel hurt and frustrated when you fail. Your work will never be perfect. The work of even accomplished writers is imperfect. As some-one has said, "A work of art is never finished, it is merely abandoned." So think of your writing as always in a state of becoming. If it starts out poor, it can be revised and made better; if it starts out good, it still can be revised and made very good. The basis of the writing process is working on successive drafts and slowly improving them.

Some writers freeze because they try to do too much at once: They try to think of ideas, plan organization and strategy, write a rough draft, and edit for style—all simultaneously. This is difficult if not impossible. These steps use different skills, and sometimes you have to complete one step before going on to the next. For most of us, writing comes more easily if we do these steps separately. In particular, don't try to edit as you write. You will quickly cut off the flow of ideas if you keep rejecting words and sentences as not good enough. In the beginning, simply write. Form and content may be rough, but don't criticize. And don't revise. Those are separate steps that you will turn to later.

You may also have to change your attitude about writing. Look at writing as a job like any other job; you must sit down at your computer and do it. Although you may not be in the mood, you aren't "inspired," you still have an obligation—to yourself, to your instructor, to your colleagues, to your employer, to your editor—to get the job done. Setting up a routine, making a schedule for the writing project, arranging your environment so you have the minimum of distractions—these will help you to approach writing as a job. And when you write, try to concentrate wholeheartedly on writing; exclude other worries and concerns from your mind. Admittedly, this advice is easier to give than to follow; it requires self-discipline. But then writing is a job that requires self-discipline.

Let's Solve It!

Writers sometimes lose sight of their goal when they work on rough drafts. Here's how to stay on track.

Problem: Correcting Typos Instead of Writing. Even though you save major revisions for a later stage of the writing process, your rough draft still proceeds slowly because you constantly stop to correct typos, spelling errors, and punctuation errors. Your thoughts race ahead, but your writing bogs down.

Solution. Discipline yourself to ignore little mistakes. As long as ideas are coming freely, don't interrupt them or lose your train of thought by stopping to make corrections, even minor ones. If the urge to perform "micro-editing" becomes too strong, simply remove the source of temptation: Dim the light on the screen so you can't see the words while you type. Constantly making minor corrections can become a form of procrastination.

Problem: Drifting Off the Topic. You start out with a clear enough thesis and outline and keep these in view as you write, but even so, your work loses its focus. The finished draft rambles, or it doesn't say what you want it to.

Solution. After you finish the draft, let it sit—for a few hours or even days. Then look at it with fresh eyes. Review your planning notes and compare them with your draft. What did you want to say? What does your draft actually say? Outline the draft; write notes in the margins. Compare these with the original outline. Where did you lose your train of thought? Did you leave out material or add irrelevant or trivial material? Did you go off on a tangent? After you answer these and similar questions, rewrite the draft. Chapter 6 will give you help.

Problem: Running Out of Ideas. Midway through the project you run out of things to say. You find yourself counting words after each paragraph to see if you can quit yet. You start inflating your sentences with extra words to pad out your writing. In desperation, you consider setting unusually wide margins and even printing the text triple spaced.

Solution. Gather more information about your topic and do much more prewriting, twice as much as you think you will need. (Undoubtedly you have underestimated the amount of brainwork needed for this project.) Add more examples. Go into the subject more deeply; don't be satisfied with a superficial, obvious treatment. Use analysis/classification, breaking down large elements into their component parts and investigating the relationship among the parts. Classify your material into groups, categories, kinds, or types. Be concrete and specific as well as abstract and general.

Problem: Writing Far Too Much. A one-page memo becomes three pages; a 750-word paper or article grows to 2000 words. You want to say everything possible about the topic, or you fall in love with your own words and refuse to delete them, or your style is wordy and diffuse.

Solution. Remember your readers and the demands on their time; write to meet their needs. They are not interested in a definitive treatment of the topic, nor are you required to provide one. Discuss what is most important, and don't repeat yourself. Ruthlessly cut out even striking or beautiful passages if they are not absolutely necessary and to the point. When your project has a length limit—and most projects do—use a word counter to keep track of the number of words you have used. Study one of the masters of conciseness like Ernest Hemingway or John Steinbeck. And consult Chapter 6 of this book for tips on curbing a diffuse style.

Computer Writing Tips

Be sure that your word-processing skills keep pace with your writing skills.

- Just because you are becoming a proficient computer writer, don't ignore the most elementary rule of all: Save frequently, every twenty minutes. In addition, make a habit of saving whenever you pause in writing your rough draft or are interrupted by a telephone call or visitor. Never leave your computer, even for a few minutes, without saving.

- At the end of your document, create two headings: "Wastebasket" and "File for Future Reference." Under "Wastebasket," put any substantial material (phrases, sentences, paragraphs) that you decide to delete from your draft. Later, you may want to use such material after all. Under "File for Future Reference," jot down any bright ideas and sudden flashes of inspiration that can be used later in the draft. Insert a page break to separate this material from the main text. (You can also open another window for such notes, or you can write them in an electronic notebook if your computer has this feature.)

- If you are going to *write* on a computer, in contrast to entering data mechanically, you should be able to type fairly quickly and confidently, so that your fingers keep up with your ideas. Improve rusty typing skills with a computer typing tutorial; if you are a poor typist, you will find yourself rapidly becoming a competent one. (And note that as more and more people use the computer, the word "keyboarding" is starting to replace the word "typing.")

- If you are a good typist already, learn to use all the shortcuts and exploit all the capabilities of your word-processing program. Review the user's manual from time to time; you always pick up tidbits of information you skipped earlier. Also read computer magazines; articles and letters to the editor give helpful hints. Talk to others who use your program, or join a user club or invest in a book that explains the program to novices. Ideally, a word processor should become transparent, so that you are not conscious of a barrier between your ideas and the moving words on the screen. You should feel confident about drawing on all the enormous power the computer has put at your disposal.

I was asked to contribute an autobiographical piece for a reference book on contemporary authors, and at the same time I got an idea for a children's book. I suddenly realized I didn't have time for both. So I bought a computer on Friday, and by Monday I was able to use it—the typewriter part, at any rate. I was so fascinated by the machine that I finished the manuscript in six weeks, though I had promised it to the publisher in four months!

A computer is an absolutely wonderful tool, but like everything else, it has to be used intelligently. I always start by writing the first draft on the computer. Then I print out a draft and scribble all over it with a pencil.

Once I have the beginning, I write a certain number of pages each day, then read them the next day on the screen and add some more. And as I read, I edit on screen. The first time round is the messy time. I keep going over and over my work; I must read a piece fifty to a hundred times before it sees the light of day.

When I come to the end of a chapter, I print it all out and then there is more scribbling. I write all over it. I find that with the computer, I have a much cleaner first draft—often only one, though sometimes I have to do a second printing. At first I thought I could go from the screen to the finished copy, but you can repeat yourself if you don't print your work and read it. You'll get some word or phrase stuck in your subconscious and keep using it as you write.

I've learned computer tricks, too. In one novel, I wanted to change a character's name from "Martin" to "Michael," so I just used the "find and change all" command. I like being able to search forward and backward. Sometimes I find a page by remembering an unusual word I've written and locating that. With a computer, all the physical pain and labor has gone out of writing. I do a lot more now.

Eilís Dillon
Novelist

The Electronic Art of Building Paragraphs

Building paragraphs
Writing introductions
Writing conclusions

Today we take paragraphing for granted, but it wasn't always used. Medieval manuscripts simply ran text together in one unbroken flow. Eventually, scribes in monasteries began making a line or penstroke in the margin to signal the beginning of a new section or idea. This habit of making marks next to the text gave us the word "paragraph"—from the Greek *para-*, "beside," and *graph*, "to write." Since the coming of the printing press, visual signals to indicate the start of a new thought or paragraph have taken the form of blank space: indention of the first line of each new paragraph or an extra line between paragraphs.

No matter what they look like, paragraphs are a convenience to both readers and writers. They reflect our need to divide long works into smaller parts and to present material in logical, easily digested units. For example, we divide a long work like an encyclopedia into volumes, a book into chapters, a chapter into sections, and sections into paragraphs. Or you can look at paragraphs another way: They are the building blocks used to construct the whole edifice. Each block is carefully structured—that is, each paragraph develops and supports a main idea; follows a plan of organization; and has a beginning, a middle, and an end. When properly arranged and combined, the individual blocks form a unified whole, the complete document.

Computers have given writers new power and more options when it comes to paragraphing. In fact, one of the first things people praise about word processors is their ability to move whole paragraphs quickly and easily. This ability means that you can truly build a document, block by block, from the ground floor up. You carefully construct paragraphs on screen and move them around until you find the most logical and effective order for them. If you are the kind of writer who dashes off a freewheeling draft, the computer lets you rearrange individual sentences and virtually carve out and mold paragraphs from a mass of unstructured words. Once paragraphs are constructed, the computer allows you to format them in a variety of ways.

The computer also helps you to analyze the inner workings of your paragraphs, that is, to take them apart physically and see what makes them work or not work in your piece of writing. This chapter begins with an analysis of a paragraph from Charles Darwin's *Autobiography* and then goes on to discuss the hallmarks of all good paragraphs—unity, completeness, and coherence.

Putting a Paragraph Together

Type the following sentences on your computer screen and move them around until they form a well-organized paragraph that describes a favorite activity of Darwin when he was a student at Cambridge University. Keep the original scrambled list of sentences in view while you reconstruct the paragraph.

1. It was the mere passion for collecting, for I did not dissect them, and rarely compared their external characters with published descriptions, but got them named anyhow.
2. I was forced to spit the beetle out, which was lost, as was the third one.
3. Then I saw a third and new kind, which I could not bear to lose, so that I popped the one which I held in my right hand into my mouth.
4. But no pursuit at Cambridge was followed with nearly so much eagerness or gave me so much pleasure as collecting beetles.
5. I will give a proof of my zeal.
6. Alas! It ejected some intensely acrid fluid, which burnt my tongue.
7. One day, on tearing off some old bark, I saw two rare beetles, and seized one in each hand.

When you are finished with your reconstruction, look at the answer at the bottom of the page. Does your paragraph match Darwin's?

How did you decide which sentences to put where? What clues did you find in the original list? Analyze your decision making by going back to the individual sentences and highlighting the clues you found. (Use bold or underlining.)

First you probably looked for the general topic of the paragraph and found it in sentence 4 — "collecting beetles." Moreover, this is an activity Darwin enjoyed above all others — "But no pursuit... was followed with nearly so much eagerness or gave me so much pleasure." The word "but" signals that sentence 4 is a transitional, or *bridge*, sentence, and we can reasonably assume that paragraphs immediately preceding this one described other pursuits Darwin enjoyed at the university.

The theme of enjoyment is defined more specifically in sentence 1 — it is a "mere passion for collecting." Then Darwin announces he will give an example of what he means — "I will give a proof of my zeal" (sentence 5). The structure of the paragraph is now clear: main idea, definition of idea, example illustrating definition. But note that

(4) **But no pursuit at Cambridge was followed with nearly so much eagerness or gave me so much pleasure as collecting beetles.** (1) It was the mere passion for collecting, for I did not dissect them, and rarely compared their external characters with published descriptions, but got them named anyhow. (5) I will give a proof of my zeal. (7) One day, on tearing off some old bark, I saw two rare beetles, and seized one in each hand. (3) Then I saw a third and new kind, which I could not bear to lose, so that I popped the one which I held in my right hand into my mouth. (6) Alas! It ejected some intensely acrid fluid, which burnt my tongue. (2) I was forced to spit the beetle out, which was lost, as was the third one.

Darwin's language also links the first three sentences together—"so much eager-ness," "so much pleasure," "passion," and "zeal" all are variations of the same theme.

As you looked for organizational clues in the remaining sentences, you undoubt-edly noticed that Darwin tells a chronological anecdote, so you looked for time signals, words like "one day" and "then" or numbers like "two rare beetles" and "a third and new kind." But more important, you looked for logical order in the narrative, a buildup to the climactic moment—"Alas! It ejected some intensely acrid fluid, which burnt my tongue"—and the final result—"I was forced to spit the beetle out, which was lost, as was the third one." The last sentence (2 in the original list) brings the anecdote to a close and gives the reader a sense of completion. But also notice the subtle language links that give the reader a sense of continuity: The pronouns "one" and "it" and the demonstrative adjective "which" all refer back to the beetles Darwin has been collect-ing; he cannot "bear to lose" the third beetle, but in the end, two of them are "lost."

Try this experiment on one of your own paragraphs: Break it down into a scrambled list of individual sentences and see if you (or a willing friend) can recon-struct it. Look for clues that signal the main idea, a logical plan of organization, and a method of development; try to find language links that provide continuity and direction.

Conveying the Main Idea: Paragraph Unity

Think of a paragraph as a miniature composition or document. Like any piece of good writing, the paragraph has unity; it is about a central, unifying idea. This idea is ex-pressed in a specific statement, the *topic sentence,* which is the equivalent of the thesis statement. The topic sentence may be preceded by a brief introduction (perhaps one to three sentences), or it may be followed by one or two sentences or clauses that clarify or limit the central idea. All the other sentences in the paragraph support, expand, prove, illustrate, or explain the idea expressed by the topic sentence.

In the following paragraph from her book *The White Album,* Joan Didion describes the power of Hoover Dam to haunt her imagination. The topic sentence states this idea; all the other sentences elaborate it, either by describing the dam or giving exam-ples of its sudden intrusion into Didion's mind. (Note that the topic sentence is under-lined; throughout this chapter, underlining, italics, and bold are used to emphasize elements in quoted passages.)

> Since the afternoon in 1967 when I first saw Hoover Dam, its image has never been entirely absent from my inner eye. I will be talking to some-one in Los Angeles, say, or New York, and suddenly the dam will material-ize, its pristine concave face gleaming white against the harsh rusts and

taupes and mauves of that rock canyon hundreds or thousands of miles from where I am. I will be driving down Sunset Boulevard, or about to enter a freeway, and abruptly those power transmission towers will appear before me, canted vertiginously over the tailrace. Sometimes I am confronted by the intakes and sometimes by the shadow of the heavy cable that spans the canyon and sometimes by the ominous outlets to unused spillways, black in the lunar clarity of the desert light. Quite often I hear the turbines. Frequently I wonder what is happening at the dam this instant, at this precise intersection of time and space, how much water is being released to fill downstream orders and what lights are flashing and which generators are in full use and which just spinning free.

Although Didion makes the first sentence her topic sentence, a topic sentence can be placed at the beginning, middle, or end of a paragraph.

- You can announce immediately what you are going to talk about and follow through with supporting material.
- You can gradually introduce the main idea.
- You can lead the reader through details and evidence to a final discovery or conclusion at the end of the paragraph.

Call up a typical paragraph from one of your disk files and move the topic sentence to various locations within the paragraph. Which one is most effective? Some writers don't discover exactly what they want to say until they get to the end of the paragraph, but their readers may need more guidance at the beginning. If you fall into this category, try moving your last sentences to the beginning of your paragraphs.

You can omit a topic sentence altogether if the rest of the paragraph clearly and accurately implies your main idea. For example, the theme of a narrative or descriptive paragraph is frequently implied rather than spelled out, and a paragraph that describes a series of steps or stages in a process may simply have as the implied topic sentence "These are the next steps in the process." Nonetheless, you ought to be able to state this implied sentence in words; as you practice writing paragraphs, write any implied topic sentences in hidden text (if your word processor has that capability) or embed them in bold or capitals (to be removed before you print).

If your paragraphs lack unity, the reason is probably easy to pinpoint. You may include irrelevant material, information that is off the subject announced by the topic sentence. Or you may try to pack the paragraph with too many ideas and end up with a grab bag. Perhaps you jam two paragraphs together as one. In the worst case, you have no central idea at all; sentences simply ramble on, getting nowhere.

To avoid these problems, focus on one particular idea when you write a paragraph. Don't let your attention—or your readers'—wander. To keep your attention focused, underline your topic sentence. Everything else you say in the paragraph should be closely and directly related to the controlling idea of this sentence. Delete any extraneous material. Don't try to say too much in one place. Move any material on a different idea to a new paragraph.

Getting from Beginning to End: Paragraph Completeness

How long should a paragraph be? Long enough to do its job. It needs to satisfy the readers' need for supporting detail and evidence so that they have a sense of development and completeness. It must be short enough, though, to hold their attention; it can't drag on or be wordy and repetitious. Admittedly, these are vague guidelines that don't give you a specific word limit to follow. But in practice, you will find that readers have fairly specific expectations—depending on the type of document and its difficulty—for how long a paragraph should be. Thus, readers expect paragraphs in business writing to be relatively short; but in scholarly treatises involving difficult and abstract material, they expect paragraphs to be correspondingly longer.

Collect samples of the types of documents you write. How much information is included in a typical paragraph? How detailed is it? What is the extent of development? Count the words in several paragraphs. What is the average for a single paragraph? Then analyze typical paragraphs from your own writing. How do their length and complexity compare with the length and complexity of paragraphs in similar documents? The more practice you get in writing, the more accurately you will be able to meet readers' expectations about what constitutes a complete paragraph in a particular type of document.

Some computer style checkers count the number of sentences in your paragraphs and give you the count for the longest paragraph, the shortest paragraph, and the average paragraph. This should help you spot possible inconsistencies or problems in your paragraphing. But you still must base the length of paragraphs on readers' expectations and needs.

You will also find it easier to write complete paragraphs if you pay attention to the organizational plan and the method of development.

Organizational Plan

The particular organizational plan of a paragraph often gives you a natural way to gauge its completeness. Like organizational plans for the whole document, these fall into basic types, although there are many variations:

General to specific
Specific to general

Pivoting or zigzag
Spatial
Chronological
Climactic or anticlimactic

General to Specific. With this organizational plan, you announce the central idea at the beginning and then go on to support it with details and evidence. The paragraph is not complete until you have provided enough material to support the opening generalization. Alice Walker writes such a paragraph in "The Black Writer and the Southern Experience." (The main idea is underlined.)

What the black Southern writer inherits as a natural right is a sense of *community*. Something simple but surprisingly hard, especially these days, to come by. My mother, who is a walking history of our community, tells me that when each of her children was born the midwife accepted as payment such home-grown or homemade items as a pig, a quilt, jars of canned fruits and vegetables. But there was never any question that the midwife would come when she was needed, whatever the eventual payment for her services. I consider this each time I hear of a hospital that refuses to admit a woman in labor unless she can hand over a substantial sum of money, cash. (Alice Walker, *In Search of Our Mothers' Gardens*)

CREATING SPECIAL EFFECTS WITH PARAGRAPHS

A paragraph's length is sometimes determined by the effect it is designed to create.

Dialogue (conversation). The words of each new speaker (along with any related description) go in a separate paragraph, even if only one word is said. Dialogue paragraphs are often short and staccato.

Newspaper reporting. Newspaper paragraphs must hold the attention of busy readers. Typically they present a single idea and brief supporting details in two or three sentences.

Visual emphasis. Some paragraphs are deliberately very short— perhaps only a sentence long—so that they call attention to themselves and emphasize what is being said. They function almost like an exclamation point.

Transitions. Transitional paragraphs form bridges between major sections or different ideas in a document. Or they signal a turning point in the development of an argument. They can be any length but are often short for greater emphasis.

Not only does Walker move from a broad generalization to specific examples, she also contrasts the sense of community in the past to the alienation of the present. Search your disk files and find a paragraph you think goes from general to specific. Underline the most general statement. Is it the topic sentence? Does it appear at the beginning or near the beginning? Do the rest of the sentences support the generalization with specific details and concrete examples? Underline or italicize those that do.

Specific to General.   You can also start with specific details, amplify them, and at the end draw some deduction or general conclusion. In this case, your paragraph is complete when you have provided enough details or evidence to support your generalization. Stephen Jay Gould, a science writer, uses this structure with an ironic twist in an article of his in the August 1983 *Vanity Fair*. He has just identified as a fad the "overextended, even silly, speculation" that the left side of our brain is "rational" and "reflects linear and logical Western culture," while the right side is "intuitive" and reflects "contemplative and integrative Eastern thought." Here is the next paragraph. (The conclusion is underlined.)

> For example, neurologists have long known that a curious crossover occurs between brain and body, so that the left brain regulates the right side of the body, while the right brain controls the left side. Our culture also displays a lamentable prejudice toward right-handedness, a bias deeply embedded in nearly all Western languages, where right is dexterous (from the Latin *dexter,* or right), *Recht* (or justice in German), *droit* (or law in French), and, well, just plain right—while left is sinister (from Latin for left) or gauche. If we overextend the theme of cerebral asymmetry, we might be tempted to trace this prejudice to our Western bias for rational over intuitive thought, since the favored left brain controls the valued right side. (Stephen Jay Gould, "Left Holding the Bat")

Gould doesn't believe the conclusion that might be drawn from this evidence, that we can trace the prejudice for right over left to Western bias for rational over intuitive thought. Therefore he clearly signals that the generalization is false by introducing it with words like "overextend" and "might be tempted." This clever twist to the organizational plan gives Gould's argument more punch.

Find one of your paragraphs that goes from specific to general. If you can't find one, write a sample paragraph on any subject you are interested in. Underline the generalization. Now try moving it to the opposite part of the paragraph. Does it work as well there? Why not? Check the supporting details: Will they convince readers? Revise and strengthen them if necessary.

Pivoting or Zigzag. Some paragraphs have a turning point or a zigzag structure. Broad statements or assertions within the paragraph signal definite changes or turning points in your ideas. Paragraphs developing an argument, a comparison/contrast, or a problem/solution are likely to use this structure, although it can be adapted for a variety of other paragraphs. Zigzag paragraphs are complete when they provide enough detail to justify the turning points. Lewis Thomas, in his introduction to *The Search for Solutions* by Horace Freeland Judson, tells how our increasing scientific knowledge has made us less sure of our place in the universe. (The turning point is underlined.)

> That is, to date, the most wrenching of all the transformations that science has imposed on human consciousness—in the Western world, anyway. We have learned that we do not really understand nature at all, and the more information we receive, the more strange and mystifying is the picture before us. <u>There was a time, just a few centuries back, when it was not so.</u> We thought then that we could comprehend almost all important matters: the earth was the centerpiece of the universe, we humans were the centerpiece of the earth, God was in his heaven just beyond what we have now identified as a narrow layer of ozone, and all was essentially right with the world; we were in full charge, for better or worse.

The pivotal sentence—"There was a time, just a few centuries back, when it was not so"—introduces the contrast between past and present.

Underline the pivotal sentence in one of your paragraphs that has a pivoting or zigzag structure. Does it come at a logical point? If not, move it elsewhere. Are other pivot points needed? If so, insert them. Are enough supporting details given? Add more if necessary. If you can't find a zigzag paragraph, write one for this exercise.

Spatial. In a descriptive paragraph you would probably use a spatial plan to organize details. You might describe objects and scenes from a fixed viewing point in space, or take a sweeping look across or above or below or behind the object or scene, or group details around a focal point. This kind of paragraph is complete when you have written down all the relevant details in the space surveyed and created the image or mood you want. For example, in a nostalgic description of his childhood home in Missouri, Mark Twain moves around the family room but centers on the fireplace. (In this paragraph all the spatial references—including the fireplace, the focal point—are underlined.)

> I can see the farm yet, with perfect clearness. I can see all its belongings, all its details; the family room of the house, with a "trundle" bed in <u>one corner</u> and a spinning-wheel <u>in another</u>—a wheel whose rising and falling wail, heard from a distance, was the mournfulest of sounds to me, and

made me homesick and low spirited, and filled my atmosphere with the wandering spirits of the dead; the vast <u>fireplace</u>, piled high, on winter nights, with flaming hickory logs from whose ends a sugary sap bubbled out, but did not go to waste, for we scraped it off and ate it; the lazy cat spread out on the rough <u>hearthstones</u>; the drowsy dogs braced against the jambs and blinking; my aunt in one <u>chimney corner</u>, knitting; my uncle in the other, smoking his corn-cob pipe; the slick and carpetless oak floor faintly mirroring the <u>dancing flame tongues</u> and <u>freckled with black indentations where fire coals had popped out and died a leisurely death</u>; half a dozen children romping in the <u>background twilight</u>; "split"-bottomed chairs here and there, some with rockers; a cradle—out of service, but waiting, with confidence; in the early cold mornings a snuggle of children, in shirts and chemises, occupying the <u>hearthstone</u> and procrastinating—they could not bear to leave that comfortable place and go out on the wind-swept <u>floor space between the house and kitchen</u> where the general tin basin stood, and wash. (*Mark Twain's Autobiography*)

Even when Twain moves from the family room to the outside wash-up place, his description is written in terms of leaving the cozy hearth. Thus he also uses contrasts to shape his paragraph—contrasts between warmth and cold, evening and morning.

Look at a descriptive paragraph you have already written, or write one now. What is the organizational plan? Underline words and phrases that indicate location. Do other elements—like comparisons and contrasts or the passage of time—help structure the paragraph? Highlight these.

Chronological. You can also arrange material in sequence, putting down what happened first, what happened second, third, and so on. The chronologically organized paragraph continues until you cover the necessary steps or stages in the sequence. Barry Lopez, in his book *Of Wolves and Men,* writes a chronological narrative of a typical afternoon in the life of a wolf. (References to time are underlined; words that move the action forward are italicized.)

<u>It is now late in the afternoon.</u> The wolf has *stopped traveling,* has *lain down to sleep* on cool earth beneath a rock outcropping. Mosquitoes rest on his ears. His ears *flicker.* He *begins to waken.* He *rolls* on his back and *lies motionless* with his front legs pointed toward the sky but folded like wilted flowers, his back legs splayed, and his nose and tail curved toward each other on one side of his body. <u>After a few moments</u> he *flops* on his side, *rises, stretches,* and *moves* a few feet to *inspect*—minutely, delicately—a crevice in the rock outcropping and *finds* or *doesn't find* what *draws* him

there. <u>And then</u> he *ascends* the rock face, *bounding* and *balancing* <u>momentarily</u> before *bounding* again, *appearing* slightly unsure of the process — but *committed*. <u>A few minutes later</u> he *bolts* suddenly into the woods, *achieving* full speed, almost thirty miles per hour, for forty or fifty yards <u>before</u> he *begins to skid, to lunge* at a lodgepole pine cone. He *trots* away with it, his head erect, his hips slightly to one side and out of line with his shoulders, as though hindquarters were impatient with forequarters, the cone inert in his mouth. He *carries* it for a hundred feet <u>before</u> *dropping* it by the trail. He *sniffs* it. *He goes on.*

Notice all the phrases indicating passage of time: "It is now late in the afternoon," "After a few moments," "And then," "momentarily," "A few minutes later," "before." The narrative action of the paragraph is driven forward by dynamic verbs, usually of movement. And the last sentence, "He goes on," promises more narrative action in the next paragraph.

Call up one of your chronologically structured paragraphs and underline all statements indicating the passage of time. Italicize other devices or words that propel the action forward. Does your paragraph move dynamically from beginning to end?

Climactic. Arrange your material in order of importance and build up to a climax. A paragraph organized in this way must include enough steps in the progression to make the climax convincing to readers. Sometimes the progression toward a climax is signaled by enumeration: "first, second, third." Other times verbal cues tell readers the climax is coming: "most important," "finally," "at last," "the most serious thing is . . ." However, in the following paragraph by Edward Abbey, the progression is much more subtle: Abbey goes from the overwhelming silence in which he is lost, to great stillness, to overwhelming peace, to suspension of time, to the final realization that he is very much alone. (This progression of awareness is indicated by underlining.)

But for the time being, around my place at least, the air is untroubled and I become aware for the first time today of the <u>immense silence in which I am lost</u>. Not a silence so much as <u>a great stillness</u> — for there are a few sounds: the creak of some bird in a juniper tree, an eddy of wind which passes and fades like a sigh, the ticking of the watch on my wrist — slight noises which break the sensation of absolute silence but at the same time exaggerate my sense of the surrounding, <u>overwhelming peace. A suspension of time, a continuous present</u>. If I look at the small device strapped to my wrist the numbers, even the sweeping second hand, seem meaningless, almost ridiculous. No travelers, no campers, no wanderer have come to this part of the desert today and for a few moments <u>I feel and realize that I am very much alone</u>. (Edward Abbey, *Desert Solitaire: A Season in the Wilderness*)

The progression toward a climax in this paragraph is intuitive rather than logical, and its purpose is to describe how the desert environment affects Abbey's inner awareness. Thus details are held together by phrases like "I become aware," "I am lost," "exaggerate my sense," "I feel and realize."

Some paragraphs start with the most important point and progress to the least important, thus using the anticlimactic organizational plan. In your anticlimatic paragraphs, clearly indicate that the first item is most important and the others increasingly minor. To emphasize the first item's importance, you may want to return to it at the end of the paragraph.

Choose a paragraph of yours that builds to a climax and underline the most important statement. Italicize the words and phrases that mark stages on the way to this climax. Is the progression logical or intuitive? Are the stages emphatically or subtly signaled? Do any of the stages need to be rearranged? Move the sentences around if necessary.

Methods of Development

So far in this section we have focused on one aspect of building paragraphs—your plan of organization. Remember, though, that many variations can be made in the basic plan and that any plan of organization goes hand in hand with rhetorical methods of development. Thus Alice Walker and Lewis Thomas write paragraphs that also depend on comparison/contrast; Barry Lopez writes a narrative; Mark Twain and Joan Didion give descriptions; Stephen Jay Gould formulates an argument.

Like the complete document, individual paragraphs, too, can follow a particular method of development:

> Narration
> Description
> Exemplification
> Process
> Comparison/contrast
> Analysis/classification
> Cause/effect
> Definition
> Argumentation/persuasion

Deliberately using one of these methods will help you write a more complete, as well as a more organized, paragraph, although many of your paragraphs will use a combination of methods.

The material on organizing and developing paragraphs closely mirrors the discussion in Chapter 3 on planning the whole document. This similarity is to be expected, because paragraphs are like miniature compositions or documents. If you keep this similarity firmly in mind, you will find the task of writing much easier.

Making It Flow: Paragraph Coherence

In addition to unity and completeness, a good paragraph must also have coherence. Literally, "to cohere" means "to stick together, to hold fast, to be connected." Thus a coherent paragraph holds together. It has smooth connections between sentences and logical transitions, or bridges, between ideas. There are no gaps in the development or abrupt jumps in logic; the style is neither disjointed nor choppy. "Coherence" is what you mean when you say something "has continuity" or "flows." You can achieve coherence in your paragraphs by paying attention to content, structure, and style.

Content and Structure

First and foremost, be sure that your paragraph makes sense. If you are writing nonsense, it is foolish to worry about coherence. Of course, you don't set out to write nonsense, but if you don't know your subject well or are unsure about your purpose, the coherence of your writing will suffer. Fuzzy thinking leads to fuzzy writing.

Next, be sure that your paragraph has unity. If your writing goes off in several directions at once, if you try to jam too many ideas into one paragraph, or if you include irrelevant material, achieving any kind of coherence is going to be very difficult if not impossible.

Finally, be sure that your paragraph is clearly and logically organized. Your paragraph won't achieve a smooth and logical flow if sentences are misplaced. This chapter's earlier discussion on completeness should help you to arrange sentences in the best order.

Style

Even if your paragraphs are models of clarity, unity, and organization, you may still find that their style is choppy. Transitional writing techniques help solve the problem.

Transitional Words and Phrases. Smooth, logical bridges between ideas and sentences, transitional words and phrases also act as signposts, telling your reader where you are going next. A few common transitional expressions are given in the following list , but there are many, many more.

Place: above, below, beyond, farther
Time: when, before, after, then, since
Sequence: first, second, third, next, finally
Amplification: in addition, furthermore, besides, moreover
Causation: therefore, thus, consequently, because
Contrast: on the other hand, however, but
Similarity: also, too, just as, similarly
Example: for example, for instance, in this case
Admission: of course, although, despite

Although these expressions are indispensable for achieving coherence, don't use them too frequently or too obviously. Choose from the many other transitional techniques available.

Repetition of Key Words. Repeating key words can be a powerful device for linking ideas and sentences, as long as the repetition is functional and not boring or unnecessary. Repeat the same word or different forms of the same word: "walk," "walking," "had walked." Or use synonyms: "stroll," "amble," "wander." Or use related words: "path," "journey." "He *dashed* across the bridge and *ran* down the *path. Running* quickly, he soon caught up with the jogger."

Omission of Key Words. Just as you can repeat key words and link ideas and sentences, you can also omit them, as long as you make clear to readers exactly what word they must supply mentally. Take the following example: "Three training seminars on spreadsheets for beginners will be held on Tuesday afternoons. Three others, for advanced users, will be held on Wednesday mornings." The phrase "training seminars" is left out of the second sentence, but readers know from the first sentence that they should insert it mentally as they read. Such omissions force readers to make logical connections between sentences.

Pronouns. Use of pronouns—"he," "she," "it," and so on—also provides transition, especially when the pronouns refer to key nouns or agents of action in the paragraph. "Robots are a fast-growing segment of the American work force. More and more, *they* do the jobs that are repetitive, boring, dangerous, or delicate. *They* paint and weld on the production line, go in after radiation leaks, and assemble miniature electronic components." Pronoun links like these are stronger if the pronouns are also combined with parallel sentence structure. (See below.) But it is crucial that pronouns clearly refer to the correct noun; a vague "it" or "they" is worse than useless.

Demonstrative Adjectives. Demonstrative adjectives like "this," "that," "these," and "those" act as verbal arrows, pointing back to previously mentioned material and thus providing links between sentences and ideas. For example, "W. B. Yeats claimed in his *Autobiography* that poets write 'in little sedentary stitches as though we were making lace.' *This* kind of painstaking craftsmanship is evident in his poetry, which he revised extensively even after it had been published." Again, it is crucial that demonstrative adjectives clearly refer to a specific noun or noun phrase; a vague "this" unconnected to a specific noun only weakens your writing and makes it vague.

Other adjectives — "another," "each," "both," "such," "the same" — can also act as transitional signposts.

Summary. Briefly sum up, in a few words, what you have just said before going on to the next idea or subpoint. For example, in a paragraph on the qualities of a successful writer, this sentence introduces the last point: "*In addition to creativity and perseverance,* successful writers need a thick skin when the critics savage their work."

Parallel Sentence Structure. A sophisticated technique for gaining paragraph coherence is writing sentences that are balanced and parallel in wording and structure. Martin Luther King, Jr., in his famous "Letter from Birmingham Jail," contrasts just and unjust laws in parallel sentences.

> An unjust law is a code that a numerical or power majority group compels a minority group to obey but does not make binding on itself. This is *difference* made legal. By the same token, a just law is a code that a majority compels a minority to follow and that it is willing to follow itself. This is *sameness* made legal. (Martin Luther King, Jr., *Why We Can't Wait*)

Parallel structure tends to be more formal than the other techniques we have discussed, and it can result in dramatic, memorable statements.

These techniques can also be used to build bridges *between* paragraphs. By convention, transitional devices are placed at the beginning of the next paragraph, even though the previous paragraph may indicate what you are going to discuss next.

Your attempts to achieve stylistic coherence will be more effective if you use transitional techniques subtly rather than obviously and mechanically. Don't overdo them. It is highly unlikely you will use all of them in any one paragraph; generally you will rely on one or two techniques and use several others in a minor way.

Running a Computer Check on Paragraphs

How well do you construct paragraphs? Do they have unity, completeness, and coherence? If you are using this book in a writing class, your instructor may be telling you in no uncertain terms what he or she thinks of your paragraphs. Or perhaps an employer, a colleague, or an editor has complained that your paragraphs are choppy or rambling or undeveloped. But you can analyze your writing on your own, using the computer to provide a graphic picture of the inner workings of your paragraphs. You can see what you are doing correctly and what needs to be improved. Try the following exercise.

Call up a sample document from your disk files and choose a typical paragraph (not the introduction or conclusion, which are special paragraphs with their own special features and problems). Test for unity first. Underline or put in capitals the topic sentence of the paragraph. Now ask yourself, Are all the other sentences in the paragraph related to this sentence? Underline other words and phrases throughout the paragraph that deal with the central idea. If the paragraph also has a block topic sentence (discussed on p. 104), use a distinctive style option such as bold or double underlining to highlight it. (If your word-processing system doesn't show all these style options on the screen, you can still carry out this graphic analysis, but you will have to wait for the printout to see the results.)

Test for organization. Open a second window or a new file and write a brief item outline of the paragraph; outline exactly what appears on the screen in the precise order it occurs. (Even if your word processor has automatic outlining, write your own for this test.) Next, analyze the outline. Is the overall plan of organization clear? Are ideas arranged in the most effective order? Are minor ideas subordinated to the main ones? Have any ideas been repeated? Has anything been left out? Is the method of development effective?

Test for coherence. Look through the paragraph for writing techniques used to gain coherence; change these to italics. Does a network of linkages appear? Are they subtle, or are they too mechanical and obvious? Do gaps occur between sentences? Mark these with bold brackets.

Check for transitions between paragraphs and change these transitional words, phrases, or sentences to bold. Is a strong link with the preceding paragraph established at the beginning of the paragraph? Does the ending subtly point to the next paragraph?

Print out this graphic analysis and study it; print your item outline, too. The highlighting in your paragraph should be similar to that in this paragraph, from *Places,* by James Morris. (Here, the topic sentence and other phrases that develop the main idea—the search for class and splendor—are underlined; repeated key words are italicized; and transitional elements are in bold. An item outline appears next to the paragraph.)

I. Chicago's quest for class and splendor

A. City's majestic views
B. Example: view from lake

1. Foreground—park

2. Middle distance—expressway, railroad, Lake Shore Drive

3. Background—skyline

a. Glorious jumble of styles

b. Examples

II. Builders "unappeasable giants" [implied: "who sought class, splendour"]

But if Chicago's *yearning for tradition and urbanity* is sometimes ridiculous, **in other ways** it is noble. It is **not only** a *search* for *class,* it is a *hunger* **too** for *splendour*. Thanks partly to the pretensions of the Mrs. Windleshams, trying so hard to keep up with the Cabots or the Cecils, this is a city of *majestic presence*. Consider the view on a spring morning, **for instance,** from the shore of the Lake beside the Planetarium. A belt of green parkland fills **the foreground,** plonked about by tennis balls, spashed with tulips and cherry blossoms; **then** a moving strip of traffic, streaming relentlessly along the expressway; **then, behind** the sunken railroad tracks, the tight-packed facade of Lake Shore Drive, which reminds me of Prince's street in Edinburgh. **Above and behind all this** rises the skyline of downtown Chicago, and there it all comes true. It is one of the grandest of all silhouettes. It is a *glorious jumble* of styles and conceptions— **here** a cylinder, **there** a pyramid, Gothic bobbles and Victorian scrolls, bumps, domes, cubes, towers like the lattice masts of old battleships, gables, even a steeple—a *tremendous congeries* of buildings, *without balance or symmetry,* which properly suggests a metropolis *thrown together* in an enormous hurry by a race of unappeasable giants.

Other devices give this paragraph coherence: parallel structure in the first two sentences; logical links between the words "Chicago," "city," "Edinburgh," and "metropolis"; the mention of specific places in Chicago—"the Lake beside the Planetarium," "Lake Shore Drive"; even the use of the pronoun "it." A computer analysis like this one graphically reveals exactly how to go about constructing a paragraph. Probably you won't do such a detailed analysis more than once or twice, but if you have trouble writing focused and unified paragraphs, routinely underlining topic sentences is easy and helps enormously. And some people find they are more careful about transitions between paragraphs if they temporarily mark them in bold. Try visual aids in your rough draft, then switch to regular type before the final printing.

Writing Special Paragraphs for Special Jobs

Some paragraphs play specialized roles, especially in expository or argumentative writing—that is, writing that explains or demonstrates something or argues a point. You can guide readers through your document and help them understand it with overview, summary, and transitional paragraphs and with paragraph blocks.

Overview Paragraphs

Overview paragraphs do precisely what their name implies: give readers a concise survey, or overview, of the material to be covered. Such paragraphs come at the beginning of a report, a chapter in a book, or a major section in a long document. The paragraph below previews material to be covered in a report entitled *Comprehensive Needs Assessment for the South Coast Regional Beach Erosion Control Group*.

> The report is divided into several sections, the first describing the South Coast littoral cell. The second section details the major causes of beach erosion along the South Coast, while the third describes specific beach erosion (and accretion) problems within the cell.

And here is an overview paragraph from the beginning of a chapter on computer printers in Cary Lu's *Apple Macintosh Book*:

> Printers come in many forms. After a brief look at the elements of print quality, I will take up conventional designs and some considerations about their use and then describe more sophisticated units such as the LaserWriter. For test information and a comparison of many printer models, see Table 16-3 at the end of this chapter.

Readers find overview paragraphs at the beginning of the main text very helpful, especially in long technical or informative documents. They act as a mini table of contents and give readers a context for the information they are about to receive. (But you can preview text in other ways, too; Chapter 8, p. 168, shows you how.)

Summary Paragraphs

In a long or complex document, you can help readers to understand and remember your main ideas by summing them up at strategic points along the way. Write a summary paragraph when you finish explaining a particularly difficult concept or when you come to the end of a major section. For example, Jeremy Bernstein, in an article entitled "Calculators: Self-Replications," explores an abstruse scientific question: Can a machine such as a computer create a new organism like itself out of simple parts contained in its environment? Before he continues the article, he sums up thus:

> Where does all of this leave us? The point I have been trying to make is that, as far as I can see, the most profound impact of the computer on society may not be as much in what it can do in practice, impressive though this is, as in what the machine *is* in theory—and has less to do with its capacity as a calculator than with its capacity for self-replication. (Jeremy Bernstein, *Experiencing Science*)

End-of-chapter summaries, especially in textbooks and how-to manuals, review the material presented and highlight the most important information. At the end of chapters in his book *Running MS-DOS,* Van Wolverton actually lists the main points in a paragraph headed "Chapter Summary":

> This quick tour of DOS may have introduced several new terms and concepts. Here are the key points to remember:
>
> ■ A computer system needs both hardware (equipment) and software (programs).
> ■ DOS (Disk Operating System) coordinates the operation of all parts of the computer system.
> ■ A file is a collection of related information stored on a disk. Most of your computer work will involve files.
> ■ Besides running your application programs, DOS is a valuable tool in its own right.
>
> The next chapter starts you off at the keyboard.

Note that the end of the summary serves as a transition to the next chapter.

Transitional Paragraphs

If you are moving from one large section of your document to another, the transition may be so important that it merits a paragraph of its own. For example, in *Zen and the Art of Motorcycle Maintenance,* Robert M. Pirsig finishes describing the kinds of external problems that cause people to lose their "gumption," his term for the enthusiasm that is part and parcel of achieving quality in one's life. Then he briefly sums up this section in a single paragraph and makes a smooth transition to the next section, internal "gumption traps."

Well, those were the commonest setbacks I can think of: out-of-sequence reassembly, intermittent failure and parts problems. But although setbacks are the commonest gumption traps they're only the external cause of gumption loss. Time now to consider some of the *internal* gumption traps that operate at the same time.

Such paragraphs clearly signal the end of one section and the beginning of the next; they provide smooth and logical transitions between sections and give your whole document coherence.

Paragraph Blocks

A powerful way to guide readers through your document is to write *block topic sentences*. Block topic sentences govern a block, or group, of two or more paragraphs. (Each paragraph still has its own topic sentence, however, including the paragraph containing the block topic sentence.) Each paragraph in the block expands, supports, illustrates, and clarifies the block topic sentence. Often the first paragraph in the block contains some introductory material, and the last paragraph brings the block to a close or sums up. Writing in paragraph blocks, rather than in discrete paragraphs, gives your document a more definite structure and stronger coherence; readers get a broad understanding of large sections rather than becoming mired in the details of individual paragraphs. In technical or professional documents, paragraph blocks may correspond to major divisions and so may have headings as well as block topic sentences. But any kind of long document gains from paragraph blocks and block topic sentences.

Writing the Difficult Paragraphs: Introductions and Conclusions

Introductions and conclusions can be the most difficult part of any writing project—and the most important. The opening may decide whether or not a reader continues; the impression left by the ending may color the reader's whole perception of what has gone before. If you have trouble with these two parts of a document, save them for last, when you know what you have said and how you have said it and can tailor your introduction and conclusion accordingly. Always have your thesis and statement of purpose on screen when you work on introductions and conclusions. And don't think you will get them right the first time. Try writing several alternatives, and keep the extras in a section called "Alternatives" at the end of your document (or in a separate document that you open in a second window) until you decide which one is best.

The following guidelines will help you write effective introductions and conclusions.

Introductions

The opening of a document may have to fulfill a variety of functions:

> Get and hold the reader's attention
> Establish rapport with the reader
> Introduce the topic
> State the thesis (although this can be done elsewhere)
> Clarify or limit the thesis (or both)
> Give background information
> Present your credentials to write on this subject
> Indicate the organizational plan of the document
> Set the tone and approach to be used
> Establish the value of what is to follow
> Explain methodology used, assumptions made, or models followed
> Define terms

Your particular introduction may not require all these functions; it depends on the length and complexity of your writing project. The longer the work, the longer the opening: A book may need an introductory chapter; a business letter, only a sentence or two. And certain types of technical documents, especially reports and proposals, usually have prescribed introductions.

Other kinds of work seem to call for their own kinds of introductions. For example, an article for a popular magazine or newspaper needs a journalistic "hook"—a clever and vivid anecdote, quotation, description, unusual fact, or sensational detail that "hooks" the reader's attention. A scholarly or scientific paper, on the other hand, might open with a survey of the literature in the field, and a review of a book, play, or movie might briefly summarize the work under discussion.

In addition, certain methods of development suggest the type of introduction you ought to write:

- *Process:* Give a broad overview of process before breaking it into steps.
- *Problem/solution:* Outline the problem and promise a solution.
- *Classification:* Indicate the principle of classification, the number of types, or the purpose of classifying.
- *Cause/effect:* Give some historical background, sketch the present situation, or make a prediction.

- *Definition:* Establish the need for a definition.
- *Argumentation:* Explain the context of the issue, take a strong stand, or quote the opposition only to demolish them.

You can also begin with rhetorical questions, with a bit of humor, with a paradox, with a dramatic situation, with a figure of speech, with facts and figures—the list of opening devices goes on and on. But always remember that your introduction must harmonize with the rest of the document; it should match it in tone, formality, and type of content.

You can improve your introductions by avoiding some common faults. Avoid one-sentence or two-sentence introductions in moderate to long documents. If other paragraphs are of normal length, a short opening paragraph (unless deliberately used for a special effect) will seem skimpy. Also avoid the opposite fault, the panoramic opening. Typically this is a survey reaching back to the dim past and containing such telltale phrases as "since the beginning of time," "down through the ages," "throughout the course of history." Sometimes writers start with big, broad abstract statements and, after much windy philosophizing, finally get to their subject. Or they state the obvious: "Loneliness is such a common emotion." Avoid empty windups such as these. Often you can delete the first two or three sentences of your introduction; in some cases you can cross out the whole first paragraph or even the first page. Get to the heart of the matter quickly!

And remember Disraeli's advice: "Never complain." No matter how you might feel about the writing assignment, never open with a complaint or an apology. Keep your attention on your readers: Write an introduction that will engage their attention, predispose them, if possible, to your point of view, and prepare them for the material you are about to present.

Conclusions

In discussing conclusions, it is easier to start by saying what not to do. Avoid short concluding paragraphs tacked on like an afterthought. Your ending should not read as if you were merely going through the motions. Neither do you want your ending to trail off inconclusively or to take refuge in vague generalities, obvious truisms, pious hopes, or sentimentality. (Words like "hopefully" and "sad" are often tip-offs for the latter two.) Say something definite. Don't waffle, and don't apologize. Avoid conclusions like the following:

> Traveling is something no one gets tired of. Hopefully, you will travel extensively during your lifetime and see a variety of places that you will always remember.

Divorce can be very disruptive to many other people besides the two people directly involved. It is so sad when a family is hurt, but then that is part of life.

Although many people feel, as I do, that the capital gains tax rate needs to be lowered, others do not. You may be one of the latter, but I believe everyone is entitled to his or her own opinion.

You don't want to write an ending that undercuts or even contradicts what you have said in the body of the document. Nor do you want to draw more conclusions than you reasonably can from the evidence you have presented. If you have written a relatively simple document, don't repeat yourself by retelling readers what you have just finished telling them. (This advice doesn't contradict the earlier discussion on summing up. Effective summary paragraphs fulfill specific functions: They help readers understand difficult material and absorb important information. Concluding a simple document by summarizing its contents, however, is almost always repetitious and unnecessary.) On the other hand, going off in an entirely new direction is confusing. Finally, don't write "in conclusion." Although that phrase may be welcomed in a long and windy speech, it sounds hackneyed in a piece of writing.

With a such a formidable list of "don'ts," what *can* you write at the end? There are, of course, the standard ending devices: an apt quotation, a concrete example or anecdote (if the document is general and abstract), a broad generalization (if the document is concrete and detailed), a clever analogy, metaphor, simile, or epigram, a repetition of a significant phrase or image that appeared in the opening. But these remain only devices. To write a substantial conclusion, consider the function it ought to fulfill. For example, it might do any one, or more, of the following:

- *Bring the writing project to a satisfactory close:* Give readers a sense of completion; what needs to be said on the subject has been said.
- *Stop at a dramatic highpoint:* Bring ideas, examples, or events to their logical climax.
- *Complete a process:* Explain the last step or stage in a process.
- *Decide issues:* Resolve thorny issues raised earlier; make some judgments.
- *Solve problems:* Offer specific ways to remedy a problem.
- *Answer questions:* Give answers to the rhetorical questions you posed at the beginning.
- *Make recommendations:* Urge a course of action.
- *Evaluate:* Spell out advantages and disadvantages, or declare one item better than another.
- *Draw conclusions:* Make logical deductions based on the preceding evidence.

- *Warn of consequences:* Predict what will happen if a specific course of action isn't taken.
- *Persuade:* Emotionally move people to do something: buy a product, vote for a candidate, contribute to a charity.
- *Mediate:* Soothe ruffled feathers or put the best face on things.
- *Universalize:* Point out the broader implications of your ideas or the universality of your topic.
- *Leave the question open:* Show readers what issues remain or where more research is needed.

Although incomplete, this list does suggest that the function of your conclusion is determined by your purpose in writing. Call up your thesis and statement of purpose on screen. Reread them. Reread the whole document. What is the final impression you would like to leave with readers? Do some prewriting; for example, complete this sentence: "What I want readers to remember (or do or feel) after reading this document is..." Then draft an ending that underscores this final impression and demonstrates, in a memorable and appropriate way, that you have fulfilled your initial purpose in writing. Make your endings functional, not decorative, vague, or general.

How long your conclusion should be depends on the length and type of your document. Thus certain types of routine business letters may have short, standardized closings: "Please call us if you have any questions about this matter." The ending of a technical report usually takes up a whole section (often headed "Conclusions" or "Recommendations"), and its actual form may have to follow prescribed guidelines. Long essays or articles may devote several paragraphs to the conclusion, and books may have a concluding chapter.

Checking the Complete Structure

So far we have concentrated on paragraphs as individual entities, almost as stand-alone compositions or miniature documents. But you don't want to forget that they are merely parts, or "building blocks," of a larger structure. They need to be arranged in a logical sequence, and each one must relate to the central idea or thesis of your document. Exploit the computer to ensure that the individual paragraphs do in fact add up to a unified, coherent whole.

Because introductions and conclusions are notoriously difficult, check those first. Use the split screen capability of your computer to put the ending right after the opening. Read them in sequence. Do they fit well together? Do they harmonize in tone, level of formality, and type of content? Is there a sense of unity and completion? Does the ending fulfill what the opening promised?

Be sure that the opening and ending harmonize with the whole document as well. No matter how brilliant, witty, creative, or insightful they are, if they differ in tone or level of formality from the body of your writing, or if they are not directly relevant to the point you are making, they must be changed.

To see if the rest of your paragraphs do their job, print out only the thesis statement and the topic sentences. (If your word-processing program is very sophisticated, flag these sentences so that they will be printed out automatically; otherwise use copy and move functions.) Alternatively, print out a rough draft with the topic sentences underlined and the thesis statement starred with asterisks.

When you read these sentences in sequence, they should provide a concise but comprehensive and organized summary of the whole document. If they don't, you need to do some revising. If you have printed a list of topic sentences, reword them until they do provide a good summary of the whole document. Move them around until you achieve the most effective order. Then use the new list to guide your revisions. (Detailed guidelines for revising are discussed in Chapter 6.)

Formatting Paragraphs

Formatting refers to the physical appearance and layout of text. There are three main ways to format paragraphs:

- *Indented* paragraphs are the most common. The first line of each paragraph is indented, and no extra blank lines are left between paragraphs. Indention is preferred for books, articles, academic papers, and some reports. (Word-processing programs can automatically indent paragraphs for you.)
- *Block* paragraphs are frequently used in business letters and memos and professional reports and proposals. There is no indention—the text forms a solid block. The beginning of each paragraph is signaled by extra space between paragraphs. (Word-processing programs often let you specify that an extra blank line will be left every time you press Enter to start a new paragraph.) Block paragraphs look solid and formal, but the format can cause confusion. If your document goes on for several pages, for example, the reader may not know whether material that begins at the top of a page belongs in a new paragraph.
- *Semiblock* paragraphs combine indention of first lines with extra blank lines between paragraphs. This style gives a more informal look to a document and clearly indicates whether material starting at the top of a page forms a new paragraph. This style is often used in business writing, too.

In addition, some documents, like technical reports, use a system in which paragraphs are numbered or lettered.

To find out exactly how you should format your paragraphs, look at typical examples of the type of document you are writing, or follow the guidelines in a writer's handbook or style guide. Aspects of paragraph formatting are discussed in Chapter 8 under "Arranging the Text on the Page" and in Chapter 9 under "Technical and Business Documents."

Let's Solve It!

Problems with paragraphs generally fall into four categories: lack of focus, lack of development, excessive length, and choppiness.

Problem: Unfocused Paragraphs. You write a lot but meander aimlessly; the paragraph covers many different points but never develops one particular aspect.

Solution. Do what good journalists do: Make your first sentence a strong topic sentence; assert something definite, and give it an argumentative edge if possible. Plan the rest of the paragraph carefully. Choose an overall plan of organization; if appropriate, follow a particular method of development. Briefly outline the material to go into the paragraph. When the paragraph is written, check to see that every sentence relates directly to the topic sentence; watch for sentences that gradually slide away from the central idea or actually fly off on a tangent.

Problem: Undeveloped Paragraphs. Your paragraphs are skimpy; they have significantly fewer words than average paragraphs in the type of document you are writing.

Solution. Perhaps you are simply dividing your work into too many paragraphs. Combine several short paragraphs into one fully developed one. Rearrange sentences if necessary. Eliminate any repetition, add transitional words, and be sure that the topic sentence is comprehensive enough to cover the new paragraph. Add more concrete details, examples, case studies, facts, statistics, quotations by authorities, paraphrases or summaries from relevant books and articles, or whatever else is needed to make the paragraph more specific. Or go into your main idea more deeply; don't be satisfied with a superficial or hackneyed treatment. Do more analysis; think of more causes or effects or both; include more arguments for your point of view; subdivide your main points; use classification. However, avoid wordiness and padding!

Problem: Long, Rambling Paragraphs. Your paragraphs go on and on; some continue for a page or two. They have significantly more words than average paragraphs in the type of document you are writing.

Solution. Divide a particularly long paragraph into two or three smaller ones, each with its own topic sentence. If these paragraphs are closely related, put a block topic sentence at the beginning of the first one. Also eliminate any material that wanders off the subject or isn't necessary. Cut out extra words and don't repeat ideas. Be especially on guard against saying the same thing in different words. Be sure your paragraphs are tightly organized; some repetition is caused by disorganization.

Problem: Choppy Paragraphs. Your paragraphs sound abrupt and disjointed.

Solution. First, be sure that the paragraphs are unified and logically organized and the ideas in them clearly expressed. Then try using some of the transitional devices discussed in this chapter. If the writing style is still choppy, the problem lies with the sentences; you probably need to combine sentences. (See Chapter 6, pp. 130–32.)

Computer Writing Tips

You have done so much writing by now that you need to organize your files and keep track of your work.

- As you begin to generate various subdocuments—prewriting, statements of purpose, outlines—be sure you give them distinctive and informative names. "Prewrite 1" will not tell you much after you have written Prewrites 10, 11, and 12. And names like "The Boss" or "Trivia" may be clever, but three weeks from now you won't remember what they mean. Some people use words or abbreviations for filenames; others devise a numbering system. (This chapter, for example, had the filename "05.NewWr.MS"— the fifth chapter of *The New Writer* for Microsoft Press.)

- Keep your data disk neat. Arrange your work into logical directories and subdirectories (or file folders, as they are called in some computer operating systems). Use a consistent principle for organizing your work: by writing project, by date, by client, by type of job, and so on.

- If your operating system permits, write brief descriptions of what is in each document. Even with a distinctive name, it is easy to forget exactly what a particular file contains.

- If you use many data disks or have many directories on your hard disk, be sure that at the bottom of each important document you write a short code identifying its disk location. (Put this code in a small type size so it will be inconspicuous.) Then you will be able to locate the electronic file quickly when you are working with paper copies from your regular filing cabinet.

Last year on sabbatical leave I learned word processing and also saw how computers are used in composition classes. Until then, I had never even turned on a computer, let alone imagined using one as a writer and teacher. I had a rather medieval attitude that electricity and its devices, except for the electric light and typewriter, were somehow the enemies of literacy. Surprisingly, it only took about 20 minutes to learn the basics of word processing. Later I even taught one of my sabbatical-leave colleagues how to use computers for writing; like me, he soon became hopelessly addicted to this new technology.

I was pleased to find that students showed the same enthusiasm: They *love* writing with computers. In the computer writing labs that I visited, not a single student was staring at the clock; each one was actively engaged in the writing task at hand. The production of multiple drafts is no longer an arduous chore for them—instead, it's a pleasing electronic adventure.

Using a word processor has created nothing less than a revolution in my own writing. Rather than elaborately avoiding writing as I did in the past, I now look forward to it eagerly. I see using my computer as a subtle and startling extension of my own thinking skills. As I write, I can effortlessly coordinate a protean flow of ideas with the emerging text on the computer screen. The rapid and dramatic textual transformations of word processing allow my insights and subtle shifts in meaning to appear in print almost instantaneously before my eyes. Thinking, writing, and revising are suddenly a single, integrated activity. For the first time in the history of writing technology, the mind creating the text and the text the mind is creating are virtually one. Thus the computer has done an amazing thing: It has put my mind at my fingertips.

Robert A. Isaacson
Language Arts Instructor

The Computer as Editor

Revising content, logic, and structure
Revising sentences and words
Proofreading

By the time you are this far on your writing project, you have gone through several major steps in the writing process: prewriting, planning and organizing, and writing the rough draft. Now comes the step that some writers say is the most important of all—revising.

But what does revising mean?

The word "revise" comes from a Latin word meaning "look back," "revisit." And in an important sense revising does involve "revisiting" your work, going back to look at it in a new light, with fresh ideas and perhaps a different attitude. You compare the ideal version of your project with the rough draft you have actually created and see what needs to be corrected, changed, added, or deleted. You look at ways to improve content, structure, logic, strategy, style, diction, and grammar. If necessary, you tear apart your original work and thoroughly rethink your ideas and rewrite the draft. (Notice that the easiest mistakes to correct on the computer—spelling, punctuation, and typographical errors—aren't even mentioned at this point, because mere proof-reading is not revision. In fact, you can leave proofreading until after you have finished revising your work.)

Revision is a process in itself, with various steps. Long, complex, or important documents go through several revisions. In the early stages, you critique your work yourself and make your own revisions; as part of this process, you may do more research or brainstorming. Then you submit your work to one or more critics, who may suggest further revisions. Later in the process, when the work is nearly complete, an instructor, editor, or project manager may require you to make specific changes before giving approval. Finally, if the work is to be published or widely distributed, an editor or someone else in authority may put the finishing touches on the document. (Your consent will probably be asked if anything substantial is changed.) This is only a general overview; in the case of your particular project, the revision process may be somewhat different. The point is that writing and producing a professional document usually involves group effort, especially in the revision stage. The revision process for short or routine documents is apt to be simpler, but even here you may revise your work more than once and seek outside criticism from peers or colleagues.

This chapter talks about critiquing and revising your work yourself; Chapter 7 discusses receiving and responding to outside criticism.

Being Your Own Best Critic

Before you can revise your writing, you need to see what is wrong with it—and also what is right with it. Ideally, you should put your writing aside for awhile before you critique it. For a short letter that has to go out quickly, perhaps fifteen minutes is all you can spare, but longer projects deserve several hours or, better still, several days. As your document sits, your mind will be consciously or unconsciously mulling over unresolved problems. When you are away from the computer, keep some paper handy to jot down good ideas. If you are still working at the computer, use an electronic note-pad if your machine has one, or set up a new section at the very beginning of your document and entitle it "Notes for Revision." Such jottings will help you revise. When you do go back to your draft, you will see it with fresh eyes. Defects will stand out more clearly, but you also will be able to appreciate the strong points.

Critiquing the Printout

Start your critique by reading the printout. True, you can call your rough draft up on the computer screen and make changes there. In fact, with the sophisticated features on modern word-processing programs at your fingertips, you may be tempted to do just that. Don't fall into this trap. One of the biggest errors in computer writing is trying to go from screen to final paper copy without intermediate printouts. You will be a far better writer if you alternate between working on the screen and editing paper printouts by hand. There are good reasons for working this way. Almost all writing ultimately gets printed on paper, so you need to see how your work is going to look in its final form. That is, after all, the form your readers will see. Furthermore, the paper copy is different from the electronic screen: Spreading out several pages on a desk so your eyes can sweep over large sections of text is quite different from scrolling through one small screen after another of text. You will see things in the paper copy that you miss on the screen.

The printout should be double spaced with fairly wide margins, so that you have room to make editing notes with a pen or pencil. Choose a printing mode that is easy to read; depending on your printer, the "draft" or fastest mode may be so cramped and full of dots that your eyes just skip over mistakes. Separate the pages and arrange them in order; a long roll of paper is difficult to manage.

Here are some ways to critique your own work. Experiment and see which one works best for you.

Use a Checklist. As you read, check your draft against a list of questions. At first you may want to use an actual list, but as time goes on, you should internalize the questions that are most important for the kind of writing you do.

- ☐ Can the title and introduction be more compelling? Do they invite readers to continue?
- ☐ Can the thesis be clearer, more provocative, or more persuasive?

☐ Can logic be improved, arguments made more convincing, or ideas developed in more detail?

☐ Does the writing strategy need to be changed in order to meet the demands of audience, subject, and purpose more effectively?

☐ Are there any questions that still need to be answered?

☐ Are more examples, facts, statistics, or the like needed?

☐ Can vague or general statements be more concrete and specific?

☐ Is there any unnecessary, irrelevant, or repetitious material that should be deleted?

☐ Will readers be able to follow the plan of organization? Should the order of parts be changed?

☐ Can paragraph blocks or large sections of the document be signaled more clearly and emphatically?

☐ Do any paragraphs need to be moved or even deleted?

☐ Does each paragraph have a topic sentence? Does the rest of the paragraph support, develop, prove, or illustrate the topic sentence?

☐ Should the order of sentences within a paragraph be changed?

☐ Are all paragraphs a reasonable length, neither too long nor too short for the type of document?

☐ Can the transitions between paragraphs and within paragraphs be made smoother?

☐ Can sentences be made more effective by varying their length and structure?

☐ Can wordiness be reduced or eliminated?

☐ Can diction be more precise, accurate, specific, and natural?

☐ Are there instances of slang, colloquialisms, clichés, or unnecessary jargon that should be eliminated?

☐ Can technical or unfamiliar terms be defined more clearly?

☐ Does the ending build to a climax and leave the right impression with the reader? Can it be stronger or more memorable?

☐ Does the document as a whole fulfill the statement of purpose and meet the needs of the audience?

As you answer these questions, make notes between the lines of your document or in the margins. You should mark up the printout of your first rough draft thoroughly, as if you were a writing instructor reading a freshman theme. Later on, these editorial notes will help you revise.

Write a Note to Yourself. After carefully reading your rough draft, write a note to yourself evaluating it. Write as informally as you like; use "I" and "my" frequently. Start by jotting down everything you like about your document, what you feel proud of, what came easily, what you think works well. Look at small details as well as the overall picture; praise a vivid choice of words as well as your grand design. Many, if not most, writers suffer from lack of confidence and need practice in recognizing the true strengths of their writing.

Now start describing what you don't like about your writing. What is weak or unconvincing? What did you have trouble with? What are you unsatisfied with? Be detailed and specific. Most writers, even relatively inexperienced ones, can be fairly good critics of their writing if they care about their work and if they are honest with themselves. At first you may not be able to articulate your faults precisely. You may say "my second paragraph doesn't flow" when you really mean "the sentences aren't in the right order and I need better transitions." But as you use this book and critique your work regularly, you will find yourself becoming a discerning critic.

Some writers are content to evaluate their rough drafts mentally. This may work for experienced writers and with short, routine documents, but your evaluation will be much more thorough, precise, and helpful if you commit it to writing. You will also remember it. Type your evaluation on the computer at the end of your document and use the split screen to keep it before you when you revise, or write it by hand if you feel more comfortable creating "personal notes" with a pen or pencil. Whatever its form, the critical note you write to yourself can provide an agenda for your revision.

Make a Laundry List of Faults. If you have been writing for a while, you probably have a good idea of the mistakes you usually make. Either you have seen them yourself or other people have criticized them. At the beginning of your document, make a detailed list of your common faults. Jot them down in a vertical row, like a laundry list, and number each one. Be unsparing with yourself. Don't try to deny or ignore weaknesses or problems.

Now read through the printout of your rough draft and mark instances of these faults. Write standard abbreviations in the margins or between the lines—"Wrdy" for wordiness, "Dic" for poor diction, "TS" for weak topic sentence—or simply jot down the number of the fault. When you revise, you can use a split screen to keep the laundry list in view as you make changes in the text.

Read Your Writing Out Loud. This is a fine way to distance yourself from your work. You need privacy to read out loud, of course, so this technique may not be suitable if you write in a busy computer lab or open office. Listening to how your writing sounds can reveal many weaknesses: repetition, awkwardness, choppy sentences, logical gaps, or the wrong word or tone. Your ear may catch what your eye has missed; listen carefully as you read. An alternative to reading out loud is to record yourself reading on a tape recorder and play it back, or have someone read your document to you. Try to sit as far away from the reader as possible; physical distance seems to increase critical detachment.

If you use either a tape recorder or a reader, take notes. Stop the tape recorder if you want to make extensive comments. You may also find that your reader has some valid criticisms. Listen to them. Be alert for nonverbal criticism, too. If the reader stumbles frequently, you may have constructed awkward sentences or made poor word choices; if she has to reread certain passages or sentences, they may not make sense. But if the reader reads smoothly and enthusiastically, she may be carried along by some very effective writing.

Do a Quick Fix. At times you may be working to meet a rush deadline and have only a short time to critique and revise your writing. In this case, resort to a "quick fix." Quickly review your statement of purpose and skim the document from start to finish. What are the three most important things that need changing? Work on them first, but don't spend too long on any one. If you have time left over, skim the document again and decide on the next two or three things to revise. When your time is up, what hasn't been fixed stays the way it is. But if you have worked on the most important problems first, the remaining ones should be relatively minor. Don't skimp on proofreading, though; like charity, a professional appearance can hide a multitude of sins.

Critiquing on Screen

Computer writers say that faults missed on paper are spotted on the screen. And some writers even advocate dividing up editing tasks: looking for big problems on the printout and doing line-by-line critiquing and editing on screen. My method is to switch back and forth between the two methods: I read the printout and write numerous comments in the margins and on sheets of yellow paper, then go back to the screen and revise. Then I read through the document on the screen, word by word, line by line; if no one is around, I read out loud. I embed critical comments and questions in the text; if I get brilliant ideas I want to mull over for possible development or revision, I type them in a special section — "File for Future Reference" — at the end of the document. I keep switching back and forth between paper and screen — reading, critiquing, revising, and printing out — until I am satisfied with the document or my deadline intervenes.

Before you start critiquing your work on screen, you might want to type a laundry list of your common writing faults at the beginning of the document; use the split screen to keep it in view. Alternatively, this list can go in an electronic notepad, but be sure to consult it regularly as you reread your work. You can also refer to a checklist of critiquing questions that you keep on disk.

If you have a sophisticated program that allows you to embed hidden text, use that to write critical comments to yourself. Or flag mistakes and weaknesses with standard editing abbreviations. Or write detailed notes to yourself as you scroll through your work and read it out loud. When you are ready to revise, open another copy of your document in a second window and make the hidden text invisible. Using the visible annotations in the first window as a guide, revise the text in the second window. Or print out a paper copy with all the embedded text visible and use that as a guide to revision.

If you use a relatively simple word-processing program, embed critical comments and flag mistakes in bold or underlined text. (After you have revised, you will, of course, delete these comments and revert back to regular text.) But if the comments reduce the readability of your document, make a copy of the original and open it in a second window. Then you can mark up one copy and save the unmarked one for rereading and revising. Again, you should print out the text with the embedded comments.

Using On-line Style Checkers

Style checkers are special tools for on-line critiquing and revising. They search documents for grammatical faults and stylistic weaknesses. Spell checkers are one such program, but other programs look for specific writing problems, such as those listed on the next page.

A WORD OF WARNING

Unless you are doing absolutely routine writing or are rushing to meet a deadline, always combine on-screen critiquing with a thorough analysis of your printout.

"To be" verbs

Overuse of passive voice

Sexist language

Vague words

Punctuation errors

Capitalization errors

Nominalized verbs (verbs that have been changed into nouns: "are indications that" rather than "indicate")

Commonly misused words and phrases

Redundant expressions

Repeated words

Clichés

Split infinitives

Incorrect use of articles

Missing space or excess space

If the program finds possible examples of these problems, it highlights them and may suggest alternatives, but it doesn't make changes. You must do that. In many cases, you must decide whether or not a change needs to be made; not all "to be" verbs, for example, are bad.

Style checkers also help with the more complex aspects of critiquing and revising. They can check sentence structure by pointing out where ideas are strung together with prepositional phrases. They can also count words, calculate the average length of sentences, and give you a general idea of the readability of your prose. Is it suitable for sixth-grade level? Twelfth-grade level? University or graduate school level? They can estimate how abstract (as opposed to how concrete and specific) your document is. And they can check organization by extracting the first sentence from each paragraph—or whatever sentence you designate as the topic sentence—and then arranging these sentences in an informal outline. Transitional words are highlighted, too.

These programs are not perfect, however. You may have to use the style checker's text editor rather than your own, or you may need to save your files in a special format that the style checker can read. It takes time to check a document—a long time if the check is thorough—and you may get impatient. Furthermore, few programs, to my knowledge, run all the checks listed above, and those that can need large amounts of memory. They don't always catch all instances of a particular problem, and their suggested alternatives may be inappropriate in the context of your writing. You may find a style checker that suits your computer's memory, your style of writing, and your pocketbook, but even so, it can't substitute for your critical sense of what constitutes good writing. Having got reams of information from the checker, you, and not the computer, must decide how to use it to improve your writing. You make the criticial decisions; you do the revising.

Revising on the Computer

Now that you have critiqued your document and gotten a clear idea of what needs to be done, it is time to make your first revision. (Remember, however, that revision is an ongoing process; you may critique and revise your work several times before it is good enough for distribution or publication. Each new version of your document should be printed out and critiqued.) Before you begin your first revision, however, make a backup copy of your rough draft. Then, if something happens to your revision, or if you make poor changes, you can always go back to the original. Also keep your printout on your desk and consult it frequently. Review comments you embedded in the text as you wrote the rough draft, and check the suggestions you made as you did your critiquing. These notes will guide you as you work to improve various aspects of your writing:

> Content
> Logic and structure
> Strategy
> Specificity
> Conciseness
> Sentence style
> Diction
> Consistency

Revising for Content

Call up your prewriting in a separate window or windows and scroll through it, comparing what you find there to what you put in the rough draft. Is your prewriting fresher, more natural, more vivid? Does it include important material you left out of your draft? If so, follow the wording of your prewriting more closely as you revise, or actually copy and move prewriting details and phrasing into the text draft. If the content needs substantial changing, however, you may find yourself doing more research and prewriting.

Revising for Logic and Structure

Use the split screen to keep the thesis statement of the document in view as you revise for logic and structure.

Call up your outline in a second window and compare it to the draft. Writers sometimes create logical, well-organized outlines and then disregard them as they write. If you haven't done so already, underline topic sentences and double-underline block sentences in your text (or use bold plus underlining). Do these sentences correspond to the headings and subheadings of the outline? Are they arranged in the same order? Move whole paragraphs around to improve the effectiveness of your organization. If certain passages or even whole paragraphs slide off on a tangent, delete them. Move them to the "Wastebasket" section at the end of your document, however; you might want to use them again.

Compare the wording of topic and block topic sentences to that of the thesis statement. Make the necessary changes to tie them more closely and clearly to your central idea. But also be sure that they don't repeat each other boringly. Vary them.

If you haven't done so already, use a split screen to place the introduction and conclusion side by side. (See Chapter 5, pp. 108–109). Make the necessary changes to bring them into harmony with one another and to eliminate unnecessary repetition.

If your word-processing program has automatic outlining and two-way viewing, display your document in text and outline. In the outline window, collapse all the details and subordinate material under the main headings. Organizational problems are easy to spot and change when you have only the main headings in view. Rearranging items in the outline view means that the text in the second window is quickly and easily reorganized at the same time. (Conversely, if you prefer to work in the text window, the outline view will graphically display the organizational changes you are making.) If your outliner has a sort function, you can rearrange paragraphs simply by renumbering them in a new order and then sorting them.

Revising for Strategy

Call up your audience profile in a second window and scroll through your document, looking at it from your readers' point of view. Change passages that don't meet their needs and expectations or that will bore or even alienate them. Remember that your purpose is not to flaunt your expertise, relive your experiences, pour out your feelings, or score debating points; rather, you are trying to help readers in some way or to bring them around to your point of view.

Try using the search function to see how often you say "I," "me," "mine," or the editorial "we." Perhaps these need to be cut or at least reduced in frequency. In business writing, it may be good strategy to employ the "you" approach. A global search will show graphically how often you address your readers directly or call them by name.

Revising for Specificity

Too often rough drafts are general. Their authors set down broad, abstract generalities and go into a few semispecifics but omit the concrete details. Look at the content of your document as an inverted triangle that goes from generalities to specific details. (See Figure 6-1.)

Where in the triangle have you stopped? Don't be content with only generalities and semispecifics. Include the details. Whenever possible, choose concrete nouns, nouns that refer to tangible things. Appeal to the five senses—sight, sound, touch, taste, smell—and describe movement. Conjure up specific images in the reader's mind in place of vague sketches. Use vigorous action verbs rather than relying on "to be," "to have," "to get," "to make." Provide exact information. Illustrate with specific examples.

General	Specific
Businesses today use modern communication.	Businesses today communicate via electronic mail, mailgrams, TWX, telex, facsimile, and videotext.
Breakfast pastries appeal to people.	Imagine the spicy aroma of cinnamon rolls or the warm, buttery taste of croissants.
He is not a good driver.	He recklessly switched lanes, cut in front of a pickup truck, and slowed down abruptly.
The company has been in poor financial shape lately.	Amalgamated, Inc., reported a net income of $84 million for the three months ending September 30, compared with $99 million a year ago—a 15% drop.
A miscarriage of justice occurred.	The homeless person was sentenced to two years in jail for stealing $10 worth of food.

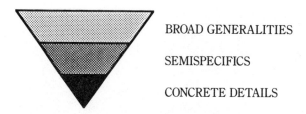

FIGURE 6-1. *From generalities to details*

Revising for Conciseness

Most people write too much. In fact, good writing often means cutting out material. So be ruthless. It may help to use a word counter to get rid of excess verbiage. How many words are in your document before revision? Type the number in the upper right-hand corner of the first page. (If you are submitting work for publication, the editor will look for a word count in this spot.) Next, type the word limit for the project; if you don't have a prescribed limit, enter a realistic limit for this type of document. Now start cutting. When you have finished, use the word counter again. The number of words should be substantially lower. Even if you are supposed to write 1000 words and have only 750, your prose may still be wordy and in need of cutting. For tips on how to *develop* your work as opposed to *padding* it, see the "Let's Solve It!" section in Chapter 5.

Some wordiness has to do with content, some with style. Let's look at problems of content first.

Saying Too Much. Instead of writing one essay or one report, you actually write enough for two. Or you try to write a definitive treatment of the subject. Or you include irrelevant material. To revise, narrow the focus of your thesis; set yourself a more limited goal and stick to it. Don't wander off the subject, no matter how interesting your remarks may be.

Repeating Ideas. Two habits lead to repeating ideas unnecessarily. One is disorganization. You scatter remarks on a particular subject in several different places and thus repeat yourself. To revise, follow the rule of putting all the material on the same subject in the same place.

Another kind of repetition stems from saying the same thing twice but in different words. Usually this happens when you write an idea in one sentence, then repeat it in the following sentence because you aren't sure you were clear the first time. To revise, eliminate the weaker sentence and clarify the remaining one.

Repetitious

Researchers in artificial intelligence are trying to work on ways in which a computer can learn from past experiences and make analogies to the present problem so it knows how to solve the problem. The computer has to be able to see similarities between the past and present and use some method from a past situation to solve the problem it is facing in the present.

Clear and Concise

Researchers in artificial intelligence are working on ways to have a computer draw analogies between past and present situations so that it can choose the best method for solving the current problem.

Padding. Some writers add extra words to beef up content or to make themselves sound more like experts. They pad their writing with filler words, jargon, and bureaucratese. If you are tempted to use empty, pretentious words to fill up space or make your writing "sound good," don't succumb. To revise, state your ideas in clear, plain English. Develop content with more insights, reasons, examples, and details.

Padded and Pretentious

Because revenue derived from the sale of company products and sales has been severely impacted by the current downturn in economic performance, it is our recommendation that the board implement a reduction in funds to be allocated for transportation and accommodation expenditures.

Plain and Concise

Because the current recession has lowered company profits, we recommend that the board cut the travel budget.

Some filler words look innocuous at first glance but nonetheless pad your prose. Often you can cross out fillers like "aspects," "fields," "areas," "factors," "basically," "ultimately," "essentially," "actually," "in essence," "virtually," "type," and "in the final analysis." Phrases that indicate your point of view—"I think," "I believe," "I feel," "in my opinion"—are usually fillers, too. The search function will help you eliminate this kind of padding.

Padded with Fillers

I believe some industrial accidents cause *virtually* crisis-*type* situations in public confidence.

Plain and Concise

Some industrial accidents cause crises in public confidence.

The problems discussed so far have to do with content; the ones below have to do with style, that is, using three words where one will do.

Weak Intensifiers and Qualifiers. To emphasize your statements, you resort to unnecessary and overworked intensifiers like "very," "so," "completely," "definitely," "really," "incredibly." To revise, eliminate most intensifiers and depend on sentence structure and concrete, vivid words to make your point. Usually the terser statement gains in emphasis.

Weak Intensifier	**Terser Statement**
At that time I was *incredibly* idealistic and naive.	I was idealistic and naive then.

By eliminating "incredibly" and changing "At that time" to "then" and placing it at the end of the sentence, you focus attention on "idealistic and naive," strong words that don't need intensifying.

A related fault is hiding behind wishy-washy qualifiers like "quite," "pretty," "rather," "sort of," "somewhat." You beat around the bush. To revise, eliminate the qualifier and say something definite.

Unnecessary Qualifier	**Definite Statement**
The City Council found the proposal *quite* feasible.	The City Council found the proposal feasible.

Never qualify "unique" or other absolute words like "crucial" or "universal." Either something is unique or crucial or universal or it is not; there is no halfway house.

If you have favorite intensifiers and qualifiers (mine are "clearly" and "rather"), use the search function to ferret them out.

Waffle Words. Writers add to their excess verbiage by prefacing statements with "it appears," " it seems," "I think," "I guess," "it seems to me." Often you can eliminate such phrases and take a definite stand.

Waffles	**Takes a Stand**
It seems that Hemingway is a more popular writer than Faulkner.	Hemingway is a more popular writer than Faulkner.

Circumlocution. Circumlocution means talking around a subject rather than coming to the point quickly and directly. To revise, recast the statement in short, simple language. Try to use one or two words instead of a phrase.

Roundabout	Short and Simple
The company came to the decision that	The company decided
They are of the opinion that	They think
Concerning the matter of	About
It is often the case that	Often
At this point in time	Now

Redundancy. Being redundant means that you double up on words meaning the same or nearly the same thing: "autobiography of my life," "square in shape." Some redundant phrases slip by because they are used so often: "prove conclusively," "basic fundamentals," "close proximity," "connected together," "the reason why is because." To revise, eliminate hackneyed redundancies ("true facts," "free gifts"); be wary of doublets ("feelings and emotions," "expensive and costly"); cut out restatements of the same thing ("his attitude of contempt," "a period of time").

Redundant	Concise
Throughout the entire year he tried to *justify and excuse* his poor management policies.	Throughout the year he tried to excuse his poor management policies.

Verbal Repetition. Avoid repeating the same word unnecessarily. Repetition can be a powerful rhetorical device, but only if it is used carefully and deliberately for effect. Reading aloud often reveals annoying repetition like the kind found in the following passage.

Repetitious	Concise
If we are unduly influenced by *others,* our *lives* won't be full of the wisdom that can be gained only by going through *life* and making our own decisions without being intimidated by how *others* say we should lead our *lives.*	We will gain wisdom only if we make decisions for ourselves, without being unduly influenced or intimidated by others.

Substitute synonyms, related words, or pronouns for repeated words, or try restructuring your sentences to omit them. If you know you have favorite words that you tend to use often, use the search function to find and change them.

Overuse of the Verb "To Be." Although "to be" plays a vital role in the English language, it is a bland, passive verb that can make your writing bland and passive—and wordy as well. Whenever possible, choose strong, action verbs; they are the driving force in dynamic prose. Use the search and change commands to find instances of "is," "are," "was," "were," "being," "been," "to be." You will probably be able to change one third to one half of these to terse action verbs. Or circle in red ink every form of "to be" on the printout; seeing your prose look like a bad case of measles will shock you into writing with action verbs.

Overuse or misuse of "to be" usually falls into five patterns:

"To Be" plus a Participle

She *was visiting* Europe last summer.

Action Verb

She *visited* Europe last summer.

"To Be" plus a Noun

The large deficit and farm credit crisis *are indications* that the U.S. economy still hasn't recovered.

Action Verb

The large deficit and farm credit crisis *indicate* that the U.S. economy still hasn't recovered.

"To Be" plus an Adjective

Images of snow and darkness *are suggestive* of death.

Action Verb

Images of snow and darkness *suggest* death.

Passive Voice

The difficult questions at the news conference *were answered* smoothly by the senator.

Active Voice

The senator smoothly *answered* difficult questions at the news conference.

The revised sentence in the last example gains in power because the doer of the action—the senator—is now the grammatical subject of the sentence.

Two or More "To Be" Verbs in One Sentence

Tidepools *are* a place which *are* often studied by marine biologists because they *are* the habitat of mollusks, crabs, anemones, starfish, and many other sea creatures.

Action Verbs

Marine biologists often study tidepools, habitat of many sea creatures, including mollusks, crabs, anemones, and starfish.

Too Many Sentences, Clauses, or Phrases. Always try to use the smallest grammatical unit possible. Never use two sentences when you can combine them into one; never use a clause when you can reduce it to a phrase; never use a phrase when you can make do with a single word. Construct your sentences economically.

Unnecessary Sentence

Juan Rodriguez Cabrillo discovered California in 1542. *He was a Spanish conquistador.*

Economically Constructed

Juan Rodriguez Cabrillo, a Spanish conquistador, discovered California in 1542.

Unnecessary Clause

Hurricanes, *which are the kind of storms that occur over the North Atlantic Ocean,* are characterized by high winds and torrential rain.

Economically Constructed

Hurricanes, storms occurring over the North Atlantic Ocean, are characterized by high winds and torrential rain.

Use the search function to find clauses beginning with "who," "which," and "that." Often you can reduce them to shorter phrases.

Unnecessary Phrase

The vase, *made of delicate porcelain,* dated from the Ming Dynasty.

Economically Constructed

The delicate porcelain vase dated from the Ming Dynasty.

Empty Beginnings. Like a pitcher winding up but not throwing the ball, some writers start their sentences with unnecessary and empty phrases, usually beginning with "There is (are)," "It is," or "This is." Frequently these are combined with wordy "who," "which," and "that" clauses. (In the following example, the first sentence also contains unnecessary and wordy "to be" verbs.)

Empty Beginning

There are three concepts *that are* frequently used in discussions of corporate taxation; these concepts are the statutory tax rate, the average tax rate, and the effective marginal tax rate.

Concise and to the Point

Discussions of corporate taxation frequently make use of three concepts: the statutory tax rate, the average tax rate, and the effective marginal tax rate.

As you critique and revise your writing, try to identify the specific types of wordiness that weaken it. List them in a second window and keep them in view. (Fortunately no one is guilty of all types of wordiness at any one time!) Keep track of your progress with a word counter if your computer has one. With practice, you will begin to avoid wordiness when you write rough drafts. But even professional writers cut and prune in the revision stage. They know that concise prose is powerful prose; it moves at a faster pace and has a more dynamic impact.

But when you look at your revised document, you may suddenly realize it looks not merely lean but positively emaciated. Those extra words had hidden how undeveloped, superficial, or general the content really was. Now that you have the space, delve into your subject more deeply and add more details, examples, and facts. Your aim in writing should be to say more in fewer words.

Revising for Effective Sentences

You may discover that sentences pruned down to their bare minimum sound choppy; suddenly your style is disjointed rather than fluid. The solution is not to pad sentences with extra words again but to construct them in more sophisticated and effective ways. Try the following techniques.

Combining Sentences. We briefly touched on combining sentences in the "Revising for Conciseness" section. As the term suggests, combining sentences involves making several short sentences into one. The result should be a tautly constructed sentence that is fluent rather than choppy, and concise rather than wordy. This writing technique also offers you a good way to vary the length of your sentences.

Sentences are good candidates for combining when they have any of the following characteristics:

- *Loose and wordy:* Information is spread out over two or three sentences when it could be confined to one.
- *Repetitious:* Two sentences have the same subjects or same objects, or one sentence ends with the same word that begins the next sentence.
- *Choppy:* Sentences are short and their length doesn't vary.
- *Simplistic:* Sentence structure doesn't vary; simple declarative sentences use little or no subordination.

When you combine sentences, use the techniques of coordination, subordination, and embedding.

Coordination. Combine two sentences by joining them together with conjunctions like "and," "but," "or," "nor," "yet," "either...or," "not only...but also," "both...and." Or use a semicolon and start the next clause with an adverb like "however," "nevertheless," "hence," "thus," "for example," "furthermore."

When you combine two sentences by coordination, you transform them into *independent clauses*. That is, each retains a subject and a verb, and each could stand alone as a separate sentence.

Choppy

He forgot to save his work on the computer. His whole document disappeared when the power went out.

Fluent

He forgot to save his work on the computer, *and* his whole document disappeared when the power went out.

Subordination. Make one sentence the main clause. (This clause has a subject and verb and could stand alone as a separate sentence.) Then subordinate the second, less important sentence and join it to the main one with a subordinating conjunction: "if," "although," "because," "so that," "unless," "when," "while," "before," "after," "than," "until," "as long as," "whether," "unless." Or use a relative pronoun such as "who," "which," "that." (Sometimes these are omitted, however, and merely understood.)

Loose and Repetitious

Poinsettias were introduced to the United States in the nineteenth century by J. R. Poinsett. Poinsettias grow easily in California's temperate climate. They blossom profusely in December.

Taut and Concise

Poinsettias, *which* were introduced to the United States in the nineteenth century by J. R. Poinsett, grow easily in California's temperate climate and blossom profusely in December.

The subordinating conjunction or relative pronoun indicates the logical relationship between the two clauses. Note that the subordinate or dependent clause cannot stand on its own as a separate sentence.

The computer can help you combine and subordinate short, choppy sentences. Underline the core part of each sentence. This will graphically isolate the important information from the wordy surroundings and help you decide on the logical relationship between the main clause and the subordinate clause. Then use the move function to transfer elements from one sentence to the other.

Choppy and Wordy

Modern life involves a great deal of stress. Some people are overwhelmed. They turn to alcohol and drug abuse. They may even commit suicide.

Concise and Fluent

Some people turn to alcohol and drug abuse or even commit suicide because the stress of modern life overwhelms them.

Embedding. In this technique you reduce one sentence to a few words (or even to one word) and embed this material in the other sentence. Again the computer helps.

Underline the core part of each sentence. Usually you will see that one sentence, the main one, has a great deal of information and the other has very little. You may be able to simply delete the core information from the minor sentence and move it to the main sentence without further ado. Normally, though, you will also revise and condense as you embed.

Loose and Repetitious	**Taut and Concise**
<u>Simplicity</u> is an important quality in the layout of an ad. Simplicity means that <u>readers are more likely to be attracted</u> to the ad. They will <u>remember the message</u>.	Simplicity in the layout of an ad attracts readers and helps them remember the message.

Varying Sentence Structure. The basic elements of a sentence are subject, verb, and object or indirect object (or both). When we construct a sentence, we frequently arrange these elements in this order because it seems natural, logical, and effective. Often it is. But experienced writers also vary their sentence structure to produce sophisticated effects. As you revise, experiment with sentence structure. You may want to model some of your sentences after the types discussed below.

Cumulative Sentence. In this type of sentence, you write the subject and verb at the beginning and then add details. The process is like rolling a snowball in snow; it accumulates material and grows as it rolls along. Grammatically, the cumulative sentence could be ended at any number of points. Or conversely, more details or examples could be added without disturbing the basic subject-verb construction at the beginning.

The harbor lay between two rocky headlands that curved protectively around the water with its burden of sailboats bobbing up and down on the waves, their masts and blue tarpaulins glittering in the hot sunshine.

Inverted Sentence. Normally we put the subject first and then follow it by the verb or predicate. A predicate, however, can contain other elements besides a verb—adverbs, direct objects, prepositions, indirect objects, and various other modifying words or phrases. You can construct effective sentences by placing some of these elements in front of the subject. Changing the natural order of subject-predicate can improve the rhythm and flow of a sentence, emphasize a particular idea or relationship, and smooth the transition from one sentence to another.

>*Down the stairs and out the main door flowed* a stream of panicked office workers as the fire alarm blared in the background.

Periodic Sentence. This type of sentence creates suspense by not revealing the predicate until the end or nearly the end of the sentence. The subject comes first, then other material intervenes, and finally the predicate appears. Only then do we discover the full meaning.

>*The new tax reform bill,* despite its detractors, who say it will precipitate a recession, and despite its supporters, who say it will lighten the tax burden of millions of Americans, *undoubtedly will be changed after the next election.*

Note how dramatic this type of construction is. Reserve it for material that deserves such dramatic treatment.

Parallel and Balanced Sentence. Here elements within a sentence, or even between sentences, parallel or correspond to one another in a sophisticated fashion. Items in a list parallel one another, clauses parallel other clauses, or phrases parallel phrases. If deliberate use is made of verbal repetition, comparison, or contrast, we say that the sentence is balanced as well.

>Speed allows pitchers to overpower batters, control enables them to throw strikes consistently, and style allows them to delude batters by varying the curvature of their pitches.

Parallelism and balance can be used to construct formal passages that are memorable in their stately eloquence. Thus President John F. Kennedy proclaimed in his inaugural address of 1961:

>Now the trumpet summons us again—not as a call to bear arms, though arms we need; not as a call to battle, though embattled we are; but a call to bear the burden of a long twilight struggle, year in and year out, "rejoicing in hope, patient in tribulation"—a struggle against the common enemies of man: tyranny, poverty, disease, and war itself.

Parallelism also ensures that your readers can easily follow long or complicated sentences. In fact, the rules of good grammar demand parallelism in certain situations. Lists like the one in Kennedy's speech—"tyranny, poverty, disease, and war itself"—

should always be parallel. Make the listed items all nouns, or all adjectives, or all verbs, or all noun phrases, and so on. Don't mix and match.

Do your sentences need a new look? Take a typical paragraph and visually analyze the structure of its sentences. Underline the subject and verb (or predicate) in each sentence or change them to bold. Where do you typically place them? Do you ever put any part of the predicate before the subject? Do you ever create suspense or make dramatic statements by locating the subject at the beginning and the verb at the end? Now highlight parallel and balanced elements by underlining them or making them bold. Do you ever use parallelism, repetition, comparison, or contrast to emphasize a point and make it memorable? Are lists always parallel in structure? If the answer to these questions is usually no, you need to experiment more. Revise at least some of your sentences.

But as you revise, be a savvy computer writer: If you are not sure exactly what you want to do with a particular passage, use the copy function to make a duplicate. Then play around with the duplicate while you keep the original on screen as a reference. When a revision finally satisfies you, delete the original.

Avoiding Common Sentence Faults. What if your sentences are simply ungrammatical? This book assumes that you already have a good working knowledge of basic English grammar and that you have invested in a writer's handbook that includes sections on grammar and common grammatical faults. Refer to these frequently. Look up any point you are not absolutely sure about. Murphy's Law in writing states that if you make a mistake, your document will be read by the one person who prides himself on being an expert on that particular point of grammar. When necessary, do the exercises most handbooks contain.

Revising for Effective Diction

The great nineteenth-century poet and critic Samuel Coleridge defined poetry as "the best words in the best order." That is a good working definition of any kind of writing. And professional writers are quick to admit that choosing the best word is one of their hardest tasks. If you try to do it while writing a rough draft, you may lose sight of your main purpose and even run into a writing block. Many writers find it easier and more efficient to polish diction in the revision stage.

Using a Dictionary and Thesaurus. If you are serious about words, you need the resources of a good dictionary and a thesaurus. And you need to know how to use each of them correctly.

Use the dictionary to look up the meanings of words. Don't trust your guesses about doubtful words. A dictionary tells you where a word comes from; knowing the root meaning will often fix the contemporary meaning more firmly in your mind. A dictionary also gives all the different meanings for a particular word. (You may know only one or two meanings.) It will tell you if the word is archaic and thus not suitable for contemporary prose, or if it is slang or dialect or colloquial and thus suitable only for spoken conversation. Frequently a dictionary gives antonyms and synonyms and explains the difference in connotations between them. This last feature is especially helpful in making sure the word you are choosing has the right tone and emotional associations for your document. A historical dictionary like the *OED — Oxford English Dictionary* — even gives examples of how a particular word has changed through the years. All this information helps you to choose words that are appropriate — in meaning, in level of language, in connotation — for your particular writing task. (Computer writers and dictionary buffs will be glad to know that the complete *OED* — containing half a million entries, more than 2 million usage citations, and a total of 60 million words — is to be made available on CD ROM.)

A thesaurus, on the other hand, lacks this range of information; it merely lists words that are synonomous or closely related. (It may list antonyms and contrasted words as well.) Thus, if you think someone's writing is "flowery" but want to use a different adjective, a thesaurus will suggest "rhetorical," "aureate," "bombastic," "declamatory," "euphuistic," "grandiloquent," "magniloquent," "overblown," "prolix," "sonorous," "swollen," "diffuse," "redundant," "verbose," or "wordy." It won't, however, give you the meanings or connotations of these words. That you will have to look up in a dictionary.

But if you don't use a dictionary, if you choose words from a thesaurus as if you were pulling rabbits out of a hat, you're likely to come up with some odd choices. "Thesaurus prose" is painfully obvious to the experienced reader. Had President Lincoln misused a thesaurus, the Gettysburg Address might now read, "That régime of the multitude, by the multitude, for the multitude, shall not evaporate from the terrestrial globe"! So keep in mind that the thesaurus is an excellent tool for reminding you of alternatives but a poor one for teaching you about words or helping you to make the best choice. Some computer spell checkers have a thesaurus, but since these are usually not extensive, you will probably want a printed one as well. If your computer has a hard disk, however, and if your budget will stand it, you can buy an on-line thesaurus with more than 200,000 words. Nonetheless, some critics still maintain that a printed thesaurus offers better word choices.

Writing on the Appropriate Level. The language used in writing can be divided into three broad categories or levels. The level you write on will largely determine the kinds of words you choose.

- *Formal English* is serious, eloquent, and lofty. A person writing at this level deliberately wants to exploit the beauties of language; he or she draws on a wide-ranging vocabulary and makes frequent use of rhetorical and literary devices. But the opportunities for using formal English are limited: inaugural or other solemn addresses, formal sermons, proclamations, and the like. Most writers are not likely to do much writing at this level.

- *Standard English* takes in most academic and business writing and most published writing. It draws on an educated vocabulary but doesn't try to be lofty. Grammar and structure are always correct, but the style is flexible and can be adapted to a wide variety of purposes. At its upper level, standard English approaches formal English, whereas at its lowest level, it can sound almost like conversation. Much of your writing will probably fall into this broad category.

- *Casual English* is conversation in print. It may contain slang, colloquialisms, dialect, sentence fragments, or nonstandard grammar. The style is usually loose and unstructured. You might use casual English for your personal writing—letters, journals, diaries, and the like—or you might adapt it for humor, satire, dialogue, and some kinds of advertising. Although modern business practice calls for a conversational and friendly tone in many letters and memos, this quality is best achieved with standard English rather than with a slangy, colloquial style.

As a general rule, don't try to mix these levels in a particular piece of writing. Lofty diction sounds as out of place in a personal letter as slang does in a formal document. Be sure that the level of diction is consistent throughout the piece of writing and that it suits your particular audience, subject, and purpose.

In this context, writers often worry about contractions. As a general rule, the more contractions you use, the more informal your level of language seems. Although contractions of verbs and negatives—"can't," "don't"—are often acceptable in standard written English, contractions of pronouns and verbs—"they're," "you're," "it's"—seem informal, perhaps too informal. And certain contractions sound downright ugly: "you've," "would've," "we'd."

Choosing the Best Words. When you wrote your rough draft, you may have embedded many alternative word choices, or perhaps you left some blank spaces because you couldn't think of the right word. When you did your critiquing, you may have underlined examples of clichés, jargon, or vague language. Here are some guidelines to help you choose the best words as you revise.

Use words that are as direct, clear, and specific as possible. Be accurate and correct. Don't settle for near-guesses. If you tell yourself, "Oh, they'll know what I mean," the word is not precise enough. Consult your dictionary frequently.

Choose concrete nouns and vigorous action verbs. "Cars, buses, and commuter trains" is more concrete and specific than "modes of transportation." "Zigzagged down the hill" or "careened down the hill" is more action-packed than "went down the hill."

Avoid big, showy words. There is no need to write "eschew pretentious Latinate diction." Don't try to impress readers by packing your writing with long jawbreakers. Simple, plain words are usually the most accurate and precise.

Choose words with appropriate connotations or associations to suit the tone and purpose of your writing. For example, the connotations of "stiff" fit a hard-boiled detective story but would be offensive in a newspaper story about an airplane crash.

When appropriate, use figurative language—similes, metaphors, personification, irony, hyperbole. Turn to the great writers for examples of brilliant uses of figurative language. Thus Charles Dickens, in *Great Expectations*, describes how the child Pip gradually becomes aware of his surroundings:

> I found out . . . that the low leaden line beyond, was the river; and that the distant savage lair from which the wind was rushing was the sea; and that the small bundle of shivers growing afraid of it all and beginning to cry, was Pip.

Harlan Ellison, in his short story about the twenty-fourth century, "'Repent, Harlequin!' Said the Ticktockman," graphically conjures up an ugly sound:

> There was a hideous scraping as the sound of a million fingernails rasped down a quarter of a million blackboards.

D. H. Lawrence paints a bleak picture of the Nottingham countryside in "The Horse Dealer's Daughter":

> In the distance, across a shallow dip in the country, the small town was clustered like smouldering ash, a tower, a spire, a heap of low, raw, extinct houses.

Avoiding Poor Diction. A good writer stays away from certain kinds of words. For example, never mix metaphors: "We have the bull by the horns and have safely passed through the eye of the storm." And don't decorate your prose to make it look creative and literary.

Avoid worn-out, tired, dull words. Colorless words like "pretty" and "nice" convey nothing specific; constant overuse, and misuse, of "incredible," "unbelievable," "great," "unique," and the like have drained them of meaning. By definition, clichés are trite and worn-out: "deaf as a post," "strong as an ox," "as American as apple pie," "passed with flying colors." Harder to give up, perhaps, are expressions currently in fashion: "for starters," "the bottom line," "window of opportunity," "trendy." They are on everyone's lips today and out of date tomorrow. Slang is rarely appropriate. Although vivid and amusing when first coined, it withers rapidly. Does anyone remember what "the bees' knees" once meant?

Avoid jargon and gobbledygook. Jargon is the special language of a particular group. To computer hackers, "a cold boot" is perfectly intelligible; but if you are writing for the general public, you had better say, "Turn on the computer." Keep technical terms to a minimum unless your readers are specialists, and define the terms you do use. Always avoid the pompous, inflated prose of bureaucratic pronouncements: "The interface between marketing and production is to be actualized in a time frame consistent with the goal-timetable delineated by management."

Never use offensive language of any sort. Although most writers have the common sense not to use coarse language in inappropriate contexts, and racist language is becoming a thing of the past, sexist language still litters the scene. Your audience likely includes women, and women—-and men, too—are understandably offended by patently demeaning terms like "chick" or "broad." But sexist language can take subtle forms, too. You can avoid sounding offensive and alienating readers if you remember this list of "don't"s.

- Don't call an adult female (anyone over eighteen) a "girl."
- Don't use only first names for women but last names and titles for men. ("Mr. Bradley argued for the proposal, but Janet said it was too expensive.")
- Don't give social titles (Mrs., Miss, and Ms.) to women but official titles to men. ("Premier Jacques Chirac and Mrs. Thatcher will meet next month.")
- Don't describe women in terms of appearance, domestic skills, or so-called feminine attributes. ("Mrs. Talbot, looking very chic in a pearl gray suit and pink blouse, rejected Atech's latest buyout offer for Miton Products.")
- Don't say "lady" when you mean "woman" unless you would say "gentleman" for a male in the same context.

A good rule of thumb: If you don't use such language for men, don't use it for women. Another good rule: Don't use gender-specific language when neutral terms exist: Write "letter carrier" instead of "mailman," "fire fighter" instead of "fireman," "workers" instead of "workmen," and so on. In referring to both males and females in the human race, use inclusive terms like "persons," "people," "society," "human beings," "individuals," "humanity" instead of "man" or "mankind." If you want to refer to representative persons, use plurals and gender-neutral pronouns like "they" and "their" rather than "he":

Gender-Specific	**Neutral**
A person who drinks shouldn't drive; he is a danger to others.	People who drink shouldn't drive; they are a danger to others.

In an informal context, address the reader directly and say "you": "Don't drink and drive; you're a menace to others." The formal alternative is "one," but be consistent; don't switch the point of view in a document.

If it is more appropriate to refer to a single representative person, use "she" in some paragraphs, "he" in others. Or occasionally say "he or she" and "his or her." A more radical approach (not accepted by everyone, including the publisher of this book) is to use the gender-neutral "they" or "their" with singular nouns. This solution is frequently used in conversation, and according to the *Guidelines for Nonsexist Use of Language* put out by the National Council of Teachers of English, it can be occasionally used in writing when the subject is an indefinite pronoun: "When everyone contributes their own ideas, the discussion will be a success."[1]

The main thing to remember is that you want to communicate with readers, not alienate, ignore, or trivialize them. Words are powerful; choose them carefully. To root out instances of sexist language in your draft, make a list of words you want to avoid and use the computer's search function to look for them.

Revising for Consistency

As you revise, be sure your document is consistent (or uniform) in diction, tone, and style. Consistency can be weakened by any of these practices:

- Combining words from different levels of English (using formal, standard, and casual English in the same document)
- Contracting words haphazardly (sometimes writing "do not" or "they are" and other times writing "don't" or "they're")
- Inserting unexplained technical jargon in a document written for nonspecialists (referring to the "kinked demand model of oligopolistic behavior" when you are trying to explain to ordinary people how firms set prices)

---

[1]A copy of *Guidelines for Nonsexist Use of Language in NCTE Publications* can be obtained free of charge by writing to NCTE, 1111 Kenyon Road, Urbana, IL 61801. Enclose a self-addressed, stamped envelope. For an excellent book-length treatment of how to avoid sexist language, consult Casey Miller and Kate Swift, *The Handbook of Nonsexist Writing* (New York: Lippincott and Crowell, 1980).

- Inserting patches of ornate or decorative writing in the midst of plain and simple writing (using highly figurative language or lapsing into "purple prose" when it is not appropriate)
- Unnecessarily switching tenses (moving between the past and the present or the future and the present)
- Switching point of view (starting out with "they," then switching to "you" or "we" or "I" or "he")
- Writing in different tones of voice (being factual and serious in one part of the document, satiric in another, and humorous and coy in yet another)
- Using different terms and modes of address (using different names for the same item—"USA," the "U.S.," "the United States"—or sometimes calling people by their titles and last names, other times referring to them by their first names)
- Incorrectly or inconsistently using abbreviations or capital letters (writing "corp." instead of "corporation," or sometimes writing "Chemistry Department" and other times "chemistry department")

Avoid inconsistency by drawing up a brief style guide containing the rules or principles of usage you intend to follow. A writer's handbook will help you with details. (Newspapers, publishers, business firms, and universities often have style guides for their own use.) Carefully check your document against this style guide. Also read your document aloud (or have someone read it to you) and listen for inconsistencies. Then use the search function to locate all instances of a particular problem. For example, you might look for instances of "you" in a document that is supposed to have a third-person point of view, or search for abbreviations in a document that is supposed to spell everything out.

Proofreading with the Computer

Probably you have been correcting typos and spelling and punctuation errors as you revised your document. Frequently, though, it is more efficient to leave proofreading until the end. After you have finished the last draft of the document and made a backup copy, use a spell checker to correct all misspellings. Remember the limitations of such programs, however. Many will not tell you that you used the wrong homonym ("their" for "there"). Nor will they spot that you wrote "simplistic" when you really meant "simple," or that you left out a word by mistake. And they won't know that the name of a person—Percy Bysshe Shelley, for example—is spelled correctly unless you have added this name to the dictionary. Correctly spelled words sometimes get flagged as wrong, especially if the checker's dictionary is small, and occasionally mistakes are simply missed. But despite these imperfections, spell checkers—along with the Delete key and the undo function—are a writer's best friend!

When you have finished checking for spelling, go through the document with a fine-tooth comb looking for other errors. In this case, the computer's cursor will be your comb. Slowly move the cursor through the document from beginning to end. Look at each word, each letter, each punctuation mark as the cursor moves past it. Is it correct? If not, the cursor is in position for a quick change or delete. Following the cursor letter by letter enables you to focus on the smallest details, rather than being distracted by larger problems, all of which should be taken care of by now anyway. Look most carefully at the most familiar words; those are the ones your eyes can trick you into skipping over. In fact, some writers advocate reading your document from end to beginning while you move the cursor backward; then you won't be distracted by content at all. Also double-check all numbers against your original information; a single wrong digit can wreak havoc.

And know your limitations. Get someone else to proofread your document, too. The proofreader can check for errors on screen while you read aloud from a printed version, or she can proofread on her own after you have finished a preliminary check.

The goal of proofreading is always zero mistakes in the final printed version. No matter how good the content, errors in spelling or punctuation will cheapen it. And you as a writer will make a bad impression. Unfair or irrational as it may seem, typos make you look sloppy or, worse still, illiterate. You don't seem to care about your work, so why should the readers? If your writing matters, proofreading matters, too.

Avoiding the Pitfalls of Computer Writing

If you have been using the computer effectively, it should be helping you in all your writing tasks, from prewriting to revision. Nonetheless, critics complain about serious pitfalls in writing on the computer. They charge that computer writers fall into the following traps:

- Writing too much, so that their work has length but not much substance
- Never getting a broad view of their work because the computer screen is so small
- Writing in a disjointed way and producing a collage or pastiche rather than a unified whole
- Writing prose as dull and bland as processed cheese
- Not revising thoroughly because they don't have to retype their work
- Making superficial, local revisions rather than substantial, global ones

- Never achieving finality in their prose because the electronic words can always be changed
- Losing a record of how their writing develops by not handwriting and typing various manuscript versions of their documents
- Spending a long time working on the computer but not improving their writing

Some — but certainly not all — computer writers may be guilty of some of these faults, but the computer is not to blame. Rather, writers who fall into these traps are making mistakes at various stages in the writing process, or they don't know how to exploit the capabilities of the computer to their own advantage. Thus, if the final version of a piece of writing is too long, the writer didn't use a word counter to keep the length within reasonable bounds in the rough draft stage or didn't cut ruthlessly enough during revision. Writers who never get a broad view of their work don't use the computer's split screen and multiple windows and don't print out enough copies. If the writing is disjointed, then not enough time and care went into the planning stage; or little or no attempt was made to write in blocks of paragraphs; or not much attention was paid to improving coherence during revision.

As for dull prose, computers don't turn out dull prose, dull writers do. And people who don't revise thoroughly because they don't have to retype, or who spend all their time making superficial corrections and changes instead of wrestling with larger problems of organization, logic, and development, need to learn better revision strategies. If writers are seriously concerned that they will lose the opportunity to revise if they don't retype, then by all means, let them retype their document; the computer's split screen and multiple windows will make their task easier. But for the overwhelming majority of writers, retyping as a revision strategy is an inefficient and unnecessary use of time. Critiquing and editing the paper printout, combing through the document word by word and line by line on screen, and reading the document out loud are all better revision strategies for most people.

As for achieving finality in prose, good critical judgment, and not the fixed type of a typewriter, enables the writer to say, This is finished. Finally, if writers end up with no manuscript versions of their documents, that means they tried to go directly from the screen to final printout without any preliminary paper versions. Not only did they bypass a valuable editing technique — correcting successive paper copies by hand — they also ran a greater risk of pastiche writing.

However, critics are correct when they say computer writers spend more time at writing. And the reason is clear: Computer writers enjoy what they are doing and are willing to invest the time in doing it right.

The computer isn't a magic machine: It won't automatically make you a Joan Didion or an Ernest Hemingway. What the programmers say is still true: "Garbage in, garbage out." What comes off the printer in the final version is what you put into the machine to begin with. The computer doesn't improve your writing; you do. You are the one who does the thinking, planning, writing, revising, rethinking, and revising again. But if you're a smart computer writer, you know how to use your machine as a powerful new writing tool to help you.

Let's Solve It!

Going through the motions of revising your work doesn't necessarily mean that it will be improved. Here are ways to avoid falling in love with your writing, getting frustrated, or making things worse.

Problem: Falling in Love with Your Own Words. You can't bear to revise particular phrases or passages because you love them just as they are—so witty, vivid, perceptive, intelligent, and true. Or you feel that to criticize your writing is to criticize your self-worth; having to revise means admitting failure.

Solution. Try to look at writing as a job to be done or a skill to be used rather than as an expression of individuality or a measure of self-worth. Learn to be more detached. Let your document sit longer before rereading it. Then read it from the readers' point of view. (Oddly enough, seeing your work on the computer screen often helps you to view it more objectively.) You may find that the passages you love the most are really not effective or appropriate. But if it helps you to change or delete them, save them in another file; perhaps you can use them in a different context.

Problem: Staying on the Surface. You correct spelling and typos, you even change words and perhaps some sentences, but you never go deeper than that. You make only superficial or local corrections.

Solution. Remember that revision also involves "re-vision," that is, reseeing your work and rethinking its ideas and reorganizing its structure. Don't be afraid to tear apart your document and rebuild it from top to bottom. Computer writing is not rigid and fixed, but fluid and changeable; take advantage of this quality.

Problem: Never Being Satisfied. No matter how many changes and corrections you make, you are never satisfied with your work. You want perfection, and when you can't get it, you feel frustrated.

Solution. Nothing achieves perfection in this world, including heavily revised writing. Look at your work as in a state of becoming: It can always become better if more changes are made. But you may not have the time to make them, or the project may not be worth further time and effort, or you may not be skilled enough to make the kinds of revisions that are needed. Set high standards for yourself, yes, but not impossibly high ones. Accurately gauge how much time and effort you can invest in a project and how much work the project itself deserves. Then "satisfice." That is, given the limitations of a particular project, be satisfied with work that is reasonably acceptable or sufficient to get the job done.

Problem: Making Things Worse. You work hard at revising. In fact, you go through revision after revision, but when you finish, you feel that the final draft is worse than the original. The sparkle has gone out of your writing; it sounds dull and unnatural.

Solution. Maybe you try too hard. You are like an artist who does a pencil sketch and then proceeds to erase his or her work and redraw it and erase and redraw, until nothing is left but a worked-over smudge. Do less revising. Work only on the main problems, then get outside criticism. If you can find a writing mentor—an instructor, a colleague, or a supervisor—rely on her critical judgment. When she says to stop, *stop*. Don't keep erasing or, in this case, deleting.

Computer Writing Tips

Truly revising a document, as opposed to merely keying something into the computer, goes faster and better if you employ the following techniques.

- Learn how to move around quickly and efficiently in a long document. Use your word processor's capability to go directly to a specific page. Use the printed version to guide you. (In some programs you may have to repaginate your document first if you have made substantial deletions or additions.)
- Move to a particular section by using the search function to locate a term found only in that section. Or flag different sections by placing special symbols (%, $, ?, @) before key terms. Keep a list of these symbols so you don't forget them.
- As you revise, don't delete until you have a satisfactory alternative. For words and phrases, type alternatives next to the original until you decide what is best. For sentences, move the old ones out of the way by pressing Enter a few times; see how new versions look before deleting the old. Long passages should never be deleted entirely until the writing project is finished; move them to a special "Wastebasket" section at the end of your document.

■ Print out frequent copies of your revised rough draft. Major projects should go through many revisions. Date or number each one so you know which is the latest version.

■ You may want to change the filename to reflect the state of revision, as for instance, "05.NewWrRvsd.2." If such names get too unwieldy (and if your operating system allows you to), note the state of revision in a file description.

■ Remember to back up your work again after you revise it. For major projects, don't wait until the document is completely finished; redo the backup after each revising session.

When it comes to technological stuff, I'm a dinosaur, and I wasn't anxious to embrace computers. Clearly, they're an alien life form. The crisis came with my Ph.D. dissertation—all 245 pages of it. I did one chapter my usual way: wrote it on yellow paper, scribbling all over the pages, crossing things out, drawing arrows and stars. Then I typed it, smeared it with whiteout, and gave it to my committee, who asked me to make more changes, which meant more typing.

If this is what it took for one chapter, I dreaded the remaining five. But I didn't want to be pushed or bullied into using a computer, either.

"Just try it," my husband said gently (and cleverly). In 20 minutes he showed me how to type in text, make basic revisions, move text around, and save my work. I was impressed at how much I could do with such limited instruction. That afternoon I worked for several hours; in fact, I got so engrossed I missed a hair appointment for the first time in my life!

Still, I had to work out a continuing relationship with this alien machine. I like to animate technological things. So I've given the computer a name—"Tandy"—and a personality. And I talk to it. Out loud. "Tandy, why are you doing this?" "Don't do that, Tandy!" Or I give it positive reinforcement. "Wow! Tandy! Look at what you can do!"

The result of this relationship is that my writing practices have changed. I don't worry about the quality of my typing anymore; consequently, I don't make as many mistakes. And I compose at the keyboard, something I never did before. I find the computer draws out my willingness to speculate, to pursue an idea to its limits and beyond. Then I can just dissolve it with a keystroke if it doesn't work out. So the computer encourages my freethinking side.

As for my dissertation, the first chapter took what seemed like a year, but the next five went much faster, in part because of the computer. And it was great to print out for the last time—a complete, *pretty* version I could actually hold. (I thanked Tandy for its hard work!)

Karen Cunningham
Lecturer in English

The Reader Responds

Accepting criticism
Understanding criticism
Correcting and editing
Rethinking ideas

In the early chapters of this book, you were urged to write for the reader. That is, your writing should take into account your readers' attitudes and possible responses and should meet their needs and expectations. Until now all this has been theoretical, because you have been busy writing, evaluating, and revising on your own. Now it is time to submit your writing to some readers—not all readers, because your document isn't ready for publication yet, but you do need outside critical response. Although you might omit this step with routine documents, longer or more important documents always benefit from reader response, even if it is only informal criticism from colleagues or peers.

What do other people think of your work? How do they respond to it? What suggestions do they have for changes and improvements? Do they see any unresolved issues, unconvincing arguments, inaccurate information? Do they find your strategy effective, your plan logical? What about matters of style? Tone? Grammar? Answers to questions like these enable you to look at your writing from the readers' point of view and then make revisions that convey your ideas more accurately, persuasively, and elegantly. Perhaps you will need to change your ideas or at least refine them.

Your work can be submitted to different types of readers who fulfill a variety of functions and give you different types of responses, all of them useful in their own way:

- A *technical expert* gives you the benefit of his or her expertise and tells you whether or not your content is correct and complete.
- A *skilled writer* comments on the quality of your writing and discusses craft and style.
- A *test driver* sees if your directions are clear and your ideas practical (especially important if you write how-to documents).
- A *supporter* provides encouragement and appreciation.
- A *team member* works with you on a collaborative writing project, checking your work in terms of group aims and standards.
- A *mentor* plays the role of teacher, giving advice and showing you how things are done.
- A *judge* evaluates your abilities as a writer and decides if you have met the requirements of the writing assignment.

If you have only one critic, ideally he or she would play all these roles to some extent. But often you will submit your work to a variety of people who will read and criticize it from different points of view. This chapter discusses how to accept and understand their criticism and how to translate it into a plan for further revision. And remember that, depending on the complexity, length, and importance of the writing project, these two steps in the writing process—getting reader response and making revisions—can be repeated many times.

Submitting a Printout

Many, if not most, critics will want to read your work in printed form. Print a fresh copy for them, but first be sure that your text is ready for public exposure. Don't be seduced by the beautiful appearance of your manuscript; bad writing that looks pretty is still bad writing. Polish your prose before submitting it to others.

If you are going to incorporate visual aids in your document—tables, charts, diagrams, artwork, and so on—you may want to have them in place, too, if only in rough form; in that case, read Chapter 8 before going on with this one.

When content is complete, be sure that the physical appearance of your document makes a good impression and enhances readability. Remove the embedded comments you wrote to yourself, as well as any alternative word choices. (If you want to keep these for your own reference, make a copy of your computer file in its original form and save it.) Before you print out the document, set the margins wide enough so that your critic has room to write down comments. Use a new ribbon; choose double spacing and good quality printing. No one likes to read faint and poorly formed letters of draft printing, and it is difficult, if not impossible, to write comments on single-spaced text. Date or number the document and give it a descriptive title; you may even want to use the word "draft" in the title.

In some cases it may be appropriate to attach a cover letter or memo or informal note, reminding your reader of the purpose and scope of the document, describing its current status, and calling attention to certain parts. Or perhaps you have specific questions you hope your critic can answer. You may also want to include your outline so the critic can check your proposed plan against the actual result. If several people are reading your work, provide individual copies for each one. Exceptions to this rule might be short, routine documents that can be circulated quickly and won't be marked up heavily, or very long documents, like a full-length book or long report, which would cost too much to duplicate.

Different critics have different ways of voicing their criticisms, and they may do any one of the following:

> Write comments in the margins of your printed copy
> Write comments on a separate page
> Use a series of standard editing abbreviations and symbols in the margins
> Write a paragraph or two of comment at the end of the document
> Incorporate criticisms in a letter or memo
> Fill out an evaluation form
> Hold a personal conference

Combinations and variations of these methods may also be used. In any event, be sure you understand the system; it might be necessary, for example, to get a key to the editing abbreviations your critic uses. Also try to find out your critic's standards for judging a piece of writing. This is not always easy to do. Some instructors (or editors or supervisors or project managers) make clear what they are looking for at the beginning of the assignment, but often you simply learn by experience what your critic expects. The better you get to know your critic, the better you will be able to interpret and understand his or her remarks.

Submitting a Computer File

If your critic prefers to critique on screen, you may be asked to submit your work on a disk. However, because reading text on a screen is so different from reading it on paper, you should probably provide a printout as well. Never give your original disk; always submit a backup. Alternatively, you may be asked to transfer the relevant file or files to your critic's disk. Or you may be connected to other workstations through a network, so you can simply send your work to your critic's computer. Perhaps you and your critic share a hard disk; in that case, he or she can access your work there. Whatever the method of transfer, provide your critics with a brief description of the purpose, scope, and status of your work; you can append this to the beginning of the file. You may also want to embed comments in the text, asking the reader questions, pointing out problem areas, or giving alternatives. Use a distinctive style option or hidden text for these comments.

On-line critics can let you know their responses in much the same way as "paper critics" do; they can write their comments at the end of your document or in a separate file. (Few computer systems have the capability to produce marginal comments.) And of course they can fill out a paper evaluation form, write a letter or memo, or hold a personal conference. But there are also special methods for computer critiquing.

If the word-processing program is sophisticated enough, on-line critics can write their comments in hidden text and make them invisible when others read the file. In certain group situations—for example, when several people are trying to decide whether or not to accept a manuscript for publication—editorial readers may want to embed comments for their own information but not print them out when a paper copy of the document is circulated to others. Or members of a group project may want to read a document without being influenced by what others have said. Once they finish critiquing the document, however, they can make the hidden text visible and respond to previous critical comments.

On-line critics can make detailed changes in certain passages and then ask you to revise other parts of the document along the same lines. They may actually change the text of your file or simply embed suggested revisions in hidden text.

If your word-processing program does not have hidden text capability, your critics can still use some of the techniques described above by embedding comments or making changes to the text in capitals, bold, or underlining. In that way, their comments will stand out clearly from the original text.

On-line critics can also design an evaluation form that is opened in a second window and filled out while they read the document in the first window. Or they could read a paper copy of the document but fill out the form on the computer. This form can be very simple, like that in Figure 7-1. To fill out the form, the critic merely places the cursor at the end of each question and starts writing a response. (This is, of course, only a model; questions for specific types of projects could vary widely.)

All these comments assume that you are the writer and someone else is the critic. In some cases, however, and especially in group writing projects, you may be the critic. And one of the things you will quickly find out is that critiquing someone else's writing teaches you a great deal about your own. The faults you spot in their work may be the very faults you are most guilty of, and the revisions you suggest may be the very ones you need to try yourself. Thus reading and critiquing another person's work makes you much more aware of the qualities of good writing.

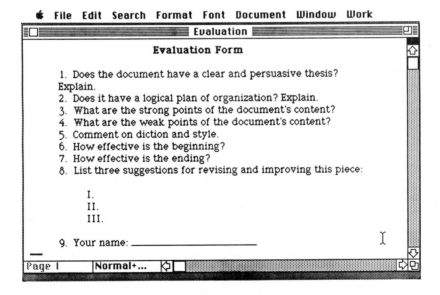

FIGURE 7-1. *A sample on-line evaluation form*

Accepting Criticism

After you get your disk or printout back from your critics, what next? The first step is acceptance.

It is not always easy to accept criticism of one's writing. Often, how well you accept and use criticism depends on your attitude toward writing and your assessment of yourself as a writer. Thus, if you persist in seeing your finished work as a measure of your self-worth, or if you fall in love with your own words, you will be defensive or even angry about criticism and it won't help your writing very much. On the other hand, if you have no confidence in your abilities as a writer, negative criticism might only confirm your worst fears and make writing even more difficult for you. Realistically knowing and appreciating your abilities as a writer will make criticism easier to accept.

Accepting criticism also becomes easier if you are realistic about the present status of your piece of writing. See it for what it is—a first draft, a preliminary report, a tentative approach to accomplishing a particular writing task. Recall where you are in the writing process. You haven't reached the last step yet, you haven't produced a finished document, so you should expect people to find weaknesses in your writing.

It is also helpful if you realize that different steps in the writing process can be approached in different ways. For example, some of the time you need to be free and unfettered and creative. Prewriting and writing the rough drafts are usually times to explore your options, try out ideas, be innovative. At other times—when you are planning strategy, for example, or organizing materials, or revising—you need to exercise your skills as a writer. You evaluate, judge, make decisions, follow the rules. And finally, there is a time for learning. You need to listen to your readers and understand what they are saying; you need to accept their criticism with an open mind and use it to improve your writing. Learn from your mistakes.

When your writing is being criticized, consciously switch to your learning mode. Don't be defensive. Listen. Think about other situations in which you readily accept criticism. If you play sports, for example, you probably welcome criticism from your coach and use it to improve your performance. Or if you take music lessons, getting criticism from your instructor becomes a valuable method of learning. Writing is no different; criticism can teach you new skills and improve the ones you already possess.

But avoid concentrating solely on the negative statements your critics make. Look at the positive ones, too. Recognizing the good points of a document and building on them is just as important as revising the weak points.

Finally, view your writing as part of a larger, two-way communication process. You are not writing in a vacuum, but rather communicating with others. Expressing your ideas initiates the process; getting feedback completes it. Until you know your readers' response, you are not really communicating. Try to put yourself in your readers' shoes.

Understanding Criticism

Once you're ready to accept criticism, the next step is understanding it and doing something positive about it. Look for patterns or trends in what your readers tell you and draw some practical conclusions. Do all your readers make the same criticisms? If everyone says a specific passage is too flowery, you can be sure your style needs to be plainer. Do their criticisms correspond to the misgivings you had about your document? If you had a sneaking suspicion your writing was disorganized, and your critics complain about the same problem, you know you have to do some rearranging. Do comments scattered throughout the document add up to a persistent problem? For example, if critics repeatedly ask for more examples and details, you should realize that you frequently fail to support your general statements.

And even if you disagree with a particular criticism, can you see the grain of truth in it? For example, you may decide that a reader is absolutely wrong when he says an argument is no good and ought to be scrapped; nonetheless, his criticism should alert you that you have not presented the argument convincingly enough.

Also understand that different types of criticism call for different courses of action. First are straightforward matters of right and wrong, good and bad. For example, no one will dispute that "ain't" is nonstandard English, or that "enviroment" is misspelled, or that "Disruption of the schedule being due to an unavoidable accident" is a sentence fragment. Your writing may also be indisputably weak or lacking in some areas: Everyone, including you, agrees that it is disorganized or undeveloped or choppy or whatever the problem is. Clear-cut faults like these seldom generate arguments. The critic merely points them out and you agree: They have to be corrected.

In other cases, the critic asks for improvement rather than correction. Your writing is already satisfactory or even good, but you can make it better. Here your critic is not disparaging what you have achieved but rather is pushing you to strive for excellence. You are being told not to be satisfied with the merely adequate. Make your writing fulfill its potential.

Finally, there are judgment calls. Your critic and you may legitimately disagree about the value or effectiveness of a particular passage or the whole work. Call this a matter of taste and judgment; there are no clear-cut answers. Much criticism is like this. Read several different reviews of the same movie or book and see how widely critics disagree. Even Shakespeare has had his share of mixed reviews: An English periodical in 1808 complained bitterly about the "undisguised, palpable grossness and obscenity" in *Othello,* and George Bernard Shaw called the play "pure melodrama." You will have to make informed decisions about judgment calls, but be sure these decisions are solidly based on principles of good writing.

If you know what kind of criticism is being made, you can understand it better and choose appropriate action—whether it be correcting clear-cut mistakes, improving your work, or making informed decisions about matters of taste and judgment.

Responding to Criticism

Criticism is made by people, and interacting with people always presents difficulties of one sort or another. Follow commonsense guidelines when you respond to your critics.

Keep Personalities Out of It. Good critics are objective and helpful; they sincerely want to help the writer improve. But being only human, critics can also have private agendas; they may try to exert their power, even old scores, vent personal frustrations, or even curry favor. Personality clashes can develop among members of a group project; a supervisor can be more interested in office politics than in your writing. However, it is wise to remember that you may have your own private agenda, too! Be honest about the situation. Sometimes a forthright discussion will clear the air. At other times you may simply have to develop a thick skin. Ideally, though, critic and writer should concentrate on the professional writing task at hand and leave personalities out of it.

Separate the Dross from the Good. Not all criticism is equally good. You may run into someone who has a tin ear or makes poor suggestions. Beware of the person, for example, who tries to change active verbs to passive ones or substitutes pretentious diction for short, simple words. The more you know about writing, the better you can judge the value of criticism and decide which suggestions to follow and which to ignore. But be careful: don't reject criticism merely because you have difficulties accepting it or because you dislike the critic.

Learn to Compromise. Your critics may be in a position of authority over you as instructors, editors, supervisors, or project managers. Consequently, their criticism may sound more like demands than suggestions. If you disagree, learn how to compromise: Give way on little matters so you can stand up for the big ones, or defer in matters you know are important to them and follow your own judgment in other cases. What matters differs from writer to writer. Some writers are willing to make extensive stylistic changes and delete whole passages as long as their controversial ideas remain intact, whereas others want to fight to the finish over single words. Nonetheless, intelligent compromise can be squared with artistic integrity. Compromise works well with peer critics, too, especially if you are working on a group project; it is a quality that goes hand in hand with cooperation and productivity.

Learn to Let Go. The notion that our writing is proprietary, that what we write is somehow distinctively and privately ours, is a cherished belief, perhaps stemming from our view of how solitary poets and novelists write. But there are many situations in professional life where the individual must contribute his or her writing to a collaborative project—academic research, reports and proposals of all kinds, technical manuals, handbooks, some types of journalism, anthologies, directories, encyclopedias. The writer must merge a distinctive style or even a creative imagination into a group effort. This may not be easy to do at first, but you should learn to let go of your work gracefully and to allow the requirements of the group to take precedence over your personal wishes.

Get a Second Opinion. If possible, get more than one person to read your work. Your first critic may not see everything, may be too positive or too negative, may have standards radically different from yours, may be unable to criticize in a constructive way, or may be otherwise inadequate. Give some thought to what role or roles you want your critic to play: technical expert? skilled writer? test driver? supporter? team member? mentor? judge? Often it is wise to choose someone who regularly writes the kind of document you are wrestling with. Choosing a second opinion wisely and listening to several different critics will give you a broader perspective on your work.

But even if you privately think your critics are insensitive, capricious, and demanding, remember that your reading public at large is also insensitive, capricious, and demanding. They may very well raise the same kinds of objections your critics have, so you had better be prepared to meet them. And if you are a student writing for a single instructor, remember that his or her response may be typical of the response your document would receive if it were widely distributed or published. Making the changes critics suggest is part of writing for the reader.

Translating Criticism into Revision

The practical point of getting outside criticism, as noted earlier, is to enable you to look at your writing from the readers' point of view, refine or rethink your ideas if necessary, and then revise your work some more. There are tricks of the trade for translating reader response into an effective program for further revision.

One of the best tricks I have found is letting the critiqued document sit for a while. First I skim it briefly, just to make sure no land mines are lurking in the marginal comments; then I put it on my shelf and go about my business. During this time I subconsciously mull over any big problems my critics have identified, but basically I am detaching myself from my document. When I sit down with it again, I want to be able to look at it objectively and professionally. As a writer, I now have a professional job to do—revise a piece of writing. True, as a professional, I don't want to compromise my standards of good writing, but understanding and meeting my readers' criticisms is also part of my job. So if you have the time, let your critiqued document sit for a while. Then approach it as a professional with a job to do.

Read all the criticisms from start to finish. As you study individual comments, write down your reactions. You can handwrite them on the printout or embed them in the computer file, using hidden text or a special type style. It may also help to rank the criticisms. What are the most serious problems your readers point out? These must be taken care of at all costs. There is no point in correcting minor problems if the major ones remain untouched. Also look for repeated mistakes. Do you always get hung up on the spelling of certain words? Do you tend to make the same grammatical errors over and over again? Make a list of these types of errors. (You may be able to use the computer's search function to correct them.) Also look for weaknesses or mistakes your readers have missed; by this time, you should be able to read your work with a much more critical eye.

Next, draw up an agenda for further revision. Jot down, in an electronic notepad or at the beginning of the document, a list of changes you want to make and perhaps some notes on how to make them. If your critics have shown you how to revise certain passages, plan to use these as models for changes in other passages. Also consult Chapter 6 of this book, or talk to people you consider good writers. And of course, keep your dictionary, thesaurus, and writer's handbook close by.

Before you make changes in the disk file, however, be sure you have a backup copy of the original. In fact, you will do a better job of revising if you open two windows at once; keep the original version of your document in one and make changes in the other. If your readers have embedded comments in your text, make these visible in the first window as you work on the second. Also keep the printout next to the keyboard; by now you know the value of switching interactively between paper and screen.

As you make various changes, tick off the relevant critical comments or items on your agenda. With long projects especially, this will help you keep track of your progress. After you finish revising, print out a fresh copy of your work, and don't forget to number or date it.

For a long, complex, or particularly important writing project, the steps of revising and getting reader response are likely to be repeated a number of times. If you submit your writing for another review, briefly summarize for your reader the changes you have made. It may also be useful to point out how these changes meet specific criticisms; alternatively, you may want to explain why certain changes were not made. This kind of explanation is easy to generate if you open a new file and write a brief running commentary as you revise. Later you can edit the commentary for distribution to your critics.

At this stage of the writing process, you are learning how to listen to other people's responses to your writing. Let these responses help you to rethink your ideas and your method of presenting them. You want to look at your writing from the readers' point of view, rather than your own, and to be sure you are writing for your audience and not only for yourself. You also want to become your own best critic. Try to develop your own standards for writing. (My standards, for example, are simplicity of style, clarity, and conciseness.) Your revisions should reflect these standards; in time, even your rough drafts will reflect them, at least in part. Also learn how to anticipate your readers' responses; meet potential objections before you submit your writing to outside criticism. And when you get your work back, learn from your mistakes. A good writer is a good learner.

Let's Solve It!

Sometimes, special problems arise when your work gets criticized. Here is how to handle them.

Problem: Not Understanding Criticism. Although you are open-minded about criticism, you honestly don't understand what your critic is trying to tell you. You can't read the handwriting, or you don't understand the terms used, or the comments seem vague, contradictory, incomplete, or unclear.

Solution. The best solution is a personal conference. Meet with your critic and ask specific questions. And remember the old saying, "There is no such thing as a dumb question, only a dumb answer." People often explain themselves more completely in a face-to-face meeting. Personal conferences also give you a chance to present your side of the case. Letters or memos are usually second-rate solutions to this problem.

Problem: Understanding Criticism but Not Knowing What to Do About It. You understand the criticism all right—you can see that your writing is disorganized or choppy or vague—but you don't know how to correct the problem.

Solution. Sometimes personal conferences are helpful; your critic may be willing to show you what to do. Other resources include this book (especially Chapter 6), a dictionary or thesaurus, a writer's handbook, examples of documents like the one you are writing, other writers, or even a tutor if you are a student. The more you learn about the writing process, however, and the more you analyze your writing and understand its particular strengths and weaknesses, the less you will have to worry about this problem.

Problem: Disagreeing with Criticism. You have solid reasons for thinking your reader's criticism is unjustified or that the revisions she suggests aren't good.

Solution. Communicate with your critic. Explain why you disagree and see if she will reconsider. Or give your own version of what needs to be done and show her a sample revision. If your revision is good, the critic will frequently accept it even if it doesn't follow her recommendations. Finally, if serious disagreement persists, agree with your critic to get a second or even third opinion.

Problem: Getting Conflicting Opinions. Various people have read your work, and while they agree on some points they disagree, perhaps seriously, on others. You don't know what to do about the conflicting advice.

Solution. Some conflicts have to be resolved on a pragmatic basis: Which critic has the most authority? If you are a student getting conflicting criticism from your peers and your instructor, most likely you will decide to follow the instructor's advice. If you are in a professional situation, you may have to follow your supervisor's suggestions rather than your colleague's, because the supervisor is the one who must approve your projects. Sometimes you can bring conflicts to your critics' attention and come to a mutually satisfactory compromise. But, ideally, you will learn how to evaluate the criticism you get and will be able to follow the best suggestions while disregarding the poor ones.

Problem: Resenting Having to Change. When you get back a piece of writing that has just been critiqued, you complain to yourself, or to others, "Every time I find out what a particular teacher (or supervisor or editor or project manager) wants, I get a new teacher and have to start all over again. I'm forced to change my style to suit her." Or "I have to write to please my teacher; I can't be myself."

Solution. This kind of resentment sounds as if you don't understand the relationship between writer and reader. A few writers may write only for themselves, but most have to reach a particular group of readers for a particular purpose. Different audiences and different occasions require different writing approaches and styles. Effective writers know this and learn how to adapt their strategy accordingly. They also realize that the individual who criticizes their work is really a stand-in for a much larger audience.

Problem: Getting Discouraged. Every time someone critiques your writing, you get discouraged. Your work never seems to improve. If you compare yourself to others, you feel stupid. You begin to think that when it comes to writing you are naturally no good.

Solution. Remind yourself that writing is a skill to be learned; nothing in a person's makeup makes it impossible to become a competent writer. If you conscientiously follow the steps outlined in this book, you will see progress. In the meantime, recognize your good points as a writer and give yourself some praise. Don't compare yourself with others in your group (unless you find it to be a good learning technique). Remember that they probably feel unsure of their abilities, too.

Computer Writing Tips

These tips will help you make a good impression on your readers and prevent your work from being lost or damaged.

- If you are asked to submit printed copy for criticism, be sure the pages are numbered. To prevent them from getting lost or mixed up, create a running head that includes your last name, the title of your work, its status ("first draft," "final draft"), and the date.
- After you print your work, separate the pages. Be careful not to tear the paper. And never submit half pages! Arrange the pages in order and clip or staple them together.
- If you are asked to submit your work on a disk, prepare a special disk containing only the material the critic is interested in; he or she may not have time to rummage through a series of directories and subdirectories looking for a particular file. And you don't want to run the risk of losing or damaging other material.
- Clearly label the files on the disk. Filenames should be self-explanatory so your critic doesn't have to wonder what "X2-31.RSO" means.
- Write-protect your disk so that people can't change your work or accidentally erase it.
- Clearly label your disk. Your last name should be part of the disk's name, and the paper label should include your full name and address.
- Save the original version of an important document; you may want to consult it when critics return your work or when you revise again.
- As you make further revisions to your document, regularly back up the revisions.

Technical writing and computers ought to go together. And they do . . . well, most of the time they do. The problem sometimes is, What is technical writing?

Increasingly, where I work, technical writing is what engineers do when they're not "engineering." Communicating about their work often takes as much time as the designing and testing, and much of the communication is in written form. Almost all the technical staff here use personal computers for writing and for preparing masters of overhead transparencies. And this is where PCs clearly stand out: Drafts can be prepared more quickly and accurately, and the visual quality of overheads has improved noticeably.

This very ease of preparation, however, is the source of a new problem. Drafts of reports and presentations printed in Helvetica on a laser printer look good, and it's easy to forget that they are still rough drafts and need every bit as much editing and rewriting as a pencil draft. While the appearance of our presentations and papers has improved, the grammatical and proofreading errors that have crept in have occasionally been embarrassing.

The moral is that we shouldn't let ourselves be beguiled by this snazzy and convenient new writing tool. Computers for word processing are just that—another tool. Clear thinking and high standards are as necessary as ever to produce appropriate, lucid prose.

Hugh Marsh
Technical Editor

Visual Communication

Using typography
Designing layout
Providing graphics

So far in the writing process, you have been concerned with text, with words and sentences—their meanings, connotations, style, and structure. If you thought at all about the visual aspects of writing, it was probably on a basic level: to produce a document with adequate margins, proper spacing, and a neat appearance. Perhaps you even experimented with headings and subheadings. Writing, however, is part of a larger communication process that involves visual signals as well as verbal ones. These visual signals—produced by the choice of type and the arrangement of text and graphics on a page—make their own impact on readers and convey meaning, too, sometimes subtly, sometimes dramatically.

In the past, writers didn't worry too much about visual communication. They produced a handwritten or typewritten manuscript that someone else set in print. But today's computer writers have potential printing presses sitting on their desks. Richard Lanham, a professor at the University of California, Los Angeles, has predicted the changes this potential will bring to writing:

> We are so used to the convention of print—linear, regular left-to-right and top-to-bottom, black-and-white, constant font and type size—that we have forgotten how constraining it is. It is remarkable not only for its power in expressing conceptual thought but for all the powers it renounces in doing so. No pictures, no color, no perspective. Up to now these things have been just too expensive. No longer. On the electronic screen you can do them all and a lot more. And as electronic memory gets ever cheaper, they will come within the reach not only of graphics designers but of us everyday wordsmiths as well.
>
> The constraints of conventionally printed prose will slowly dissolve. If we can use color, font size and shape, three-dimensional effects like dropshadow and the like, then we will use them. If we can intersperse text and graphics with ease, we'll come to depend on the combination. All these changes will, in their turn, change how we write and indeed how we think. (Richard A. Lanham, *Revising Business Prose*)

Some of this change is apparent already, as more and more computer writers incorporate visual elements into their text. Writers are also becoming their own publishers, designing and producing the final version of their document that will then be published or given a wider distribution. And as word processing becomes more sophisticated and laser printers become more common, the pressure increases to make such documents look like professionally typeset and illustrated ones. This change has come about, not only because our high-tech culture values pictorial images, but also because visual elements in a document make it easier to read and understand. In fact, neglecting the visual aspects of communication can mean that your information will be poorly presented; as a consequence, readers may react negatively to your document or even find it unintelligible.

You want your document to make a visual as well as a verbal impact on your readers, something you can achieve by using the resources of your computer to their fullest extent. But first you need to know and follow the principles of good visual communication. This chapter deals with the new look of computer documents and shows you how to integrate typography, graphics, and text into a unified communication. You will learn how to progress beyond merely typing a document to designing it, so that its physical appearance, as well as its verbal content, contributes to meaning.

But first, a few definitions of technical terms:

- *Typography* refers to the art of printing with type; it covers the style, arrangement, and appearance of printed matter.
- *Graphics* refers to pictures, diagrams, charts, and any other visual expression of ideas and objects.
- *Layout* refers to the arrangement on a page of the various elements—both graphic and typographic—that make up a document.
- *Format* is the term computer writers frequently use when they refer to all the choices concerning typography, layout, and graphics.

VISUAL COMMUNICATION AND THE WRITING PROCESS

When in the writing process should you start thinking about visual communication? The answer depends on the nature of your writing project. You may be concerned about some aspects of visual communication as early as the prewriting stage. Especially in technical and professional writing, graphics may precede text and determine or influence both content and organization.

Making preliminary decisions about page layout and headlining could also be part of the planning or drafting stage. And if you are writing a document that relies heavily on graphics, you may want the illustrations in place by the time critics read your work.

The finer points of document design, however, are often determined after the document has gone through several revisions or immediately before it is readied for publication. In fact, revisions in the text may require revisions in typography, graphics, or layout.

The more sophisticated you become as a computer writer, the more natural you will find it to think both verbally and visually about your document in all stages of the writing process.

As you learn about typography, graphics, layout, and formatting, keep in mind the basic purpose of all visual aids: They should make your document more inviting to read and its message clearer, more informative, and more convincing. Aim for simplicity, balance, and unity rather than fancy decoration; use a few design elements well. The total visual impression your document makes should harmonize with the tone and the purpose of the text. It should also meet the expectations of your readers; that is, your document should look like other documents in its class. In fact, formatting conventions for the particular type of document you are writing may actually govern the choices you make in graphics, typography, and layout.

Arranging the Text on the Page

How you arrange text on a page—the layout, in other words—can increase readability, aid organization, and emphasize specific points. It can also enhance the aesthetics, or appearance, of your work so that people will find it more inviting to read. Computers allow you to arrange, or format, your text in a variety of ways.

White Space

Never crowd text onto a page. Leave plenty of white space around it. If you are a naturally visual person, think of the text as a solid dark block or series of blocks that need to be dramatically positioned on a light background. White space obviously enhances readability and attractiveness, but it also takes part in the communication process. Extra white space can be used to emphasize certain parts of the text, signal a change in content, or guide the reader from one part of the viewing area to another.

Start by leaving adequate margins on all sides. Remember that very long lines of text are difficult to read. For ordinary text on an $8^1/_2$-by-11-inch page, one-inch margins are fine. Special documents, however, may have special requirements. If your work is to be bound, for example, wider side margins are required. Some word-processing programs take care of this by giving you the option of printing with a *gutter margin*—extra space for binding on the left side of odd pages and on the right side of even pages.

There are other reasons for changing margins: If a business letter or memo is short, you will need to set wide top and bottom margins so that the text is centered on the page. If you are submitting a document for criticism, you may want to make one side margin very wide so people have room to jot down comments. Or you may want to improve the readability of a document by providing wider margins or by isolating sections of important text with more white space. So before you print the final copy of any document, always print out a draft and check the relationship between text and the white space around it.

Also consider the white space between lines of text. Computers allow you to choose different type sizes and line spacings. But if you make a poor choice—long lines of single-spaced small type, for example—your text will be difficult to read. In some word-processing programs, you can specify line spacing not only in terms of whole lines—single spacing and double spacing—but also in points, the same measurement that is used for type. (Among printers and publishers—including desktop publishers—the spacing between lines is referred to as *leading*—pronounced "ledding.") If your word processor lets you precisely determine line spacing, or leading, begin by choosing a type size that is easy to read (in the 9-point to 12-point range) and then experiment with spacing until your text has a pleasingly open look.

Conventionally, the left edge of text is *justified,* that is, absolutely straight, but computers allow you to justify the right edge as well, thus giving your document a professionally typeset look. On the other hand, leaving the right edge ragged, or *unjustified,* produces more white space and gives the page a more open and informal look, which you may prefer in certain cases. And because *full justification* (both left and right edges) in some word-processing programs leaves odd-sized spaces between words, you may find it easier to read unjustified text. Use your judgment.

Paragraphing

Most word-processing programs let you format paragraphs automatically and give you a choice among styles. The conventional paragraph formats are *indented, block,* and *semiblock*. (See Figure 8-1.) Your main concern is to choose the format conventionally used in the kind of document you are writing: the indented format for books, magazine articles, and academic papers; the block format for much business writing and most reports; and the semiblock format for relatively informal business writing. (Chapter 5, p. 109, discusses these paragraph formats in more detail.)

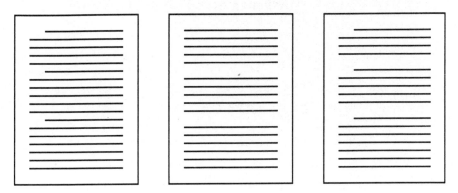

FIGURE 8-1. *Conventional paragraph formats: indented (left), block (center), and semiblock (right)*

Another useful paragraph format is the *hanging indent.* This colorful term refers to a paragraph in which the second and subsequent lines are indented, so that the first (flush-left) line *hangs* over the edge, as it were. (See Figure 8-2.) The hanging indent style is useful in résumés and some reports or brochures that need more dramatic arrangements of text than conventional paragraphs provide. Combined with an opening word or phrase in italic, bold, or capital letters, this style can visually set apart key points in a highly effective way.

FIGURE 8-2. *The hanging indent paragraph format*

If your word-processing program doesn't create hanging indents automatically, try using tab stops creatively. Type the first line the length you want it (but don't use the word wraparound feature). Set a tab stop where you want the second line to begin. Press Enter, then the Tab key, and type the second line, again not using word wraparound. At the end of the line, press Enter, then the Tab key, and type the third line. Continue in this fashion until the paragraph is completed.

Indented Blocks of Text

If you quote a long passage from another work (say fifty words or more), set it off from the main text by using an indented block of text rather than quotation marks. This block can be indented from both the right and left edges of the main text, as is done in this book. (See p. 162 for an example.) If you are submitting a manuscript to an editor, double-space both the main text and the indented quotation. However, if you are producing a document in its final form for distribution, single-space the indented material and put it in smaller type (if your word processor has this feature). Also set it off from the main text with extra white space. Remember not to use quotation marks with indented blocks; indention visually signals that the material is quoted.

Lists

Some material can be emphasized by breaking it into individual items and arranging these items in a list. The items can consist of single words, phrases, complete or partial sentences, or even short paragraphs. Keep these items parallel in grammar and wording. Thus you might list a series of nouns, or start each phrase with a strong action verb, or write in parallel sentence structure. For an even greater sense of unity, preview the list for the reader by introducing it in the text. (See the next paragraph for an example.)

Typically, lists are either indented or centered on the page. You can also start them at the left-hand margin. Whatever style you choose, be consistent throughout your document. Use white space to set off the list. You may also want to emphasize each item with a number, a letter, or a bullet. Numbers and letters are self-explanatory; a *bullet* is a small symbol preceding each item in a list. Following are common typographic symbols used for bullets:

- ● solid circle
- ■ solid square
- □ hollow square
- — dash
- * asterisk

You may have to use a Shift key plus an Option or Alt key to produce such symbols on your computer. Used sparingly and with a good sense of design, bullets emphasize certain points, make your text easier to read, and add to the general attractiveness of the page. (For examples of bulleted lists in this book, see pp. 34 and 49.)

Columns

Traditionally, the text of some documents—books, articles or short stories in journals, reports, memos, and letters—is arranged in a single column; other documents—newsletters, brochures, some manuals, magazines, and newspapers—are multicolumn. Sophisticated word-processing programs allow you to print in columns. They may be snaking columns—that is, text flows, or "snakes," down one column and then down the other—or the columns may consist of side-by-side paragraphs. It is also possible to divide whole documents or even single pages into different parts, or divisions, and then format each division differently. Thus one division could be arranged in the traditional single column of text; another, in two or more columns. (See p. 125 for an example of single and double columns together.)

Arranging text in columns makes small type easier to read, but be sure to leave enough white space: at least one-half inch between columns and three-fourths to one inch for the side and bottom margins. (The space for the top margin depends on the title or headline of your document.) Text can be fully justified or not. Paragraphs should be short when you print in columns, and different sections can be introduced by headings and subheadings. Sometimes multicolumn text is set off by *rules*—narrow vertical lines that separate different columns or horizontal lines that separate different sections. Even simple word-processing programs are capable of producing horizontal rules (consisting of dashes or underlining), but only powerful ones produce vertical rules.

Previewing Text

In Chapter 5 you saw that an overview paragraph at the beginning of a chapter or major section of your document provides readers with a survey of the material you are going to present and establishes a context for it. Overviews can also be formatted as distinct entities rather than incorporated into regular paragraphs, especially in reports, textbooks, technical manuals, and brochures. Typically, these overviews are set off from the main text by extra white space, a box, or a distinctive typeface or style option, or some combination of these elements; they may even have their own page. Overviews that preview a whole document can be alternatives to traditional introductions. Much shorter and more functional than introductions, such overviews can identify who would be interested in the document, what kinds of information the document contains, where in the document the information is located, and how the document can or should be used.

Overviews that preview chapters or major sections summarize the ideas or information to be found there. They can be put immediately before the main text or just under the title or section heading. They can also be placed on a separate page along with the chapter or section title and number, as in Figure 8-3.

Using Titles and Headings

Titles, headings, and subheadings provide strong visual and verbal signals to the reader. Learn to use them as effective communication tools.

Titles

In terms of content, titles should be both provocative and informative—you want to entice people to read your piece of writing, as well as give them a sample of what they can expect. You may even decide on a subtitle to clarify an imaginative title or give

SECTION TWO

Worksheets

The eight chapters in this section give you the information you need to create, format, edit, and print worksheets. Excel's powerful functions are covered in detail. Also discussed are features such as data tables and arrays, as well as how to link worksheets.

FIGURE 8-3. *A section title page with overview (from Douglas Cobb et al.,* Excel in Business*)*

more information about a complex subject. For example, the historian Barbara Tuchman called one of her books *A Distant Mirror* and then clarified her meaning by adding *The Calamitous Fourteenth Century* as a subtitle.

Titles are also an important part of the general layout of your piece of writing. The more serious and formal the writing, the more serious and informative the title is in content and the more decorous it is in appearance. Thus the typography of titles of articles in scholarly journals may be distinguished by nothing more than a slightly larger type size and a bold typeface. Popular magazines, on the other hand, by their very nature are more flamboyant. If you are submitting work for publication rather than producing it yourself, the publisher and printer will decide on such matters. Leaf through typical publications for examples of the conventions they will follow.

If you are in charge of designing and producing the document, however, you may be able to use creativity in the typography, graphic design, and placement of your title. For example, you might center the title or place it flush with either the left or right margin, using the appropriate computer commands. If you have a subtitle, separate it from the main title with a dash or colon, or place it underneath the main title, or put it in a smaller type size. If your name is to appear along with the title, put it in a smaller type size, above or below the title or to one side. You may use display type (large type suitable for headlines) and style options like bold or italics if these harmonize with the body text. Simple graphic elements, especially linear ones, are available in some word-processing programs; these, too, can be part of an attractive title design, as in Figure 8-4.

HAMLET *PRINCE OF DENMARK*

William Shakespeare

FIGURE 8-4. *A creatively designed title*

Even though computers make designing such titles very easy, however, you must still follow the conventions of the type of document you are producing. It may be totally inappropriate, for example, to design elaborate titles for a technical report.

Main Headings

Main headings indicate the overall organizational plan of your work, summarize the subjects of the large sections, and provide transitions between sections. These headings should be brief; pack as much information as you can into a few words. And make the words parallel: If one main heading is a noun phrase, then make all main headings noun phrases, or if one is a provocative question, then make all of them questions, and so on. Although headings form transitions between sections, it is frequently a good idea to provide verbal transitions in the text itself (but the first line of text should not refer back to the heading with a pronoun—"this," "it," "they").

Typographically, main headings should be smaller than the title but larger than the text. Choose a larger type size, put them in caps, or make them bold. Center these headings above the appropriate text or start them at the left-hand margin. Be consistent throughout the document; all main headings should look alike and have the same relative location. Headings may also be separated from text with extra white space to emphasize the distinction between sections.

Subheadings

Subheadings divide the large sections of your documents into smaller parts. They also reveal how secondary ideas are subordinate to the main ideas and indicate the logical progression of your train of thought. Usually subheadings correspond to subsidiary points in your outline.

Make subheadings less conspicuous than the main headings. You might put them in a different place, too: that is, center them if the main headings start at the left-hand margin, or start them at the margin if the main headings are centered. Some designers indent subheadings if the paragraphs are also indented. Subheadings can be the same type size as the text, but you should distinguish them by putting them in caps, making them bold, or italicizing them. (Underlining is another style option, but remember that in material going to a typesetter, underlining means "italicize this.") Again, be consistent; all subheadings should look alike, be parallel in structure, and have the same relative location. (To see one way of handling main headings and subheadings, you can simply flip through this book; p. 164, for example, contains both a main heading and a subheading.)

You can also have additional levels of subheadings for detailed material. As a matter of common sense, however, don't use any kind of subheading unless you can divide a particular section into at least two parts. Never have two headings, of whatever level, with no intervening text. And don't use too many headings or your document will be visually distracting.

You can make a side margin extra wide and put headings—called "side heads"—in this space, next to a section of text rather than above it. (With most computers this kind of arrangement requires a layout program that can print text in unequal columns.) Subheadings can also be placed within a paragraph at the very beginning (as they are on pp. 178-82) and distinguished from the rest of the text by capitalization or style choice. Called "run-in side heads," they are especially useful for categories in a classification scheme. Finally, in some kinds of technical or professional writing, main headings and subheadings are identified even further by a numbering system; follow a model for the type of document you are writing.

As you design and place titles, headings, and subheadings, remember that their primary function is to communicate with readers both visually and verbally. They can make your document more inviting to read and its message easier to follow.

Setting Off Special Text

Sometimes you have material that you want to emphasize or set apart from the main text. *Boxing* text is a graphic way to do this. If you are writing a set of directions, for example, and need to emphasize a warning, you might put it in a box, as in Figure 8-5. Some word-processing programs let you box text; if yours does not, go to a graphics program, create the boxed text, and transfer it to your word-processing document.

Don't turn off the computer until you have ejected both disks.

FIGURE 8-5. *A box used for emphasis*

A *sidebar* comprises information relevant to the main text but not easily integrated into it or perhaps not needed by all readers. Sidebars might present definitions of specialized terms used in the main text, highlights of the main text, or detailed information about topics discussed only generally in the main text. A sidebar is often presented as a long, vertical box, or "bar," placed to one side of a page. See p. 175 for an example of a sidebar in this book; you can create a similar effect with a sophisticated word-processing program.

Pull quotes are attention-getting quotations "pulled" from the main text. They are set in quotation marks or printed in larger type or in a different style and are prominently placed on the page. Pull quotes can be placed in a variety of locations: just below the title; within the main text but set off from it with boxes, lines, or extra white space; in the top margin, above the text; or in the side margin, next to the text. (See Figure 8-6.) You can easily produce pull quotes in a word-processing program, especially if you are printing in columns. Short pull quotes can also be used as headings.

Boxes, sidebars, and pull quotes, common enough in journalism, aren't suitable for all types of documents; you wouldn't use them in academic papers or scholarly articles. Used sparingly and with discrimination, however, they can give your message more visual impact, convey extra information, and emphasize certain points.

Highlighting Text

You can call attention to individual words or short passages in your text and make them memorable by *highlighting* them—that is, using a distinctive *style option* or typeface. Many computers offer a wide range of style options in addition to regular text (what typesetters and publishers call "roman")—for example, underlining, double underlining, italics, bold, superscript, subscript, and small capitals. Or you can simply use all capitals. If you want to set apart and emphasize a larger block of text, combine highlighting with extra white space.

Don't overuse highlighting, however; if too much is emphasized, then nothing stands out. And don't use style options indiscriminately. Too often inexperienced computer writers randomly sprinkle style options throughout their document; they decorate rather than highlight. To avoid such problems, follow these simple guidelines:

- Use a regular typeface for body text.
- Emphasize words sparingly by putting them in italics or underlining them.

Text Processing

Text appears in manuscripts, journals, reference works, periodicals, reports, newspapers, correspondence, and other forms. Computer methods
that aid in the creation and layout of text, such as word processing, electronic messaging, and photocomposition, have led to the increased availability of machine-readable texts. Standards work, as in the Electronic
Manuscript Project, will accentuate this trend. Attendant issues of analyzing, indexing, storing, and accessing text have been central to much of the
work in modern IR.

The simplest way for a computer to access text is to search it sequentially,
much as people scan the words on a page. When people search through
text collections they are able to decide whether located items are relevant
to their particular search need. Computerized retrieval systems should
find exactly those items that are relevant—ignoring items that are non-
relevant. That is to say, they should have high precision as well as high
recall. Clever algorithms, like that of Boyer and Moore (1977), can speed
up the search process, and further improvements are possible with special
hardware. But the simple sequential search becomes ineffective as the
query increases in complexity and the text collection increases in size.
However, creating complex models of text documents by analyzing and
indexing large collections can allow them to be efficiently searched.

Models

Much of the research in IR has been based on four different models of the
field: browsing, Boolean and p-norm, vector and probabilistic, and artificial intelligence. Traditionally, the Boolean model has been most widely
upheld. The vector and probabilistic models have shown promise in laboratory tests. With recent advances in display and pointing devices, browsing models have been advanced. Finally, due to the promise and popularity
of AI, a good deal of attention has been given to AI-based models. Each
of these models is discussed below, in order of complexity.

Browsing Models

In libraries, people work with the card catalog (or its equivalent) and/or
browse in the stacks. When using reference works, people frequently follow implicit or explicit pointers or skip around looking for particular
items. Now that large high-resolution displays are available for computers,
effective use of such two-dimensional devices, as in the Caliban system, is
of particular interest.

Computer methods that aid in the creation and layout of text, such as word processing, electronic messaging, and photocomposition, have led to the increased availability of machine-readable texts.

146

FIGURE 8-6. *A pull quote (from Steve Lambert and Suzanne Ropiequet,* CD ROM: The
New Papyrus*)*

■ Follow the conventional rules for using italics: for foreign words, for the
titles of long written works like books, plays, and long poems, and for the
names of motion pictures, artworks, and the like.

■ If your computer can't italicize, underline instead; this is the conventional
signal to the typesetter to use italics.

■ In general, save bold for titles and headings, where it may be combined with
other options like italics or underlining for increased visual effect. In some
types of highly visual documents—brochures, newsletters, manuals—you
may use bold for highlighting body text as well.

■ Emphasize only very short passages with all capitals; long lines or blocks of
text in capitals are difficult to read.

■ Reserve superscript and subscript for special cases; scientific formulas and
footnote numbers are the most common.

- Consider using small capitals in the captions and labels for your graphics.
- Use shadow, outline, and other novelty styles for display purposes only; that is, for titles and headlines, not text. And keep in mind that they are suitable only for certain kinds of documents—fliers, advertisements, brochures, newsletters, and the like.

On the whole, be sparing in your use of the various typefaces and style options; follow the general rule that the more formal the document, the more subdued it should look.

Clarifying Ideas with Graphics

In the past we gave lip service to the old proverb, "one picture is worth a thousand words," but we acted as if words alone sufficed. Today, easy-to-use computer graphics programs are making all writers, and not only technical ones, aware that graphic representation is part of the writing process. Graphics can clarify, explain, emphasize, persuade. They are another way—visual rather than verbal—that writers can use to meet the needs and expectations of their readers. As a computer writer, be prepared to convey your ideas in pictures as well as words.

Some writers naturally enjoy creating graphics; they may start a writing project by planning the graphics first and focusing their prewriting around them. Or they may be in charge of the final production of a document and supervise typography, graphics, and layout. Other writers concentrate solely on words and rely on professionals—graphic artists, document designers, typesetters, and the like—to create the visual elements in their document. But even if you fall into this last category, you will be a better communicator if you can provide your professional staff with general pictorial concepts. Just to do that much, however, you need to know the different types of graphics, what they can and cannot do, and how they can be integrated into your text. The following pages contain basic guidelines for using computer-generated tables, charts and graphs, signs and symbols, diagrams, and artwork.

Tables

Some types of information such as statistical data can be communicated most clearly if they are arranged in rows and columns; this format is called a table and is especially useful for comparing and contrasting. Tables often substitute for words by graphically presenting information that would require long-winded and possibly confusing verbal explanation. Say, for example, you are reporting statistics on electric appliances owned by Americans over a three-year period. You want to cite the number as well as the percentage of households owning each appliance, but you are afraid of losing your audience. Look how easily the table in Figure 8-7 conveys the information.

Don't expect a table to do all your work, however. Readers may interpret your material far differently than you want them to, so in your text point out the main information in the table and explain the important conclusions that can be drawn from it.

You can easily create tables with a word-processing program by setting tabs and entering information. Rows and columns should line up evenly; use the computer to align decimals automatically. If your program is powerful enough, you can also manipulate material in the table: You can add, delete, or move whole columns of data; you can automatically perform mathematical operations; or you can sort all the lines. Alternatively, you can create tables in a spreadsheet program and transfer them to your

SO YOU WANT TO BE A COMPUTER ARTIST AS WELL AS A COMPUTER WRITER

Various types of computer programs and graphic aids can make your work look professional.

Specialized graphics programs can do everything from creating paintlike effects to generating charts to producing professional drafting. Often they are fun to use, too.

Many graphics programs have an array of preformed elements that can be used to construct professional-looking signs, symbols and diagrams.

Pictorial computer typefaces provide a wide selection of miniature symbols and drawings that can be transferred to a graphics program, imaginatively modified and enlarged, and transferred back to a text document.

Portfolios of clip art on disk contain just about every kind of graphic representation imaginable. Again, these can be modified by graphics programs to meet specific needs.

Freehand drawings can be done on screen with a mouse. Some people, however, find the mouse clumsy to handle and prefer an interactive pen digitizer (the same technology in a slimmer form). Or they find it easier to move a stylus over an electromagnetic digitizing tablet.

Digitizers can transform a graphic image on paper to an electronic image on the computer screen. These digitized images can then be modified in a graphics programs.

Color printing is here—and as time goes on, the final product will get better and better! You need the right software and hardware, however. And even if you create graphics in black and white, you still need special hardware: Depending on your system, you will need either a plotter or a printer capable of producing graphics and possibly a graphics board for your computer.

Table 1: Electric Household Appliances in the U.S.					
	Million Households			**Percentage Households**		
	1980	**1981**	**1982**	**1980**	**1981**	**1982**
Total Households	81.6	83.1	83.8	100	100	100
Appliances						
TV (color)	67.0	68.4	71.0	82	82	85
TV (b/w)	41.9	39.5	38.9	51	48	47
Clothes Washer	58.4	58.4	57.9	72	70	69
Clothes Dryer	38.3	37.5	37.9	47	45	45
Microwave	11.6	14.0	17.3	14	17	21
Dishwasher	30.4	30.5	30.3	37	37	36
Separate Freezer	21.1	31.9	31.0	38	38	37
Source: U.S. Department of Energy						

FIGURE 8-7. *A table of statistical data*

word-processing program. In addition, specialized report-writing programs allow you to create and manipulate tables.

Be sure your table is easy to read and understand. Provide rows and columns with brief, informative headings in a special typeface or style option—italics, small capitals, bold—or in a smaller type size. Include the unit of measurement (abbreviated if possible): "Revenue in Millions of $." If the table has two or more levels of heads, separate the levels with horizontal rules; you might also use a rule between the bottom heading level and the body of the table. Use vertical rules or simply leave white space between column heads and between columns of figures. If the information in the table comes from an outside source, put a *source line* at the bottom of the table to the left; you might use a horizontal rule to separate this material from the body of the table. Above the table place an identifying number and descriptive title: "Table 1: Annual Revenue of the Top Ten Cookie Companies." Table numbers form their own sequence, separate and distinct from the sequence of figure numbers. But both sets of numbers may include the chapter number as well: "Table 5-1" or "Figure 8-15."

Use adequate white space around the table. If page layout permits, position the table after you mention it by number in the text. You need not mention the title, however. Alternatively, tables as well as figures can be placed in an appendix at the end of a document. Sometimes they are referred to as "exhibits" rather than "tables" or "figures."

You can also arrange text in table form (technically called "tabular format"). If you are comparing two or more items, for example, the comparison may be much clearer if you present it in tabular format. *Computers and Literacy,* edited by Daniel Chandler and Stephen Marcus, includes a tabular comparison of ways in which ideas

MS and early print culture	The spread of literacy	Networked society
Books rare	Books widespread	Books special
Authorship not important	Rise of author	Decline of author; writing more collaborative
Clerics as distributors	Rise of publishers	Writers as publishers
Changeable texts	Definitive texts	Changeable texts
Copying important	Concept of plagiarism	Death of copyright
Authority	Individualism	Communality
Reading aloud/listening	Private, silent reading	Participatory reading
Varied orthography	Writing conventions	Challenge to conventions of writing
International (Latin)	National	International

FIGURE 8-8. *Text in tabular format*

have been and may be presented, from the Middle Ages to a totally computerized future era. (See Figure 8-8.) You can use tab stops to create such a table, or you can format the columns in side-by-side paragraphs if your word processor has this capability.

Figures

A figure is any graphic representation that is not a table. A more useful way to define the term is to give concrete examples: Figures comprise such elements as graphs, charts, pictorial signs and symbols, diagrams, maps, and other illustrations and artwork. Figures can emphasize what you have already said in the text, add new information, and help your readers to understand and remember what you are telling them.

Figures are usually numbered in sequence and given a title: "Figure 1. Water Usage in Goleta Valley, 1966-86." The title, or caption, however, is positioned beneath the figure. You may also want to italicize the caption, use a smaller type size, or put it in small capitals. Because a figure should add to the overall attractiveness of the page as well as convey information, leave plenty of white space around it and position it carefully. Figures are frequently centered; you can do this with the word processor's centering function. A large figure, however, can be placed on its own page, facing the text in which it is discussed. If figures are numbered, be sure to mention them by number in the text, preferably before the reader comes to them. And if a figure has been previously published or contains information from an outside source, identify the source. Such an identification is usually placed immediately beneath the figure or at the end of the caption; note, however, that for Figure 8-8—really a textual quote rather than a conventional illustration—the source is identified in text. The important point is that you do identify sources, not how you do so.

Graphs and Charts.   Simple computer programs allow even the beginner to present facts and figures in a graphic and understandable way. Say that you want to compare wine production in California, in New York, and in the United States as a whole from 1980 through 1983. Instead of writing a tedious paragraph that begins "In 1980 California produced 439 million gallons of wine, New York produced 36 million gallons, and the total U.S. production was 486 million gallons," you merely create a chart like the one in Figure 8-9.

Neither graphs nor charts present the facts as precisely as numerical statistics do, but they often make the facts more meaningful to the average reader. (If appropriate, you can include the statistical information for your charts or graphs in an appendix aimed at the interested specialist.) Charts and graphs should convey a message you can express in a declarative sentence: "California produces about 90 percent of the nation's wine." Don't assume, however, that readers will interpret your chart the way you want them to. Guide them in the text. Spell out the information they can find in the chart and tell them what conclusions can be drawn.

Special programs let you key in information and transform it into a chart. Integrated programs that allow you to switch from word processing to spreadsheet work also allow you to convert the spreadsheet data into charts. But if you don't use spreadsheets, stand-alone chart programs let you enter information and convert it to visual form.

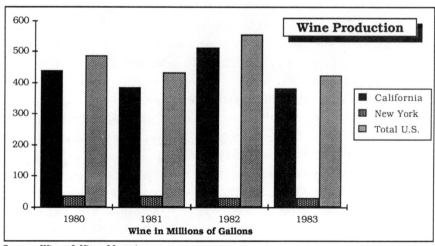

Source: Wines & Vines Magazine

FIGURE 8-9.   *A column chart*

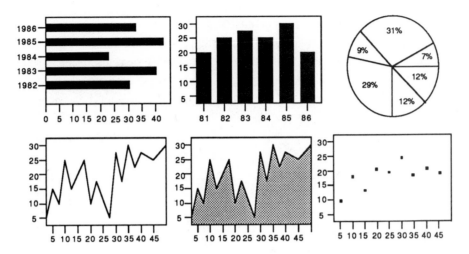

FIGURE 8-10.   *The basic types of chart: (top row, left to right) bar chart, column chart, and pie chart; (bottom row, left to right) graph, area chart, and scatter graph*

There are six basic types of chart. *Bar charts* compare the sizes or amounts of different items at the same time. *Column charts* compare the sizes or amounts of a single item at precise intervals. *Pie charts* show how parts relate to the whole. *Graphs* (sometimes called *line charts*) show how something has changed over a period of time. *Area charts,* or *surface charts,* a variation of graphs, also show how something has changed over a period of time. *Scatter graphs* plot two variables that may or may not be directly related to one another. For simple representations of these chart types, see Figure 8-10.

To be sure your readers can interpret the chart, add a legend or key to the various elements, especially if you use shading or patterns or even symbols to indicate different types of information. Give the chart the proper figure number, caption it, and label individual parts. To avoid confusion, use the same terminology in the chart that you do in text; don't depict "liters" in the chart if you refer exclusively to "gallons" in the text. If necessary, put a source line at the left, directly under the chart and above the caption.

Charts should be visually attractive, so you may want to add design elements, but don't decorate; aim for simplicity and clarity of representation. Remember that your main purpose is to convey information in an easy-to-understand and memorable form.

Illustrations.   Illustrations turn information or abstract concepts into pictures; you can illustrate, clarify, and reinforce your ideas with signs, symbols, and diagrams. In some instances, especially in scientific or technical writing, illustrations are an absolute necessity if all the information is to be presented clearly and accurately; words alone can't do the job.

Let's look at possible types of illustrations.

Signs and Symbols. Increasingly, signs and symbols are being used to convey information. (See Figure 8-11.) You can use them to convey ideas discussed in your text, too. If, for example, you talk about progressing through a series of steps in order to reach a goal, you could represent the concept graphically by using the obvious symbolism of a stairway. Or to illustrate the point that a document might reach increasingly distant audiences, you could draw a series of concentric circles around a graphic symbol of a manuscript.

FIGURE 8-11. *Several graphic symbols, indicating (from left to right) "cars prohibited"; "fragile"; "this side up"; "keep dry"; and "delete the computer file"*

Diagrams. Diagrams are explanatory line drawings or graphic designs. They range from stylized patterns or designs to fairly realistic representations of their subject. An organization chart, which represents relationships among items, is a good example of a simple and stylized diagram. (See Figure 8-12.) Flowcharts, which represent the various steps in a process or operation, are visually more complex than organization charts.[1] The flowchart in Figure 8-13 depicts a program that enables your computers to communicate with each other via a modem.

Diagrams can also depict objects and show how they are put together or how they work. In some cases, such diagrams are scientifically accurate drawings; in other cases, they are stylized representations. The example in Figure 8-14 is a highly stylized representation of a laser printer.

Using a computer graphics program, you can create diagrams such as these shown here when you want to simplify a concept; clarify meaning; explain an object, process, or relationship; and generally make your information and ideas memorable and convincing.

---

[1]For technical flowcharts, you will want to use standardized symbols. See *U.S.A. Standard Flowchart Symbols and Their Usage in Information Processing,* published by the American National Standards Institute, publication X3.5.

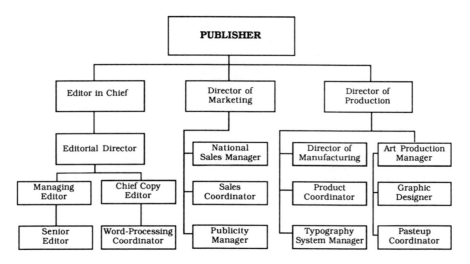

FIGURE 8-12. *An organization chart of a publishing company*

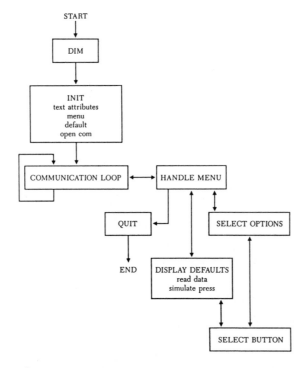

FIGURE 8-13. *A flowchart of a simple communication program (reprinted from Steve Lambert,* Creative Programming in Microsoft Basic)

181

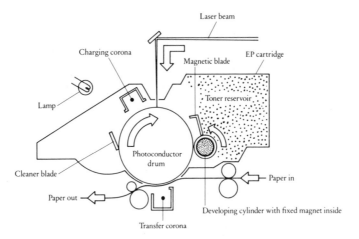

Laser beam

Charging corona

EP cartridge

Magnetic blade

Toner reservoir

Lamp

Photoconductor
drum

Cleaner blade

Paper in

Paper out

Developing cylinder with fixed magnet inside

Transfer corona

FIGURE 8-14. *A stylized diagram of a laser printer (from Cary Lu,* The Apple Macintosh Book, *2nd ed.)*

Artwork. If you are designing and producing a document yourself, you may want to include artwork that illustrates a scene, creates a mood, or appeals to readers' artistic sensibilities. Even if you are submitting a manuscript for publication, you may want to provide your editor with an artistic concept. Computer graphics programs allow you to be as creative with pictures as you are with words.

The picture in Figure 8-15 was drawn freehand on the computer. If your drawing skills are not as good, try using a digitizer. This device digitizes (translates into numeric data) a photograph or any black-and-white pictorial representation and converts it into a graphics document. Using a graphics program, you can then modify the digitized picture to suit your purposes, add design elements or even text, and finally transfer the finished product to your written document. Imagination and the willingness to experiment can produce inventive creations. Pictures like that in Figure 8-15 may or may not be captioned or have figure numbers. Positioning them on the page, however, requires thought and some knowledge about page design.

If you plan to use graphics to supplement your writing, consider starting a graphics library. Clip art disks may be all you need. And if you have a modem, you can download, or transfer, clip art from a graphics subscription service to your computer. If you create your own graphics, file them in a special directory or on a separate disk, or invest in a simple database that allows you to file, preview, and retrieve graphics. If you have an electronic "scrapbook" in your word-processing program, you can store your most frequently used graphics there.

FIGURE 8-15. *A freehand computer drawing*

Glossaries are another storage place. Some word-processing programs allow you to copy graphics, as well as text, into the glossary. Once your graphics are stored under identifying abbreviations, simply type the right abbreviation in your text and carry out the correct command, and your graphic will appear almost like magic.

Creating Running Heads

A running head—often called a "header" or a "footer"—is a line or more of type that appears in the top or bottom margin of every page (or of selected pages) and gives set information. It might contain, for example, the name of a chapter, a page number, and a simple design element like a horizontal rule. (Look at the pages of this book for examples.) Sophisticated word-processing programs can put the same running head on every page or every other page and can include automatic pagination. Running heads are often omitted on the first page of a document or chapter.

When you are ready to create running heads, look at sample documents of the type you are writing. Some running heads might include not only the name of the document but the issuing agency and the date as well. Or they might designate the subject category or incorporate graphics (a company logo, for example). Don't make running heads too busy or prominent, however; you don't want to distract the reader from the main text. Also make sure that headers and footers are clearly separated from the main text; leave adequate white space and possibly include a rule.

Choosing Type

A judicious choice of type, or fonts, can contribute greatly to the legibility and attractiveness of your text. And today your choice of fonts is limited only by the capabilities of your printer and word-processing program. But use care; resist the temptation to decorate your document by using too many fonts or inappropriate ones.

The body text of articles, stories, business letters, memos, reports, and most scholarly documents is usually printed in one font—a clean-cut and simple one. The size of the font should be big enough to be read comfortably, although footnotes or indented quotations may be printed in smaller type. (Font size is measured in *points*. The most readable sizes for body text are 10, 11, and 12 point.) Titles and headings, on the other hand, often call for variety; in that case, choose fonts and sizes that harmonize with the body text and suit the type of document and its intended audience. As a general rule, be plain and simple. Save your flights of typographic fancy for more visually creative documents: brochures, newsletters, advertisements, and the like.

For special writing tasks you may need special types of fonts. For example, you can obtain fonts for languages that don't use the Roman alphabet—languages like Arabic, Persian, Coptic, Greek, Japanese, Korean, Russian, and Hebrew. (See Figure 8-16.) And some programs allow you to compose from right to left. Even if you don't have such exotic needs, good word-processing programs still allow you to insert various accent marks: voilà, flambée, soupçon, cañon.

מחשבים מפליאים בכל שפה

Computers are amazing in any language.

FIGURE 8-16.   *A computer font for Hebrew*

Technical writers have a wide range of symbols at their command, as Figure 8-17 illustrates. Novelty fonts abound, too, and they are fun to use, but only in special documents. Invitations to a party given by the Shakespeare Club might be written in an Old English font, for example, but for standard documents choose standard fonts.

$$EI \frac{\partial^2 \psi}{\partial x^2} + KAG \left(\frac{\partial y}{\partial x} - \psi \right) - \frac{I\gamma}{g} \frac{\partial^2 \psi}{\partial t^2} = 0$$

$$\frac{\gamma A}{g} \frac{\partial^2 y}{\partial t^2} - KAG \left(\frac{\partial^2 y}{\partial x^2} - \frac{\partial \psi}{\partial x} \right) = 0$$

FIGURE 8-17.   *A computer font that includes mathematical symbols*

Keeping the Appearance of Documents Consistent

After you print a draft of your document, you may find that although you have used various visual techniques to communicate with your readers, you have used them or formatted them inconsistently, and the appearance of your document is uneven. For example, some of your main headings might be centered, others set flush with the left margin; or you might use all caps in some but revert to uppercase and lowercase in others. Perhaps you italicized the captions of some graphics but not of all, or maybe you indented some lists 1 inch and others 1½ inch.

The cure for such problems is to plan the design carefully and draw up a style guide—a list of specifications that govern the mechanics and format of writing and publishing a document. Style guides (also called style manuals or style sheets) can be very broad and deal with subjects ranging from grammar, usage, and literary style to footnotes and bibliographies. They can also discuss the details of formatting. However, footnotes are covered in the next chapter, and grammar and style are discussed in Chapter 6, so this section addresses only the formatting aspect of style guides.

There are two kinds of formatting style guides: a written list of specifications and a computer routine that automatically formats for you. Because the term "style sheet" is now firmly associated with computer programs, I will use the term "style guide" to refer to the paper product. This should avoid confusion.

Written Style Guides

Various sources can provide you with specifications for the appearance of documents. Your instructor or editor or the company you work for may give you a style guide, or you may have to write to the journal or magazine you hope will publish your work. Consult a book like *The Chicago Manual of Style*—the standard reference guide for authors and publishers and an invaluable tool for the serious writer. You can also draw up a list of your own specifications. After you decide on a design for your document, carefully note all formatting, graphic, and typographic choices you will be making. List such elements as these:

- The size of margins for main text, lists, and indented blocks of text
- Font, font size, and style option for the title, subtitle, and various levels of headings and subheadings
- Font size and style option for captions
- Use of capitals and of uppercase and lowercase
- Amount of white space (whether measured in number of lines or leading) to be left between lines, between headings and main text, between graphics and captions, and between running heads and main text

- Symbol to be used for bullets
- Location, font, and font size of page numbers and running heads

There are, of course, many other specifications you may want to record.

Keep this information at the very beginning or very end of your document and consult it whenever necessary by using the split screen capability of your computer. Alternatively, make your style guide a separate file and open it in a second window. You may find yourself adding to this list as you write your document and make increasingly complex formatting decisions. And you may even revise the formatting specifications as you revise the text.

Computer Style Sheets

Truly powerful word-processing programs have electronic style sheets as one of their regular features. These style sheets consist of a list of formatting specifications that govern how the characters (letters and numbers) in your document look, how paragraphs are formatted, and how pages are laid out. All the formatting commands you choose as you write your document are automatically carried out by the style sheets. This is how they work: Your word-processing program comes with sample style sheets. You electronically "attach" one of them to your computer file, and the commands in the style sheet format various parts of your document in the way you specify.

To take a simple example, you could specify that your document is to have block paragraphs, two blank lines between paragraphs, bold main headings in 14-point type, bold subheadings in 12-point type, and double spacing between lines. If you decide to change the formatting to indented paragraphs, single spacing, and capitalized main headings, you simply alter the style sheet rather than the document itself. Or you remove the old style sheet and attach a new one.

Computer style sheets can be extremely intricate, giving a host of different directions for different paragraphs or for different parts of a particular document. For detailed instructions, read the user's manual for your word-processing program. Later, when you become more proficient, you can copy one of the sample style sheets and modify it to suit your needs, or you can create your own style sheet from scratch.

The benefits of computer style sheets are obvious. They vastly speed up the process of formatting and make revisions easier: You change the style sheet once instead of making the same change over and over again in your document. And you can be sure of consistency: You attach the same style sheet to the different sections of a document or to different documents, and it never forgets to apply the correct format where it is supposed to.

But whether you simply make a list of format specifications or attach a computer style sheet to your document file, using a detailed style guide is important—in fact, almost a necessity—when you are doing any of the following:

Writing a document with complex formatting
Writing a document with several sections or chapters
Producing or publishing the document yourself
Planning to write other documents that must resemble the present one
Contributing to a group writing project

Style guides make your documents look professional.

Glossaries

If you can create glossaries, you may be able to store certain kinds of formatting commands in them. Assign a brief abbreviation to the formatting command and store it in the glossary. To format text, simply type the abbreviation and expand it. This trick is particularly useful when long and cumbersome formatting commands must be embedded in the text or when formats are stored in a visual symbol. For example, in most versions of Microsoft Word for the IBM PC and the Macintosh, you can store complex formatting instructions in a paragraph mark (¶) and save the mark in the glossary until you want it.

Let's Solve It!

If you are a novice, you may be tempted either to ignore visual communication or to run wild. Here's how to avoid both extremes.

Problem: Ignoring the Visual Aspects of Communication. In the past you worried only about margins when you typed your document and relied solely on words to tell your story. You see no reason to change now that you write on a computer.

Solution. Don't get trapped by old habits and rigid preconceptions. Visual communication does matter; researchers are finding that readers respond more favorably to documents with graphics. Visual signals, in the form of graphics, layout, and typography, help your readers understand and remember your message.

Problem: Decorating with Typography. Having discovered the variety of computer fonts and pictorial elements available in a word-processing program, you proceed to fill your text with as much visual embroidery as you can. Every other word is in bold, italics, or a novelty font. You are like a toddler let loose with finger paints.

Solution. Follow the basic guidelines about typography in this book and then read more detailed treatments. Also study professional examples of the type of document you are producing and follow the conventions they follow. Keep in mind that your main purpose is to communicate, not to show off typographically.

Problem: Producing a Crowded, Busy Document. Everywhere the eye looks, something is going on in your document. Boxes and pull quotes vie for attention with tables and multitudes of headings, subheadings and sub-subheadings. The page is so crowded that the reader can hardly find the main text, let alone concentrate on it.

Solution. Because you now have the resources of computer graphics and layout at your command doesn't mean that you have to use them all. It is better to do a few things well. Design the total document rather than working on it piecemeal. Be restrained in the number of graphic or typographic elements you use; leave plenty of white space. If you number any graphic artists, document designers, or printers among your friends, talk to them about their trade; even a casual conversation will give you professional tips you can use in your computer page design.

Computer Writing Tips

Becoming a pro in computer graphics, typography, and layout involves paying attention to little details.

- For most, if not all, word-processing programs, don't use the space bar or tabs to set paragraph indention. This can limit your ability to use the superb formatting ability of a computer.

- If you use a lot of tab stops to create a table, you may be able to use a special function in your word-processing program to keep the table as one paragraph. In that case, you can later change all the tab stops in a column by changing only one tab stop.

- Save frequently when you are creating graphics; it is easy to slip and draw the wrong line. Some graphics programs have an undo or erase function that lets you revert to the last version you saved.

- Give each graphic a filename that both describes the contents and identifies the chapter or section number—for example, "04.CPU.Dia" for a diagram of a central processing unit in Chapter 4. When you have decided on the final figure number, add that to the filename: "04-7.CPU.Dia."

- When you transfer a diagram or graph or chart to your text document, save as soon as the transfer is made.

- To facilitate the transfer of graphics and charts into text documents, use integrated programs that include word processing, spreadsheets, and graphics. Or use software that allows you to switch rapidly from one program to another.

- Write figure or table numbers and titles to graphics in your word-processing program; then, if you want to change the order of the graphics or reword their captions, you won't have to go back into the graphics program to make the changes.

- Because figure and table numbers are often changed in the revision stage, begin by labeling graphics with "00." When you are ready to print the final copy of your document, use the search function to locate all instances of 00 and change them to the correct numbers.

- Before printing a document, check where page breaks occur. You don't want to start a new page with a "widow," jargon for a short line of two or three words. Nor do you want a graphic to be separated from its caption or a heading separated from its text. Section breaks or indented material should not begin on the last line of a page. Sometimes you can correct a bad page break by subtly increasing or decreasing white space between sections or in the margins. Alternatively, you can shorten or lengthen the text by slightly changing the wording. Many word-processing programs, however, have a function that lets you keep indicated lines or paragraphs together.

  Another kind of bad page break occurs when a graphic, too large to fit at the bottom of a page, moves to the top of the next page and leaves a gaping space behind it. To correct this situation, you might reduce the graphic (either in the graphics program or the word-processing program), position it earlier or later in the text, or place it on a page alone facing the text that discusses it. Or if the graphic almost fits, you might simply adjust the bottom margin to make room.

  In some cases, however, a ragged bottom margin is a design element that can be attractively incorporated into the total page layout.

- Before you attempt a final printing of your document, print out several drafts in order to check all the details of typography, graphics, and page layout. Even with computers that claim "what you see is what you get" (WYSIWYG), the printed document can look subtly different from the screen version. Be prepared to make many minor adjustments.

When I first worked on a computer, I had a "poetical" thought: I would be writing with light. There's something nice about that. And something pretty corny, too. I also liked those metaphors in computer language: *mouse, menu, path, scrap, scroll, jump, home.* They seemed to animate the whole business.

The poet X. J. Kennedy told me why he likes writing poems with a computer: "Great fun to rearrange riming lines and to zap those adjectives like enemy space scouts." You can also see the poem on the screen and experiment with changing the layout—indenting, centering, spacing. You can even set the lines flush to the right margin. (I've found only one occasion to do that.)

There's an easy command in my word-processing program to make a "New Line," and that's a pretty good definition of what a poem does. J. V. Cunningham wrote that "prose is written in sentences, poetry in sentences and lines." You have to read a poem one line at a time, and little changes in layout affect how you see the line; they may nudge the meaning. For one of my long poems I gave each section a short subtitle printed in bold. The bold separates the sections and guides the readers through the poem. It also stops them at each section so they can't read straight through.

Layout on the page becomes especially important when you're not working in traditional forms. For one poem I invented a new stanza with different lengths and indentions for various lines; these were easier to play with on a computer than on a typewriter. Next time I do something experimental like this, I'll master style sheets—maybe.

Actually, I'm a Computer Wimp when it comes to trying out new commands. I figure I'm using about 2 percent of the capacity of my word-processing program. That's probably why I only revise on the computer. When you discover a new process, it's very exciting, though. For example, just this morning I discovered one called "Anagram." I thought it might work as a rhyming dictionary and I was right! *Tureen, umpteen, unforeseen, unseen, velveteen, ween, wintergreen!*

John Ridland
Poet

Getting Ready for Publication

Formatting academic papers
Formatting manuscripts for submission
to publishers
Formatting business and technical documents
Managing long documents

At this point you are nearing the end of the writing process. Your document is almost ready to be "published"—that is, to be be sent to its final destination or officially distributed. But first you need to format it correctly, and "correctness" depends on the type of document you are writing. Most likely your work falls into one of three categories, each of which has its own formatting requirements:

> Academic papers
> Manuscripts submitted for professional publication
> Technical and business documents

The first category comprises the writing you submit to instructors for review and criticism as part of your course work: term papers, reports, essays, research projects, theses, and dissertations. In the past, all that instructors expected from you was a neat, legible manuscript that followed some basic formatting conventions. And unless you were writing a thesis or dissertation for an advanced degree, your work was rarely published or distributed to a wider audience. Computers, however, will be changing all that. The spread of computer writing and the rapid evolution of computer printers, from dot-matrix to laser printers, are going to encourage much more in-house publication of student work. Desktop publishing may become a standard feature of all composition courses, whether in elementary school or in the university. And students will have to pay increasing attention to the correct formatting of their work.

The second category consists of documents submitted for professional publication: articles submitted to scholarly or professional journals, or fiction or nonfiction work submitted to a publishing house or popular magazine or even to a newspaper. In the past, all that was required was a neat, legible manuscript that the publisher turned into a professionally formatted product and then distributed. But the computer is increasingly affecting how writers format their manuscripts and prepare them for submission. And for some writers, self-publishing with a computer and laser printer allows them to bypass an outside publisher altogether.

Finally, there are the business or technical documents you write on the job, most commonly letters, memos, and reports. You may be wholly in charge of these documents—that is, you not only write and format them but also oversee their physical production and final distribution—or you may simply write them and then collaborate with others on their production. Large companies sometimes have in-house publishing departments. But in either case, the computer allows you to specify the documents' final form. And you will be expected to follow the formatting requirements for the type of document you are writing.

You probably won't have to deal with all the types of documents mentioned here, but most likely you will write some of them. Read the sections in this chapter that seem most relevant now; consult the other sections if you find yourself working on other types of writing projects. (See the chapter table of contents below.) And remember that the discussion in one section may pertain to another section as well: Thus business and technical reports as well as academic papers may have footnotes, and all long documents are likely to have tables of contents.

Academic Papers

For any kind of academic writing project, always follow the prescribed format, whether it is laid down by an instructor, academic department, university library, professional society, or scholarly journal. Even if you are accustomed to another procedure, follow the new directions. Instructors often provide formatting guidelines in the form of a handout, or they will direct you to a manuscript preparation section in a writer's handbook. Unfortunately, older handbooks—and some instructors—assume you will be typing your paper and make suggestions that aren't applicable to computer papers.

Computer Formatting Instructions

General formatting instructions for computer papers might read like this:

1. Prepare a title page if required. (If one is required, its form is usually specified by the instructor.) Insert a page break after the title page text.

2. If no title page is required, place the title on the first page of text, paying attention to the principles of good document design. (See Chapter 8, pp. 168–70.)

3. Identify your paper with your name, the name of the course, the assignment number, and the date (or whatever other information the instructor requires). If a special title page is not required, this information is typically placed in the upper left-hand corner of the first page. Some word-processing programs let you date and time the paper automatically.

4. Use your word-processing program to do the following automatically:

   Leave adequate margins. (Margins of 1 inch to $1\frac{1}{4}$ inches are standard.)

   Indent paragraphs one-half inch.

   Indent block quotations 1 inch on each side.

   Position footnotes at the bottom of each page or at the end of the document.

   Justify both edges of text or leave the right edge unjustified (ragged).

   Double-space the text.

   Provide a top running head (header) with your last name and the page number in the upper right-hand corner for every page except the first one: "Brown: 2."

   Insert a bottom running head (footer) for the first page only and place the numeral 1 in the center of the bottom margin.

5. Insert a page break at the end of the paper; start the bibliography or reference list on the new page.

6. Follow correct guidelines for using computer typefaces or style options; for example, don't underline if you mean to italicize.

7. Proofread carefully, preferably using spell checker and style checker programs; there should be no handwritten corrections whatsoever on computer-printed papers.

8. If you use a dot-matrix printer, be sure the ribbon is fresh and the printer is set to near-letter-quality.

9. Use fairly heavy $8\frac{1}{2}$-by-11-inch white paper, preferably "laser perfed." (Laser-perforated strips are easy to tear off and leave a smooth edge.)

10. Carefully remove the perforated strips, separate the pages, and staple or clip them together in order.

You should remember, however, that individual instructors may give slightly different instructions.

Computer Footnotes

Footnotes are an integral part of academic papers, but when done on the typewriter, they can be sheer agony. I vividly remember my own typewriting days: trying to estimate how much space to leave for footnotes at the bottom of the page and inevitably estimating wrongly—and then trying to squeeze the notes in. Could I get away with a bottom margin of one-eighth inch? In desperation, I would retype the whole page only to discover I had omitted a footnote at the very beginning of the paper, so the rest of the notes, all forty-five of them, were misnumbered. Computers, of course, have done away with such horrors and saved many an academic career. Now computer writers merely have to know how to take advantage of their word-processing programs and what form their footnotes should have. This section discusses creating footnotes with a word-processor; the next section, "Footnote Styles," addresses the subject of footnote form.

Automatic Footnoting. In a powerful word-processing program, you simply give a footnoting command and the computer automatically places a correctly superscripted number in your text. Then it lets you type in footnote information. You may have to embed this information in the text or write it in a special footnote window. The computer scrupulously keeps track of your footnotes: If you add, delete, or rearrange material, it renumbers both the notes and the material in the text.

You can also specify where you want footnotes printed. The computer will "float" them to the bottom of the page and separate them from the main text with a short line and some white space; in this case they are technically called *footnotes*. Alternatively, the computer can put your notes at the end of the document; in this case they are technically called *endnotes*. (For the sake of convenience, I use the word "footnotes" in this book even though I am referring to both endnotes and footnotes.) If you choose endnotes, insert a page break after the last line of the main text. Title the new page "Notes" and press Enter two times to insert blank lines. The computer now treats this page as the end of the document or division and automatically places the first footnote after the blank lines.

If you don't want to use numbers for footnotes, preferring symbols like an asterisk instead, the computer lets you do that, too. Footnotes can be edited just like any other text, so you can make textual changes in them as you revise your document, or you can change their typography and spacing when you format your work. In some computer programs, for example, you have to specify that the first lines of footnotes are to be indented.

Nonautomatic Footnoting. But what if your word-processing program doesn't have automatic footnoting? Your job is a little more difficult, but the computer still makes it easier than using a typewriter. Simply follow these tips:

- Eliminate all unnecessary footnotes. Your reader may actually appreciate it if there is more of you and less of outside sources. In any case, you don't want to write a "scissors and paste" paper — one that is merely a pastiche of other people's work.
- Use the simplest type of documentation you can. You may be able to give internal references rather than write full-blown footnotes. (Various ways of documenting outside source material are discussed in the next section.)
- If possible, use endnotes (at the end of your document) rather than footnotes (at the bottom of each page).
- After you have footnoted a book or article the first time, put subsequent references to the same work in parentheses in the text of your document, rather than writing another footnote.
- Most word-processing programs have superscript capability; use it for writing footnote numbers in the text and in the list of footnotes.
- Number footnotes successively and then use the search function to be sure you haven't skipped or repeated any numbers.
- Be sure the numbers in the list of footnotes correctly match the numbers in the text; this is especially important if you add, delete, or rearrange footnoted material. Again, use the search function to double-check.

Footnote Styles

Once you know how to write footnotes on your computer, the next problem is knowing what style, or form, they should have. Not all footnoting systems are alike. Each of the main academic disciplines has established its own set of standards, and each set differs somewhat from the others. Your instructor or academic department may give you the relevant formatting instructions to follow (in a handout or writer's handbook), but your best source of information is the library. For example, the library at the University of California, Santa Barbara, publishes a brief pamphlet entitled *Style Guides for Technical Reports, Journal Articles, Dissertations, Term Papers, Publications, Theses.* Inside are listed individual style guides for a wide variety of academic disciplines, from archaeology and art to engineering and medicine. If you were writing a paper on music, you would be told to consult Demar Buel Irvine, *Writing About Music: A Style Book for Reports and Theses*. This guide, according to the pamphlet,

> includes not only information on footnote and bibliography format but also a section on suggestions for improvement of literary style. Valuable guide to particular forms of citations such as letters, documents, iconographic items, recordings, autographs, manuscripts and microfilm.

A few of the more important style guides are listed in the bibliography of this book. An important benefit from following such professional guides is the certainty that your work is absolutely correct down to the last detail.

If you haven't had much experience in writing footnotes, or if you aren't up to date on the latest trends, here is a brief overview—and this is truly an overview, not a substitute for the style guides. I will discuss the traditional footnote first—when to use footnotes, how to number them, what to put in them, how to write and format them, and where to put them. Then I will discuss the latest trends in footnoting and different types of footnoting systems (or, more accurately, "referencing" systems, because sometimes you don't have to use a footnote at all).

Traditional Footnotes—The Modern Language Association (MLA) Style. The style of footnote you are probably most familiar with is the traditional one codified by the MLA and widely used in high schools and universities. Many of the MLA's general guidelines concerning when, what, how, and where apply to all referencing systems.

When to Footnote. In writing an academic paper, you are obligated to provide a footnote whenever you use a direct quotation from an outside source: a book, magazine, recording, lecture, electronic document, personal communication, and so on. You must also footnote any paraphrases (material that you put in your own words) or summaries (material that you condense). Footnotes can also be used to give readers information that is important but doesn't quite fit into your main text.

How to Number Footnotes. Footnotes are signaled by numbers placed in the text directly after the material quoted, paraphrased, or summarized. For easier reading, put the footnote number at the end of the sentence, after the last punctuation mark.

What to Put in a Footnote. Footnotes give readers all the information they need to look up the source of your material. For example, if you are quoting from a book, you need to include, at the very least, the author's full name, the complete title of the book, the place of publication, the publisher, the date of publication, and relevant page numbers. Depending on the book, you might also have to include several authors' names, an editor's or translator's name, the edition number, the volume number, the year of reprinting, and so on. Footnotes to other sources—encyclopedias, periodicals, newspapers, government publications, letters, unpublished dissertations, lectures, recordings, computer software, computer information services, interviews, performances, movies, TV or radio shows, videotapes, maps, charts—require still other information. Professional style guides help with these details.

How to Write a Footnote. Footnotes follow strict formatting conventions; you must follow them all, down to the placement of the last period. Style guides give models for all types of footnotes. In general, simple ones (for a book by a single author or for an article in a magazine) look like this:

[1]William Golding, *The Spire* (London: Faber and Faber, 1964) 10–12.
[2]Lionel Trilling, "Of This Time, of That Place," *Partisan Review* 10 (1943):72–73.

More complicated footnotes have more complicated formats. The best course to follow is to have a style guide beside you as you write. Find the correct models for your footnotes and follow them exactly.

How to Write a Second Footnote to the Same Work. You don't want to repeat information you have already given readers, so subsequent footnotes to the same work are always shortened as much as possible. In the past, Latin abbreviations were frequently used, and footnotes such as these were common:

[4]Ibid., p. 5.
[5]Golding, *op. cit.*, p. 21.

This kind of notation is going out of favor, however, and more and more people are using simply the last name of the author (and the work's title, if they are quoting from more than one work by the same author) in second references:

[4]Golding 15.

You can also put the page numbers of second references in the main text. Put these numbers in parentheses at the end of the sentence and follow them with the appropriate punctuation, like this (Golding 15). If you make clear in your text that the quoted material comes from Golding, you can omit his name in the parentheses and simply write the page number, like this (15).

Choose one method for writing second references—either the short footnote or the parenthetical reference—and use it consistently. A style guide will give you models to follow, but let your computer eliminate some of the drudgery. Make glossary entries for frequently used authors' names or titles of works and merely type in the glossary abbreviation or code rather than the full name or title.

Where to Put Footnotes. Footnotes can be placed at the bottom of the page on which the quoted material appears or at the end of the document or division, on a special page titled "Notes." Unless you are specifically told where to put footnotes, the choice is yours. For a few short notes, the bottom of the page is fine, but large numbers of long notes belong at the end. (As mentioned before, these notes are technically known as endnotes.)

How to Format Footnotes. Indent the first line one-half inch and raise the footnote number one-half line ("superscript"). Do not put a period or a space after the footnote number, but begin the text immediately. Sometimes you are told to double-space footnotes; in other cases you can single-space them and put them in a smaller type size. For easier readability, however, double-space between footnotes. Use the same margins for the endnotes pages as for text pages.

Other Styles in Footnoting. Many disciplines in the humanities tend to use some form of the MLA system for referencing outside source material, but other academic disciplines use other systems, and even the MLA is changing.

MLA Parenthetical References. The latest style guide from the MLA recommends giving up the traditional system. Instead, outside source material is to be referenced in parentheses in the text itself. Directly after the sentence containing quoted material, put in parentheses the author's last name, the volume number of the work (if relevant), and the page numbers. You may also need to give the act, scene, line, chapter, book, or stanza number if you are quoting from a piece of literature.

> Hamlet can also be seen as a drama of political crime, in which Hamlet "puts on, in cold blood, a mask of madness in order to perform a coup d'état; Hamlet is mad, because politics is itself madness, when it destroys all feeling and affection" (Kott 62).

A bibliography at the end (titled "Works Cited") will give all the other details that used to go in the footnote. The entry for the example above would read like this:

> Kott, Jan. *Shakespeare Our Contemporary*. Trans. Boleslaw Taborski. New York: Doubleday & Co., 1966.

Ordered References Method. Engineering and some of the sciences favor a system of internal references called the ordered references method. In papers written in such areas as engineering, mathematics, chemistry, or physics, one or more Arabic numerals is placed in parentheses or square brackets after the quoted material; these numbers refer to numbered works in a reference list at the end of the paper.

The normal modes and natural frequencies for numerous vibrating beam systems can be found in several books [1–6].

The numbered reference list contains complete bibliographic information; for example, the first two items for the above citation would read as follows:

1. Blevins, R. D., *Formulas for Natural Frequency and Mode Shapes*. Van Nostrand Reinhold Corporation, New York, 1979.
2. Harker, R. J., *Generalized Methods of Vibration Analysis*. John Wiley and Sons, New York, 1983.

Small variations in this system will be found, however.

Author-Date Method. Subjects like botany, geology, and zoology (life sciences) and psychology, sociology, and economics (social sciences) follow the American Psychological Association (APA) style. In this system, called the author-date method, the author's name and the date of publication are put in parentheses.

Within our own middle-class culture, the "polite smile" is used as part of a norm to manifest positive affect in public situations. The norm appears to be particularly strong for women—especially when they are in a care-giving role (Bugental, Love, & Gianetto, 1971).

The work referred to in parentheses is described more fully in a reference list at the end of the paper.

Bugental, D., Love, L., & Gianetto, R. (1971). Perfidious feminine faces. *Journal of Personality and Social Psychology, 17,* 314–18.

Again, there are variations to this system—and legal writing has yet another system.

Confused at this point? The solution is simple: Follow a style guide for your academic discipline and forget the others. On the other hand, if you have one of the super word-processing programs, you can simply select from a formatting menu the footnote style you want and write in the bibliographic information. The computer formats it in the correct footnote style. This system is as close to paradise as the academic researcher is likely to come!

Bibliographies and Reference Lists

When you use footnotes, you may be asked to provide a bibliography as well, that is, a list of the works you consulted. (If the footnotes list all the works you consulted, the bibliography can often be omitted.) With an internal referencing system, however, you *must* provide a reference list.

Bibliographies. Usually the items in a bibliography are alphabetized according to the last name of the author. (If a work was written anonymously, use the first significant word in the title, disregarding an initial "The" or "A.") Bibliographical entries look a lot like footnote entries, but there are significant differences: Numbers are not used; the author's name is inverted; items are often separated by periods rather than commas; parentheses generally do not appear; and the second and subsequent lines are indented. A typical bibliography would look like this:

Abrams, Meyer Howard. *The Mirror and the Lamp: Romantic Theory and the Critical Tradition.* London: Oxford University Press, 1953.

Bornstein, George. *Yeats and Shelley.* Chicago: University of Chicago Press, 1970.

Ellman, Richard. *Yeats: The Man and the Masks.* New York: Macmillan, 1948.

Keith, W. J. "Yeats's Arthurian Black Tower." *Modern Language Notes,* LXXXXV (February 1960), 119–23.

And just as with footnotes, offbeat bibliographic items—recordings, lectures, personal letters, interviews, and the like—require special treatment. A style guide will provide models.

The computer makes creating bibliographies much easier than it used to be. You have three basic options: writing the bibliography from scratch as part of your document; transforming your list of endnotes into a bibliography; and creating a bibliography in a database program.

If you choose the first option, clearly the easiest for a short or simple paper with few outside sources, do the following:

- Separate the bibliography from the last page of text (or from the list of endnotes) by inserting a page break.
- Title the new page "Bibliography."
- Leave some blank lines, then begin the list of works you want to include.
- Type in all the necessary bibliographic information for each entry in the correct format.
- If instructed to do so, group entries into "primary sources" and "secondary sources"; use subheadings to identify each section.
- If you have a sort function, use it to alphabetize the entries; otherwise, use the move function.

■ Use hanging indent paragraphs so that the first line of an individual entry is flush with the left margin and its subsequent lines are indented.

■ Single-space or double-space the bibliography, depending on the instructions you have been given.

If you choose the second option, transforming endnotes into a bibliography, copy your notes to the end of your document or put them in a new file. Delete all second references and then construct a bibliography from the remaining material. Follow the relevant procedures listed above.

The third option, creating a bibliography in a database, is the obvious choice for a long or complex research paper. With even a simple standard database, you can easily and accurately keep track of the bibliographic information for each reference. You can also jot down a brief summary and evaluation of the contents or approach of each work, as in Figure 9-1.

Eventually you will sort and print these entries as a complete bibliography. A database allows you to select only those entries you want to print. Perhaps not all the works you put in the database need to go into the bibliography; in that case you will be creating a "selected bibliography." A database also makes it easy for you to print comments about each work; in that case you will be creating an "annotated bibliography."

Choose a database that gives you flexibility in formatting, so when you print your bibliography, it is in the standard form. Otherwise you will have to transfer database

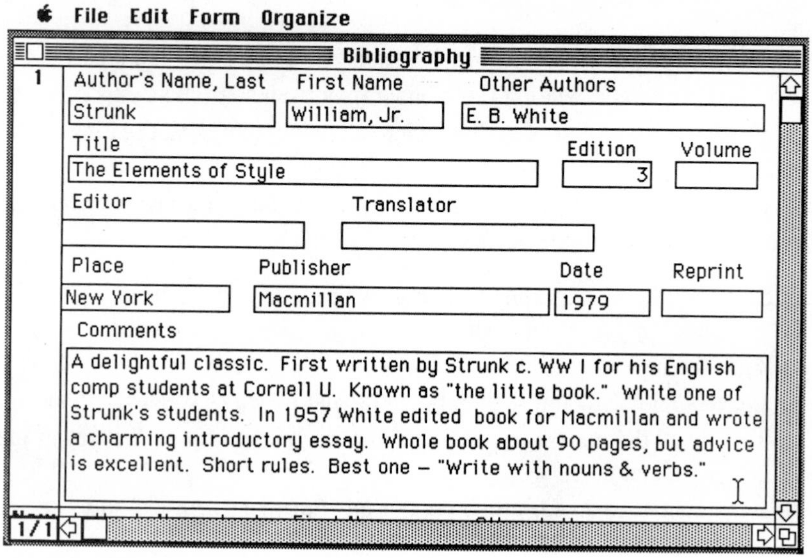

FIGURE 9-1. *A database record of a bibliographic entry*

files to your word-processing file and manipulate the text there. If you are a serious researcher, however, consider buying a special bibliographic program. Such programs provide predesigned data forms to fill in and let you choose the format style of the printed bibliography or reference list. Additionally, with the right program accessory, you can download files from specific databases you subscribe to (such as Dialog, BRS, and MEDLARS) and convert them into correctly formatted bibliography entries.

Reference Lists. A reference list follows many of the formatting guidelines for bibliographies, and you can use most of the computer procedures discussed above. (Simply title the page "References" or "Reference List.") However, individual entries in a reference are treated somewhat differently than they are in the traditional bibliography. For example, in the APA system, only initials are used for authors' first names, the date is put in parentheses, and only the first letter of the title and subtitle is capitalized. The following example is a typical APA reference list.

> Baumeister, R. F. (1982). A self-presentational view of social phenomena. *Psychological Bulletin, 91,* 3–26.
>
> Birdwhistell, R. L. (1970). *Kinesics and context.* Philadelphia: University of Pennsylvania Press.
>
> Feldman, R. S., Devin-Sheehan, L., & Allen, V. L. (1978). Nonverbal cues as indicators of verbal dissembling. *American Educational Research Journal, 15,* 217–31.
>
> Weiss, F. (1983). *Simulated vs. posthypnotically induced expressions of emotion: A validation study.* Unpublished master's thesis, University of California, Santa Barbara.

Other styles for reference lists differ somewhat. You could be required, for example, to number the items in the reference list, arrange the items by date rather than author's name, or give only the title of the journal rather than the title of the article. The variations are legion; consult a style guide for your discipline.

Theses and Dissertations

Formatting a master's thesis or doctoral dissertation is much like formatting any other academic paper. For footnotes and a bibliography or reference list, follow the style guide for your academic discipline. In addition, because a thesis is a long document divided into chapters or sections, you will have to provide a table of contents; see pp. 223–25 of this chapter for general guidelines on generating and formatting such a table on the computer.

Your best source of information on all formatting details, large and small, is your academic department or university library. The library at the University of California, Santa Barbara, for example, provides graduate students with a booklet entitled *Instructions for the Preparation and Submission of Theses and Dissertations.* This publication gives specifications for everything, from what kind of paper to use and how to copyright your thesis to how wide to make the margins and where to place the page numbers. If you are a typical graduate student, you will spend sleepless nights worrying about format requirements: If you don't meet them, the library won't accept your work, and library acceptance of the physical artifact is usually a prerequisite for getting your degree. Libraries are fussy because they often bind dissertations and put them on their shelves, so essentially you are producing the pages of a book.

Your computer will take care of many of the special formatting requirements for theses, but three items may be of special concern to you as a computer writer:

Paper. To prevent deterioration, libraries frequently specify that dissertations be printed on 100-percent cotton paper. Finding 100-percent cotton tractor-feed paper is extremely difficult. Most likely you will have to feed single sheets of cotton paper into your printer or get your printout photocopied onto 100-percent cotton paper.

Font Size and Style Options. Academic personnel are used to accepting theses produced on typewriters; the design and size of computer fonts and the variety of style options (like bold and italics) may seem too different (and hence unacceptable) to some of them. Before you print out the final version of your work, show a sample to the person in charge and get official approval. Come to an agreement about all details of the document design.

Printing Quality. Your library or academic department may accept dot-matrix printing; check first. But in the future, more and more dissertations will be laser printed; they will resemble professionally typeset books. In fact, laser printing will someday be a requirement, not an option.

Manuscripts Submitted for Publication

Manuscripts submitted for possible publication have their own formatting requirements. These manuscripts can be divided into two main categories: articles for scholarly and professional journals, and fiction and nonfiction for books, magazines, and special sections of newspapers. (Requirements for certain specialized types of writing—plays or television scripts, for example—are beyond the scope of this book.)

Articles for Scholarly and Professional Journals

In submitting an article to a scholarly or professional journal, follow the specific formatting directions laid down by the society or publication. Often you will find these spelled out in the journal itself. Try looking on the inside of the cover.

As an alternative, you can write for a style guide. For example, the *American Economic Review* has prepared a two-page handout outlining its specifications for textual divisions, footnotes, tables, figures, mathematical equations, symbolic notation, use of mathematical appendixes, quotations, spelling, references to individuals, references to organizations, the reference list, and so on. You can also deduce formatting requirements by studying the appearance of articles in the latest issue of a journal.

These formatting requirements are similar to the ones for academic papers. Unfortunately, each journal follows slightly different guidelines; if you submit an article to several places, you will probably have to create several versions. The changes are easy enough to do on a computer, but to simplify your task, save the master of your article and make a copy each time you must change the formatting in order to resubmit it to a journal. Include the journal's name or abbreviation in the filename of the new copy. Alternatively, if you regularly submit work to particular journals, create a computer style sheet for each journal (if your word-processing program allows you to do so.) Write your article, duplicate it, and then attach the appropriate style sheet to the copy.

In terms of physical *appearance* of manuscripts, editors of scholarly journals prize legibility and neatness. The basic requirements are simple: use one-inch margins, double-space your text, use good-quality paper and a dark ribbon, and print in letter-quality or near-letter-quality. Even dot-matrix printing should be perfectly acceptable if you meet these criteria. Be forewarned, however: Laser printing is going to place enormous pressure on all writers to upgrade the appearance of their work. No typed manuscript or even a computer-printed one can compete with laser-printed work, especially if it includes computer-generated graphics. Be prepared to compete.

Usually you can laser print your computer files fairly cheaply if you take your disk to a computer store or copy shop with a laser printer and do all the work yourself. Your files should be correctly formatted beforehand. Some stores have a stiff per-hour charge for any editing done on their machines. Stores that don't have self-service may charge a flat fee for converting your files to their system and a per-hour fee for doing editing and formatting, all this in addition to the per-page printing charge. Another alternative is to send a backup disk to a mail-order printing service. Never send the original disk! And write-protect the disk you do send, to guard against accidental erasure. Finally, universities and colleges are increasingly making laser printers available to the academic community or even to the general public.

Fiction and Nonfiction

To submit a piece of writing to a commercial publisher—a book publisher, magazine editor, or newspaper that accepts freelance work—follow the formatting guidelines set down in a book like *Writer's Market* or in writing magazines like *The Writer* or *Writer's Digest*. Often you can get specific guidelines by writing to the publication itself. And although they may vary a little, the basic ones boil down to these:

- Use reasonably heavy white paper; 20-pound bond is preferred, but 16-pound is adequate. (Tractor-feed paper with a 25-percent cotton fiber content is available.)
- Use a fresh black ribbon.
- Double-space throughout.
- Leave adequate margins. (Again, one inch is fine.)
- On each page, provide a running head that includes your name and the page number.
- If your work is a book, include a shortened version of the book title and the chapter number in the running head. (Store the text and formatting of such a running head in your glossary so it will be available for each chapter; merely change the chapter number.)
- Format the first page correctly:

    Put your name, address, and telephone number in the upper left-hand corner; use four single-spaced lines.

    Put an approximate word count (rounded off to the nearest hundred), the rights you are offering, and your copyright notice in the upper right-hand corner; use three single-spaced lines.

    Center the title one third to one half of the way down the page; put it in capital letters or bold, or make the font size larger.

    Put your name, in regular type, underneath the title.

    Skip three double spaces and start the text.

- Do not staple, clip, or otherwise fasten the pages of your manuscript together.

In general, editors merely want neat, legible manuscripts; they are the ones who will decide on document design and formatting after they accept your work for publication. Nonetheless, nonfiction manuscripts especially benefit from the careful use of headings, subheadings, and other typographical features. Commercial articles are unlikely to have footnotes, but if you use material from outside sources, acknowledge your debt by weaving the name of the author and the title of the book, article, survey, or the like into the text of your article. If appropriate, include computer graphics, if only as conceptual suggestions to the editor. Books should have tables of contents that follow the principles described on pp. 223–25; you may be asked to provide an index after the manuscript is accepted, or the publisher may generate one for you. (See pp. 226–27 for a discussion of indexing.)

Computer writers have a particular problem with some tradition-bound publishers, however. They can be a conservative lot. Only recently did they agree to accept photocopied manuscripts, and they are still leery of computers in general and of dot-matrix printing in particular. The current *Writer's Market,* for example, lists many publishers who will not state that computer printouts are acceptable; others say "computer printout submissions acceptable; no dot matrix" or "prefer letter-quality to dot matrix." There is no reason whatsoever that near-letter-quality dot matrix shouldn't be acceptable, but I recommend that you send a query letter with a sample of your printing before sending off your manuscript. Laser-printed manuscripts are another story. They are not a necessity, but they outshine typed or dot-matrix-printed documents in appearance and make their own statement about the professionalism of their authors.

As we move rapidly into the electronic publishing age, writers should be prepared to submit their work on disk as well as on paper, so editors can make the necessary editorial and formatting changes on their own computers before transferring the files to an in-house electronic publishing system or to an outside vendor with a page makeup system. The manuscript for this book, for example, had to be submitted both in hard copy and on an ASCII readable disk. (ASCII values are the universally-agreed-upon computer codes for letters and characters; with the proper linkups, files generated in a program using ASCII can be read by other ASCII programs on other machines.) And some writers are already transferring their files directly from their computer to their publisher via a modem and computer network link.

If you submit manuscript on disk, be sure all the files are clearly labeled and neatly organized. (See "Computer Writing Tips" at the end of this chapter for specific suggestions.) You may also be asked to submit graphics separately from text. Again, label these files clearly and organize them neatly. Never submit your original disk; always submit a backup. Label it with your name, address, and the name of the writing project. And write-protect it so your work can't be accidentally erased or damaged.

Technical and Business Documents

On the job or in volunteer work, you can expect to write, at the very least, three basic types of document: letters, memos, and reports. (Your writing may also involve more complicated projects—handbooks, manuals, brochures, newsletters, advertisements, fliers, and the like—but these go beyond the scope of this book. Increasingly, these documents are going to be written on computers; by 1990, experts predict, there will be a computer on every business desk in the United States. More and more managers are going to write and produce their own documents. This section will give you a head start.

Letters

Conventions govern the content and form of a business letter; readers will expect your letters to follow these conventions. This section first covers the individual parts of a business letter and then addresses overall format; it concludes with a discussion of special computer aids to letter writing.

Individual elements. Although a seemingly simple document, the standard business letter usually contains at least seven elements and often more than ten. (See Figure 9-2.) The individual elements are described below.

Return Address. This consists of your address or the letterhead of your company or organization; it should give the complete address and zip code. If you have a laser printer, you might consider creating your own letterhead and storing it in your computer's glossary or electronic scrapbook.

Date. The current date conventionally follows the return address. Write out the name of the month.

Inside Address. This comprises the name, organizational title or position, and address of the receiver. The person's name may be preceded by a courtesy title, such as Dr., Professor, or Ms., but in most cases the first and last names are sufficient. Government officials, members of the judiciary, members of the clergy, and royalty have special titles that should be used correctly; a good writer's handbook or the appendix of an up-to-date dictionary will give you the correct form.

Salutation. This standardized greeting to the receiver is followed by a colon. Often the salutation consists of "Dear" plus the courtesy title and the last name of the receiver; other variations may be more appropriate, depending on the situation.

- Many professional women consider their marital status irrelevant in a professional context; it is usually better to write "Ms. Atkins" rather than "Miss Atkins" or "Mrs. Atkins."
- There is a trend to address receivers by their first and last names and omit courtesy titles altogether: "Dear Mary Henderson." This solves the question of courtesy titles for women or for people whose name could be either male or female: "Dear Meredith Kramer" or "Dear T. R. Marbury."

- If the name of the individual is unknown to you, address the person in terms of his or her position: "Dear Editor," "Dear Personnel Director."
- If you are writing to a group, use a generalized greeting, but do not use "Sirs" or "Gentlemen" unless you know the group is all male. Use "Ladies and Gentlemen," "Colleagues," "Fellow Citizens," or some other non-gender-specific term.
- If you are writing to a totally unknown person such as a functionary in a large company or agency, don't write "Dear Sir" unless you know the person is male. Write "Dear Sir or Madam."

Body. The body, or text, of the letter can comprise one or many paragraphs. Like all business and professional writing, the body should reflect the principles of good writing. Before you write, carefully analyze your audience and your purpose in addressing them, and set a specific communication goal for yourself. As you write, pay

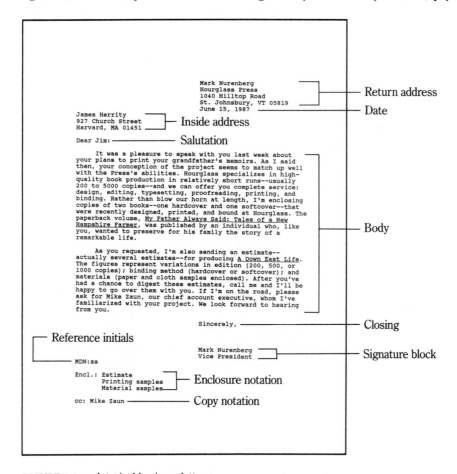

FIGURE 9-2. *A typical business letter*

special attention to being concise and achieving a fluent style free of jargon and pretentious diction. Increasingly, business correspondence aims for a friendly and conversational tone without, however, resorting to colloquialisms, clichés, or slang.

Closing. This is a standardized leave-taking like "Sincerely yours," "Cordially yours," or simply "Sincerely" or "Cordially." The closing is followed by a comma.

Signature Block. The signature block consists of your handwritten signature with your name and position typed underneath. Courtesy titles are usually omitted.

In certain situations, other sections may be required in a letter:

Addressee Notation. This message to the receiver notes that the contents should be handled in a special way. Typical notations, placed in capitals above the inside address, are "Please forward" or "Confidential."

Attention Line. The word "Attention" is followed by the name of the person who should read the letter: "Attention: Darlene Robinson." This line is placed underneath the inside address, usually in place of the salutation. The attention line is often used in conjunction with a subject line.

Subject Line. This is a brief but informative description of the letter's contents: "Subject: Investment Opportunities in the Food Industry." Place it directly under the attention line or inside address.

Reference Initials. At the left-hand margin, below the signature block, your initials in capitals are followed by a slash or colon and the initials of the word processor or typist: "JPM/ik." You will not use this code if you type your own letters.

Enclosure Notation. This indicates that other materials are included with the letter. Below the reference initials write "Enc.," "Encl.," or "Enclosures," and follow it with the number of enclosures or a brief list or both: "Enclosures (2)" or "Enc.: Résumé."

Copy Notation. The letters "cc" (for carbon copy or courtesy copy) are followed by the names of people receiving the photocopies of the letter: "cc: Cynthia Benson." Place this below the enclosure notation. Sometimes "pc" (for photocopy) is used instead. Blind copies—copies sent without the receiver knowing about them—are indicated by "bc" on the file copy but not on the original.

Computer Disk Notation. A brief notation or code in the lower left-hand corner indicates the disk and perhaps the directory or file a particular letter is stored in. For example, "Dsk:Bl:Unp" indicates the letter is stored on a disk entitled "Bills" in a directory called "Unpaid."

Running Head. If the letter runs to more than one page, provide a running head: typically this contains the receiver's name, the page number, and the date, arranged either horizontally or vertically.

Overall Format. Business letters can be formatted in various ways. Four common formats are the traditional, block, modified block, and simplified. (See Figure 9-3.)

In the *traditional* style, the return address and date, closing, and signature block are placed near the right-hand margin. (Start each of these sections at a tab stop at the center of the page.) The inside address, salutation, and body start flush with the left-hand margin. The first line of each body paragraph is indented (usually one-half inch), and paragraphs are separated by extra white space.

In the *block* style, all parts of the letter start flush with the left-hand margin. Block paragraphs are separated by extra white space.

FIGURE 9-3.   *Four basic letter formats: traditional (upper left), block (upper right), modified block (lower left), and simplified (lower right)*

In the *modified block* style, all parts of the letter except the return address and date, closing, and signature block start flush with the left-hand margin. Block paragraphs are separated by extra white space.

In the *simplified* style, all parts of the letter start flush with the left-hand margin, but the salutation is replaced by a subject line, and the closing is omitted entirely. Block paragraphs are separated by extra white space.

No matter which style you choose, format your letter by vertically centering the text on the page, taking the letterhead into account if necessary. As a rule, you should single-space the individual parts and double-space between parts, although three blank lines can be left between the date and the inside address and between the inside address and the salutation. If the letter has a typed return address rather than a printed letterhead, place the date immediately after the return address, with no blank line in between.

Find out from your company or organization exactly how your letter should be formatted; the company may provide you with a style guide, or you can look through the files for models. Eventually, however, you or your company should create a computer style sheet that will automatically format your business letters correctly. If your word-processing program doesn't have style sheet capability, consider moving up. Busy professionals who do a lot of writing need all the help they can get.

Computer Aids. Two other specialized computer aids — customized templates and mail merge — will also help you if you write large numbers of routine letters.

Customized Templates. Computer programs are available that allow you to design your own template (form to be filled in). To create a template for a business letter, you write all the standardized text that might be needed, plus the instructions for filling in the rest of the document to suit an individual client or case. When the letter is finally printed, of course, only the text and not the instructions appear. Programs for customizing templates are especially useful for highly technical writing, like legal writing, or for situations where nonprofessionals must finish the rest of the document. (Other programs purport to give the typical content as well as the standard format for various types of letters: turning down a request, asking for an interview, selling a new product, complaining about poor service, and the like. But although such letters might help the absolute novice, you will communicate much better if you compose your own letters after carefully assessing the particular needs and expectations of your readers and defining your specific purpose in writing to them.)

If you don't want to bother with a stand-alone template program, you still can create templates with your word processor. Set up a sample document; include in it as much as possible of the text, or leave blank spaces to be filled in. Also set up the formatting: margin size, line spacing, font and font size, style options, paragraph formats.

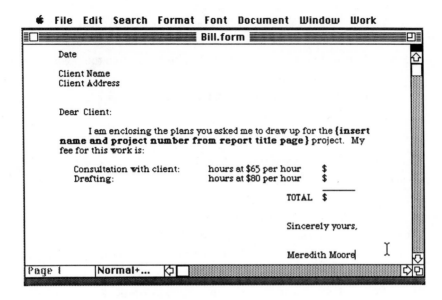

FIGURE 9-4. *A template for a routine letter*

If you want to include instructions, put them in hidden text or a distinctive typeface or style option; in the latter case they will have to be removed before printing. A template for a letter billing for services rendered might look like Figure 9-4.

Give this template a filename like "Bill. form." To use it, make a copy on your disk and fill in the relevant information. (Never work with the master.) Then print the letter on your letterhead stationery. If you use a laser printer, you can make the letterhead part of the template as well.

Mail Merge. This system may be part of your word-processing program, or you may have to invest in a stand-alone program. Mail merge greatly simplifies writing large numbers of routine letters: You store the standard part of the document in one file and the changeable parts in another and then merge the two in the printed version. Say that you want to individualize a mass letter mailing to all your customers, to all the members of your organization, or even to your friends at Christmastime. You would store most of the letter in one file and a list of each customer's name, company, and address (and perhaps other unique information) in a second. When the two files are merged, each letter has a different inside address; the salutation addresses a different person by name; and the body of the letter mentions the individual company or person by name again or makes other unique remarks.

Undoubtedly you have received many mail merge documents and already know the dangers of boilerplate letters: They can sound fake. The recipient can be painfully aware that the personal salutation of "Dear Maurice" or "Dear Susan" and the other personal touches in the body of the letter have been impersonally generated by a computer. If you write mail merge documents, be sure to write from the readers' point of view. Don't let the enormous resources of computers make you lose contact with your readers or forget the principles of honest communication.

Memos

Memos are usually brief, ranging from a few sentences to three or four pages, and serve a variety of purposes. Among other things, they can request information, give instructions, make announcements, justify or record policy, transmit (or introduce) an attached document, or give a short report.

The format of memos is fairly standard. If your company or organization doesn't have forms for memos, or doesn't provide you with a template on disk, you might begin by centering the word "MEMO" near the top of the page. (This heading, however, can be omitted.) At the left-hand margin, one inch or more below the top margin, type and double-space the headings "Date," "To," "From," and "Subject." Capitalize these headings or put them in bold or do both; follow each one with a colon. (See Figure 9-5.) Now fill in the appropriate information, using a tab stop to align the beginning text of each item.

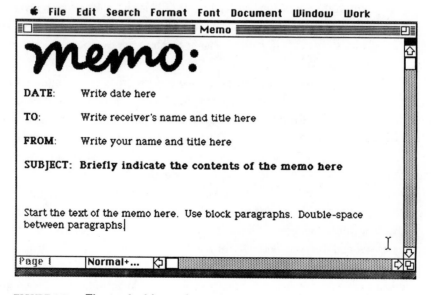

FIGURE 9-5. *The standard format for a memo*

- DATE: Write the current month, day, and year.
- TO: List the receiver or receivers. You may write the name of one or more individuals and their titles, or the name of a department or division. If you must send the memo to many people, however, write "See below" or "See distribution list." At the very end of the memo, after any enclosure or attachment notations, write "cc" and list the names.
- FROM: Write your own name and title; when the memo is printed, sign your initials in ink after your name or at the end of the text.
- SUBJECT: Write a concise but clear and informative description of the contents of the memo itself. Try to keep this to one line; emphasize it by putting it in capitals or making it bold.

Now triple-space and write the text of the memo itself. (See Figure 9-6.) Follow all the principles of good writing, with emphasis on clarity and conciseness. Busy

MEMO

DATE: June 29, 1987

TO: All managers

FROM: Mary Browning
Director of Human Resources

SUBJECT: Employee review process

During the next few weeks, Human Resources will be evaluating the employee review process. You can greatly contribute to this effort by expressing your thoughts on the subject. With the company's midyear review still fresh in your memory, please take the time to write a brief response and send it to my attention by July 16. The comments below may serve as useful guidelines.

The Review Process in General

The following are primary goals of the employee review process:

--Evaluate employee performance
--Provide a forum for productive manager-employee communication
--Update and refine job descriptions
--Set short-term and long-term goals for the employee

Is the present review process meeting these goals? Is it meeting, or failing to meet, other important goals? Is the process too shallow? Too time-consuming? Unnecessarily confrontational or anxiety-producing? Too bland? Are most of your employees satisfied with the procedure?

The Review Form

In general, are the form's instructions clear? Do your employees have trouble filling it out? Please glance through the form and comment on each section: the general evaluation, the weighted performance elements, and the future objectives. Would you like to add or delete any sections or categories?

That's All!

Thanks. In appreciation of your efforts, Human Resources promises to create, by the next review period, a bug-free, well-formatted, easy-to-use computer template for the review form. Honest.

FIGURE 9-6. *A typical memo*

people don't want to read long memos. They also appreciate a one- or two-sentence summary or overview at the very beginning. Often a memo is easier to follow if you divide it into brief sections with informative headings. If appropriate, use bulleted or numbered lists. (See Figure 9-6.)

Format the text into single-spaced block paragraphs with double spacing between them. As with letters, if the memo runs to more than one page, provide a running head with the date, receivers' names, and page number arranged either horizontally or vertically. A memo can also have enclosure, copy, and computer disk notations as well as reference initials. And when you attach your memo to other papers, use an attachment notation ("att."). Creating a computer style sheet or template, if one doesn't already exist, will eliminate having to worry about these formatting details each time you sit down to write.

Formal Reports

Short business or technical reports are often written as memos, especially when they are routine in nature, but long formal reports require a much different format. These reports are divided into separate sections. The main ones are these:

> Title page
> Table of contents
> Lists of tables or figures
> Abstract
> Introduction
> Text (body)
> Conclusion/recommendations
> Appendix
> Bibliography

Formal reports may contain other parts as well: a cover (when the report is bound); a half-title page, or title fly (a page with only the title on it); a letter of authorization (the request for the report, outlining the problem and the scope of the report); a letter of acceptance (a reply to the letter of authorization); a letter of transmittal (the transfer of the report to the reader; sometimes summarizes the main findings); a glossary (an alphabetical list of technical terms or abbreviations and their definitions); and an index (for long or detailed reports).

When you write a report, you are really addressing several different audiences in the different sections. Thus the abstract is aimed at high administrators and executives; they are probably looking for a brief but informative summary in nontechnical language. The introduction, body, and conclusion of the report are aimed at people closer to the problem who need more information and supporting data; they will welcome some technical language and details. The appendix is reserved for the specialists who want to study all the highly technical details or read supplementary materials. Keep this multilayered audience in mind as you write. Thus your prewriting should emphasize audience analysis and statement of purpose; the planning stage should emphasize blocking out the main sections and subsections in the body of the report.

When you format the report, study the layout of model reports; your company or organization should have some on file. And large organizations often provide their personnel with written guidelines or style guides. The following discussion of a report's basic sections is meant to supplement such material, not replace it.

Title Page. The title page of a report prominently displays near the top an informative title in capital letters, in bold, or in a type size larger than the text font. This title should clearly indicate the contents of the report and, if possible, the type of report: proposal, feasibility, progress, marketing analysis, and so on. Farther down the page are listed the person or group for whom the report was prepared, the author, the author's title if applicable, and perhaps the date. If your company or organization doesn't prescribe a layout, center the text between the left and right margins, and space the various items attractively on the page. (See Figure 9-7.)[1] Depending on company policy, simple design elements may also be included.

Table of Contents. Follow the guidelines on pp. 223–25 for generating and formatting the table of contents. Make the main entries and subentries specific and informative rather than vague or abstract. (See Figure 9-8.) Your purpose is to let readers preview the substance of your report and quickly find the sections that most interest them. For short reports you may be able to omit a table of contents.

Lists of Tables or Figures. If you have tables in your report, list them on a separate page. Arrange them in the order they appear in the report; include both their table and page numbers. A list of figures, similarly arranged, goes on the next page. The table of contents, list of tables, and list of figures should all follow the same format. If the report is short and has few graphics, you may be able to omit table and figure lists or to place such lists on the same page as the table of contents.

Abstract. This section is given a variety of names—abstract, summary, executive summary, introductory summary—but the purpose is always the same: to provide busy managers with the gist of your report in a highly condensed form. Sometimes the length is specified—a half page, 250 words, 10 percent of the length of the report. The longer and more complex the report, the longer the abstract is likely to be.

---

[1]Figures 9-7 to 9-13 are from Edward J. Koszalka et al., *Preliminary Evaluation of Chemical Migration to Groundwater and the Niagara River from Selected Waste-Disposal Sites*, EPA-905/4-85-001, prepared by the U.S. Geological Survey for the U.S. Environmental Protection Agency, 1985.

PRELIMINARY EVALUATION OF CHEMICAL

MIGRATION TO GROUNDWATER AND THE NIAGARA RIVER FROM

SELECTED WASTE-DISPOSAL SITES

By

Edward J. Koszalka, James E. Paschal, Jr.,

Todd S. Miller, and Philip B. Duran

Prepared by the U.S. Geological Survey

in cooperation with the

New York State Department of Environmental Conservation

for the

U.S. ENVIRONMENTAL PROTECTION AGENCY

FIGURE 9-7.   *The title page of a report*

CONTENTS

FIGURE 9-8.   *The beginning of a table of contents for a report*

You can write two different types: A *descriptive abstract* merely indicates what subjects the report covers but not what is said about these subjects; it is like an outline or table of contents in paragraph form. An *informative abstract,* or *summary,* however, is the report in miniature; it summarizes all essential information in reasonably non-technical language so that managers (rather than specialists) can easily understand it. To write such an abstract, omit background and introductory material and drastically condense the body of the report section by section; include all significant information and principal conclusions, but omit the finer points. Avoid repetition, and never add information or distort the contents of the report in any way. The style should be concise but not stilted; concentrate on making your abstract readable and informative.

The abstract begins a new page and is given a heading like "Abstract" or "Summary." (See Figure 9-9.) If the report is very short and informal, however, you may be able to include your abstract in the introduction.

The preliminary sections of a report—the sections preceding the introduction—are numbered consecutively in small Roman numerals, although no page number is actually printed on the title page or title fly. Each section will form a separate division or file in your document.

Introduction. As its name implies, this section introduces readers to the issue you are going to discuss. It can be broken down into two or three short subsections, each with an appropriate subheading. The elements that go into a good introduction might include background material, a statement of purpose, a brief definition of the problem, an indication of the scope of the report, and a concise survey of major findings or

ABSTRACT

In 1982 the U.S. Geological Survey, in cooperation with the U.S. Environmental Protection Agency and the New York State Department of Environmental Conservation, made a preliminary hydrogeologic and chemical evaluation of 138 known toxic waste-disposal sites along the United States side of the Niagara River from Lake Erie to Lewiston, approximately 20 miles downstream. The purpose of the investigation was to identify sites that are a possible source of contamination to the groundwater system.

The 138 sites were grouped into three areas--Buffalo, Tonawanda, and Niagara Falls. Results from the geologic and hydrologic investigations and chemical analyses are as follows:

<u>Buffalo area</u>. 25 sites were studied, of which 19 were drilled and sampled and 6 evaluated through a literature review. Of the 25 sites, 10 were designated as having a major potential for contaminant migration.

<u>Tonawanda area</u>. 50 sites were studied, of which 29 were drilled and sampled and 21 evaluated through a literature review. Of the 50 sites, 20 were designated as having a major potential for chemical migration.

<u>Niagara Falls area</u>. 63 sites were studied, of which 31 were drilled and sampled and 32 evaluated through a literature review. Of the 63 sites, 31 were designated as having a major potential for contaminant migration.

FIGURE 9-9. *The abstract of a report*

FIGURE 9-10.   *The beginning of the introduction to a report*

recommendations. Exactly what you say depends on the specific type of report you have to write. Keep your introduction brief; you don't want to duplicate the body of the report. But also give readers enough information so they understand what you are writing about and why. The introduction can be headed "Introduction." (See Figure 9-10.) It starts the report proper and should be numbered page 1—note the Arabic numeral.

Text.   The text, or body, of the report begins directly after the end of the introduction. Divide this part of the report into several main sections, and if necessary, divide each main section into subsections. Provide all the divisions with informative headings and subheadings. Avoid vague ones like "Section I" or "Body." Headings are vital parts of reports: They preview the contents of each section, they show readers how your report is organized, and they indicate the logical relationship between main ideas and sections and subsidiary ones. (See Figure 9-11.) Some types of reports combine a numbering system with headings.

As you format, make use of typography and layout to give your readers clear visual signals. Follow the guidelines discussed in Chapter 8. You may also want to supplement your text with figures and tables; see Chapter 8, pp. 174–83, for suggestions. If

---

EVALUATION OF CONTAMINANT MIGRATION

This report evaluates the potential for groundwater contamination from migration of hazardous wastes in a qualitative manner only; a quantitative assessment would require efforts beyond the scope of this preliminary survey. The following paragraphs give (1) criteria for the qualitative assessment of contaminant-migration potential, (2) a general method for computing the rate and quantity of chemical discharges, should sufficient data become available, and (3) suggestions for future quantitative studies to assess the regional effects of contaminant migration on the Niagara River.

Qualitative Assessment

All sites are designated as having either a major or indeterminable potential for contaminant migration in groundwater, as described below.

<u>Major potential</u>. These sites are close to the river or a tributary and (1) contain hazardous constituents or chemicals and have permeable soils or sufficient groundwater gradients for groundwater movement, as evidenced by site records, chemical analyses, and water-level or core analyses; and/or (2) have evidence that offsite migration of hazardous contaminants has already occurred.

<u>Indeterminable</u>. These sites were those for which data were inadequate to make a realistic assessment of contaminant migration; that is, where either the geohydrologic data or the chemical data were insufficient to indicate the potential for offsite migration.

Of the 138 sites evaluated in this study, 61 were judged to have a major potential for contaminant migration and are listed in table 12. The sites having a major potential may already be contaminating the rivers. The sites designated as having indeterminable potential may be reclassified as other data become available.

Quantitative Assessment

A quantitative assessment of migration rates and amount of contamination was beyond the scope of this study; however, a general procedure for calculating chemical discharges to the river, based on representative data from this study as an example, is given below. The methods presented herein should be used with extreme caution. The values would be, at best, an indication of relative differences between sites.

FIGURE 9-11. *The body of a report*

you incorporate outside source material, you will have to reference it in some way. The discussion on pp. 195–200 provides general directions for writing and formatting footnotes and internal references, but your company or organization may give you specific guidelines to follow.

Conclusion/Recommendations. This section brings your report to a close. It can have a descriptive heading — "Guidelines for Future Studies" — or can be called simply "Conclusion" or "Recommendations." (See Figure 9-12.) Sometimes you will include two sections: one or more paragraphs describing your conclusions, followed by specific recommendations (possibly in a numbered or bulleted list). The exact form of the conclusion depends on the nature of your report.

GUIDELINES FOR FUTURE STUDIES

This study indicates that some hazardous-waste sites will require further investigation to determine the potential for contaminant migration. At other sites, however, either there is no evidence of hazardous materials, or the hydrogeologic character of the site does not appear to allow for contaminant migration, so the need for further investigation may not be required.

Hazardous wastes have been disposed of in five ways: (1) in permeable deposits adjacent to the Niagara River or tributaries to the river, (2) in relatively impermeable deposits more than 15 feet thick and overlying bedrock, (3) in relatively impermeable deposits that are less than 15 feet and overlying bedrock, (4) in relatively impermeable deposits originally thicker than 15 feet and overlying bedrock but where thickness has been reduced by excavation to less than 15 feet and overlying bedrock, and (5) in relatively impermeable deposits where man-made interferences have altered site characteristics and increased the potential for flow of water from the site. Where contaminants from sites have reached bedrock, their effects have become regional. Some general guidelines for studying these five types of sites and the related regional contamination problems are given below.

Site Studies

Sites in Permeable Deposits Adjacent to the River

Where wastes are buried in or on permeable fill or alluvial sand adjacent to the Niagara River or its tributaries, contaminants can move laterally toward the river. An example of a hydrologic investigation that addressed this concern is that conducted by Dames and Moore (1981) at the Bethlehem Steel site in the Buffalo area. (See Appendix A, site 118.)

In an investigation of this type of site, the wastes produced and buried would be identified, the stratigraphy of the site documented, the quantity of groundwater and the direction of flow delineated, and mean concentrations of the contaminant plume determined. Several observation wells would be installed in the unconsolidated deposits between the site and the river and on the upgradient side of the site to determine groundwater gradients and extent and depth of geologic units. Where possible, wells would penetrate to below yearly low water-table levels. Single measurements of water levels would give only instantaneous gradient; seasonal monitoring would indicate changes throughout the year. Water-level recorders on wells would allow correlation of groundwater fluctuations with storms and river stage.

FIGURE 9-12. *The conclusion to a report*

Appendix. This section is reserved for the highly technical information that supports your general discussion in the body of the report; or it may include material too long or detailed for inclusion in the text (like questionnaires, interview questions, related memos). It is likely to include tables or figures, so follow the guidelines for these types of graphic presentations. Label each item in the appendix clearly. In some cases, this part of the report may be divided into "Appendix A," "Appendix B," and so on, with each appendix given an informative heading. Appendixes continue the pagination of the body of the report.

Bibliography. In general, bibliographies or reference lists for reports follow the same format as they do in academic documents. (See pp. 200–203.) Your company or organization may give you specific guidelines to follow. (See Figure 9-13.)

```
                        SOURCES OF DATA

American Falls International Board, 1974, Preservation and
     enhancement of the American Falls at Niagara, Appendix
     C--Geology and rock mechanics: 71 p.

Anderson, E. G., 1982, Hydrogeology review, Hyde Park
     Landfill: Toronto, Canada, Gartner Lee and Associates,
     19 p.

Buehlor, E. J., and Tesmer, I. H., 1963, Geology of Erie
     County, New York: Buffalo Society of Natural Sciences
     Bulletin, v. 21, no. 3, 118 p.

Claspon Corporation, 1977, Soils, geology, and hydrology of
     the NEWCO-Niagara Recycling site, Niagara Falls, New
     York: Claspon, 96 p., 10 figs., 6 tables.

Camp, Dresser, and McKee Engineers, 1982, City of Niagara
     Falls--Reports on Fall Street sewer tunnel, visual
     inspection and infiltration, air, and sediment
     evaluation: Camp, Dresser, and McKee Engineers, 230 p.

Cartwright, R. H., and Ziarno, J. A., 1980, Chemical quality
     of water from community systems in New York, November
     1970 to May 1975: U.S. Geological Survey Water-
     Resources Investigations 80-77, 444 p.
```

FIGURE 9-13. *The beginning of the bibliography of a report*

Tables of Contents

A table of contents can be useful, even necessary, for any long or complex document, whether it be a dissertation, a technical report, or a book-length manuscript intended for publication. The table of contents tells your readers three main things: what information is contained in your document, how this information is organized, and where it can be found. One of your primary goals is making the table of contents informative. Each of the main headings should tell readers something specific and concrete. Whenever possible, avoid vague abstractions like "Purpose," "Part I," or "Conclusion." If main sections or chapters contain subsections, give them informative subheadings in your table of contents. Subheadings allow readers to skim your ideas and information in more detail and see your organizational plan more clearly. If they want to read specific sections, page numbers will tell them where to go. Even if they intend to read your document from cover to cover, the table of contents should still provide them with a valuable overview of content and structure.

Your word-processing program may be able to generate a table of contents, or you can invest in a stand-alone program. Generating a table of contents on a computer involves "flagging" the relevant chapter titles and headings in your text—that is, putting a special command next to them. Alternatively, you can add and flag special table of content entries as you type your main text. To keep your work readable, however, put these entries in hidden text. If you want to indicate that some entries are subordinate to the main ones, the computer lets you insert indention commands and thus flag them as subentries.

When you are finished with your document, the computer will compile the flagged entries into a table of contents and automatically insert the correct page numbers next to each item. When you make later changes affecting the page numbering of your text, the computer will recalculate the page numbers in the table of contents. You can also add new entries to the table and format it however you like; a computer style sheet can be used to carry out your formatting specifications. In cases where your work consists of several sections or chapters in separate computer files, you will have to chain these files together, or merge them into one document, before you can generate a comprehensive table of contents or index. Check the user's manual of your word-processing program or stand-alone table of contents/index generator.

If your document contains more than three or four figures or tables, these must have a separate table of contents. You can title it "List of Illustrations," "List of Tables," "List of Maps," or whatever is appropriate. If you have a large number of visual aids, make one list for tables and a separate one for figures.

To create a table of contents manually, open a new document in a second window (or file) and type chapter numbers and titles, main headings, subheadings, tables, and figures and their respective page numbers as you scroll through the ready-to-print version of your document. Then use the delete and move functions to put tables and figures in their own sections at the end of this new file. Now you are ready to format this information and transform it into a proper table of contents.

The following design considerations apply to all tables of contents, whether they are generated by the computer or created manually.

- Place the table of contents in a separate division in your document so you can format it separately.
- If your word-processing program doesn't allow you to format different divisions in a document, make the table of contents a separate document.
- Center the title, usually "Contents," or place it flush against the left-hand margin. Simple linear design elements can be added, and the word "Contents" can be emphasized by your choice of type size and style.
- Separate main items with extra white space.
- Position the column of page numbers to the right (using tab stops) so it balances the list of entries to the left.
- Chapter numbers can be made part of the chapter title—"Chapter 1: Keynesian Economics"—or listed along the left-hand margin— "1. Keynesian Economics."
- Traditionally, tables of contents are very plain; however, you may want to emphasize main entries in bold or put leader characters between the entries and their page numbers. Dots, hyphens, and underlining are typical leader

characters; your word-processing program may be able to insert these automatically when you tab.

■ Table of contents pages are paginated in small Roman numerals that continue the numbering of any preceding pages, like the preface, dedication, or acknowledgments. Put the appropriate Roman numeral in the center of the bottom margin or in the same location as the page numbers of the main text. (Good word-processing programs give you style choices in pagination: Arabic numerals, large and small Roman numerals, and uppercase and lowercase alphabetic lettering.)

■ Lists of figures and tables follow the main table of contents and continue its pagination in small Roman numerals.

■ If the table of contents goes on for more than one page, place the word "Contents" in a running head. This running head should match the style and format of the running head in the main text.

Figure 9-14 depicts the first page of a table of contents that includes chapter sub-sections. For a simpler approach, see the contents page of *The New Writer*. For other samples, look at tables of contents in recently published books in your field of study.

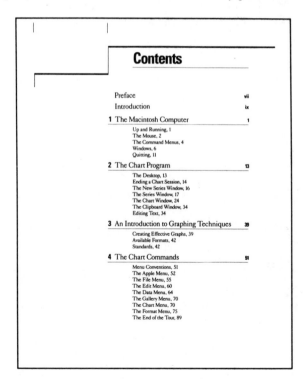

FIGURE 9-14. *A table of contents (from Steve Lambert,* Presentation Graphics on the Apple Macintosh*).*

Indexes

Generating an index follows the same general procedures as generating a table of contents. You "flag" key terms in your text (or add them as hidden text and then flag them). Next, the computer compiles and alphabetizes these terms and adds the correct page numbers. Subentries are indented under main entries. Page numbers in the index are automatically revised if you change the pagination of the main text. As with a table of contents, you are free to make additions and deletions to the index, and a computer style sheet enables you to control formatting features.

What the computer doesn't do for you, however, is decide what to put into the index. This part of a document is reader-oriented; you must make careful decisions about what information readers will want to look up and what terms they will look under. Don't try to index a document all at once; start by flagging all material on the main subject of your document and all the main headings and subheadings. Then go on to key terms and definitions, abbreviations, and acronyms. Also include synonyms for major topics ("feudalism" for "manorial system"). If a topic is two words and one word modifies the other ("imperfect monopolies"), invert the words and index the topic a second time ("monopolies, imperfect"). Tell readers where they can find related topics; good index generators allow you to insert blind entries — "see also" phrases — without page numbers. You may want to index key figures or tables. Be sure that the index directs readers to significant sections of text; they won't appreciate going on a wild-goose chase. For a particularly long or complex document, you may want to create several indexes: of subjects, of names of people, of key terms and concepts.

Consider these guidelines when you format the index:

- Give the index a title (usually "Index" or "Index of Subjects"); this can be centered or placed flush against the left margin. Simple linear design elements can be added, and "Index" can be emphasized by your choice of type size and style.

- Leave extra white space between the different alphabetic sections of the index. You may want to place the appropriate capital letter in bold above each section.

- Use style options like bold and italics to emphasize certain parts of the index. For example, put "see" or "see also" in italics; put page numbers for illustrations in italics; put page numbers for the primary treatment of a topic in bold.

- Make the index a separate division of your document and format it in two columns.

- Paginate the index as if it were a continuation of the main text. Page numbers should follow the same style and be placed in the same position as in the main text.
- Create a running head for each index. The running head should match the style and format of the running head in the main text.

This book's index is a typical example. Consult recently published books in your field for more ideas about compiling and formatting indexes.

A Word About Printers

After your document has been formatted, your next concern is printing it. Today you are faced with a bewildering choice of computer printers, from the familiar dot-matrix and daisy-wheel printers, to ink jet, thermal, and laser printers, to high-resolution photographic printers that are the equivalent of professional typesetting machines. Which type of printer you use depends on your computer system, your writing project, and your budget.

For routine or unimportant documents or for the early stages of an important writing project, you will probably use whatever printer is connected to your computer. However, if you own an old or cheap dot-matrix printer that produces squared-off letters with faint dotted lines, seriously consider moving up to something better. Certainly, any work you produce in poor dot matrix should be for your eyes only — and you may find that poor printing fools even your eyes and causes you to skip over mistakes when you revise and proofread.

Make it a rule never to give documents to others to read unless they have been printed on a high-quality printer. And don't use a dot-matrix printer unless it is capable of producing near-letter-quality print. When you get ready to print, always choose the highest quality mode: "best," "high," "near-letter-quality," "correspondence mode," or whatever term your printer employs. Don't skimp on quality because you are short of time or think printing doesn't matter. Writing is a visual art as well as a verbal one, and the appearance of your document makes a statement about the professionalism of its author. Even in a draft submitted for review, appearance conveys a subtle message about the potential of the finished work.

You want the final version of an important document to look as professional as possible. Consider using a laser or photographic printer. Laser printers are, of course, the high-tech dream of writers: small, desktop machines that produce printing nearly indistinguishable from professional typesetting—to amateurs at least; professionals can spot the minute roughness in laser type. And laser printers are becoming more and more affordable. Your office or computer lab may have one already, or you can bring your files to a copy shop or computer store. Some typesetting shops have the new photographic printers. Although the final result is of professional typeset quality, printing fees, though still reasonable, are correspondingly higher than for laser printing.

In the end, your budget may dictate which printer you use, but always choose the best that you possibly can. Good writing deserves good printing.

Let's Solve It!

At this stage of the writing process—getting ready to publish or distribute a document—you run into two main problems: when to use (or not use) footnotes, and how to format a kind of document you have never tackled before. Here are ways to solve such problems.

Problem: Unintended Plagiarism. You don't want to be accused of plagiarizing other people's work, but you don't really know what constitutes plagiarism.

Solution. Most writer's handbooks spell out what to reference and how to reference it. Follow the guidelines carefully. As a general rule, if you have a book or notebook open while you write, you probably have to make some sort of acknowledgment. There are exceptions: Often your readers will not need references for material from dictionaries, quotations from the Bible, well-known quotations from literary giants (Shakespeare, for example), proverbs, and information that is common knowledge or that appears in every treatment of the subject.

Problem: Unwanted Footnotes. You are writing an article for a popular magazine or an informal essay or a short memo or a letter, and footnotes would look far too formal and pretentious. Yet you want to acknowledge the source of your material.

Solution. Simply weave the name of the author and the title of the work into your text: "As Alvin Toffler reminds us in *Future Shock,* the rate of change in today's world is accelerating."

Problem: Scissors and Paste Documents. The document is a patchwork of other people's statements and your ideas. You haven't smoothly integrated source material into your text, and the final result is choppy and unprofessional.

Solution. Don't use too many quotations in proportion to your own words. Know your subject well enough so that you have original things to say about it. When you do use quotations, provide informative introductions for them and smoothly integrate them into your text. (Notice that ellipses—the line of dots used to indicate omitted material—are usually not necessary at the beginning or end of quotations, only in the middle.)

Write an introductory sentence that prepares the reader for the coming quotation and join the quotation to that sentence with a colon or a linking phrase like "as follows" or "as seen below."

> Almost forty-five years ago, Vannevar Bush pointed out that construction and maintenance costs keep new technologies from coming into existence: "Had a Pharaoh been given detailed and explicit designs of an automobile, and had he understood them completely, it would have taxed the resources of his kingdom to have fashioned the thousands of parts for a single car, and that car would have broken down on the first trip to Giza."[2]

Avoid repetitive or simplistic introductions: "The author says" gets boring, and "this quote states" is too informal.

Make a short quotation part of your sentence; be sure, however, that the wording of the quotation matches your sentence in point of view, tense, and grammar.

> According to Andy Hertzfeld, writing computer programs allows him to be both a scientist and an artist, because it forces him to do "precise thinking" while at the same time "it has a wildly creative side where the boundaries of imagination are the only real limitation."[3]

In addition, give your reader a relief from quotations by paraphrasing and summarizing, but remember to indicate where the paraphrase or summary comes from by using a reference in the text or a formal footnote.

Problem: Formatting the Unfamiliar. You are assigned to write a kind of document you have never tackled before. Although you're confident about content, you don't know the correct format or what the finished document should look like.

Solution. Ask your instructor, supervisor, or editor for a style guide. Consult a writer's handbook. Read a relevant section in a textbook or how-to book. Find similar documents and study them; keep them handy as models while you write and format your own document. Talk to people who have written similar documents.

---

[2]Vannevar Bush, "As We May Think," *CD ROM: The New Papyrus,* ed. Steve Lambert and Suzanne Ropiequet (Redmond, WA: Microsoft Press, 1986) 4.
[3]Susan Lammers, *Programmers at Work* (Redmond, WA: Microsoft Press, 1986) 259–60.

Computer Writing Tips

By this time, you may be writing long documents—research papers, reports, perhaps even a book. There are special tricks for managing long documents on the computer. Here are some of them.

- Plan your time carefully before you start a long project. Drawing up a time schedule is a good idea. It can be very simple: Merely list all your tasks and their due dates and cross off each one as you finish it. Or you can use a graphics program to produce more complex time lines or flowcharts that visually depict all your tasks and their relationship to one another. Finally, you may decide to invest in a project management program that tracks a multitude of activities and guides you—and others who are collaborating with you—through the various stages of a long writing project.

- Keep track of outside source material as you write your text. You may not want to interrupt the writing process to compose formal footnotes or references, but at the very least you should embed (in hidden text or bold style) a note to yourself about where the quotation or fact you have just used came from. Otherwise, you will spend hours sifting through your notes looking for stray sources that have escaped your memory.

- If possible, use a database program to keep track of all bibliographic information as well as quotations, paraphrases, and summaries of outside source material. If you have a laptop computer, record your research notes as you work in the library. If you have a modem and can access databases like Dialogue or ERIC, do some of your research at your desk. Write your bibliography or reference list by creating a report from the relevant material in your database.

- Divide long documents into separate files. For a long report or dissertation, each major section can be a separate file; for a book, each chapter definitely should be a separate file. Keeping the whole work as one document will slow up computer operations, and should the file be damaged or lost, you may lose everything. If chapters or sections become overlong, divide them into two separate computer files, or consider being less wordy or making two chapters out of one.

- If individual chapters or sections are divided into separate files, paginate them separately while you are writing and revising them: "Chapter 9-12." Use continuous pagination only when you are ready to do the final printing.

- Give each section or chapter an informative running head. Such a header might include your last name, a shortened title of the complete work, the date or draft number, the section or chapter number, and a page number, like this:

Mitchell   New. Writer   Draft. 2   Chapter 9-12

Both the wording and formatting can be stored in a glossary; simply expand the glossary and insert the correct section or chapter number. A glossary can also be used to store the running head you want to use for the final printing.

- Every time you print out a draft version of a chapter or section—and you should make frequent printouts—date it. Your word-processing program may be able to do this automatically for you.

- Rely on a word counter to keep you apprised of the length of a particular file. As your document nears its final stage, include the word count on the first page of the printout.

- Keep the formatting of the various sections or chapters consistent by using computer style sheets or templates or by following your own notes on format specifications. Keep the writing consistent by drawing up a written style guide that spells out what you will use in the way of abbreviations, contractions, capitalizations, footnote or internal references, specialized terminology, grammatical usage, and so on. Keep this style guide open in a second window as you work on various sections.

- Reread the whole document from time to time. Working on separate files, or always looking at small sections of text on your computer screen, can give you a fragmented view of your work. You need to refresh your memory from time to time and see the whole sweep of your document.

- Save your work frequently—the more important the document, the more frequently you should save.

- Back up your work frequently; keep the backup disk or tape in a separate and safe place. If your life's work depends on a single document—and graduate students feel this way about their dissertations—by all means make two backups.

- Get into the habit of backing up your revisions as soon as you complete a revising session; otherwise, you will have two or three different versions of the same section or chapter on two or three different disks or tapes.

- Keep your storage disks neat. Give all your document files descriptive names. Group related work in directories or subdirectories (or "file folders," in some operating systems) with descriptive names.

- Give numbers to the section or chapter filenames: "03Chp.Bk," "04Chp.Bk." Then they will be listed in order on your disk.

- If your operating system allows you to do so, attach a brief note to each directory, subdirectory, and file, describing the contents.

- Even if you transfer a figure generated in a graphics program to your word-processing document, save the original computer graphics file.

- Give each graphics file a descriptive name. For example, the name "03-7.Gills.Dia" indicates that the file is Figure 7 for Chapter 3 and contains a diagram of fish gills.

- Make a separate subdirectory for all the computer graphics files for each section or chapter. Label each subdirectory with the appropriate section or chapter number: "03Chp. Graphics."

- If you renumber whole sections or chapters of your document, or if you rearrange the order of figures, change computer filenames to reflect such reorganization. Be sure to change the names of backup files, too.

- Because you will generate many printouts of your document at various stages of the writing process, set up a neat and accurate paper filing system to keep track of them. For example, you can file different versions of the document in separate folders according to the stage of completion; your file folder labels might read "Prewriting," "Outlines," "First Drafts," "Second Drafts," "Revisions," "Final Changes," "Completed Project." Alternatively, you can divide the document into its component parts and file each part separately according to its stage of completion; in this case, your file folder labels might read "Introduction Prewriting," "Introduction Outline," "Introduction First Draft," "Chapter 1 Prewriting," "Chapter 1 Outline," and so on for each part.

- Make a brief notation on the printout of each document indicating what disk, directory, or subdirectory the computer file is stored on.

- If you have many computer files for a particular writing project, or if you work on many long writing projects, you may want to invest in a program for keeping track of the contents of your disks.

- Don't get suddenly virtuous and decide to clean out your disks in the middle of a long writing project. Even if you have subdirectories full of bits and pieces of early prewriting, tentative outlines and abandoned sections or chapters, and early concepts for visual aids, hang on to them until the project is finished. It's wiser to save too much rather than too little. But put such leftover files on a special storage disk to keep your regular working disks uncluttered.

- The same advice holds true for your paper files. Toss them in a cardboard box if that will keep your work area neater.

- Before you do the final printing, make a final check of your document:

    Are there any typographical, spelling, or grammatical errors? A style checker can help enormously here. Otherwise, get someone to help you proofread.

    Are the writing style, tone, and usage consistent? Double-check the whole document against the style guide you are following. Use the search function to uncover inconsistencies.

Are numbers for figures and tables in the text correct? And if you have created a table of contents or written footnotes manually, are those numbers correct as well?

Is the formatting—typography, layout, and graphics—consistent? Computer style sheets are invaluable here; the same style sheet can be attached to various sections or chapters, and the formatting will be kept consistent. Otherwise, you will have to check the document against written format specifications.

Do page breaks occur in logical places? Avoid bad breaks such as headings detached from their text; captions detached from figures; only one or two words appearing at the top of a page; or a single line of an indented block quotation appearing at the bottom of a page. Check the preliminary printout, or view the whole page on screen if your computer allows you to do so.

■ Be sure your printer ribbon is fresh and black. If the project is very long and the ribbon begins to fade after many pages, don't be a penny-pincher—put in a new ribbon. The blackness of type should be consistent from beginning to end.

■ Choose the paper for your final printout with care. Important pieces of writing deserve 25-percent cotton bond paper, in 16-pound or 20-pound weight, with laser-perforated strips. Watch the paper carefully as the computer prints out a long document. The printer is waiting for you to leave the room so it can chew up your expensive bond paper.

■ You can chain separate documents together into a final whole just before you do the last printout, but for extremely long projects it will be easier to print chapter by chapter or section by section.

■ When you are producing and distributing the final version of your document, be sure the pagination is continuous. If Chapter 1 runs from page 1 to page 30, set the pagination of Chapter 2 to start at page 31. But if you are submitting a manuscript for publication by someone else, leave the pagination by individual chapters or sections.

■ A final tip—as you go through the steps of finishing your writing project, remember that the last little things seem to take the longest while, even on a computer!

Bibliography

The following is a brief list of books you will find helpful as you write on the computer.

Introduction to Computers and Word Processing

Lu, Cary. *The Apple Macintosh Book*. 2nd ed. Redmond, WA: Microsoft Press, 1985. Even though this book is about a particular machine, it contains marvelously clear and easy-to-understand sections on how computers work in general. Many informative but simple graphics. A must for Macintosh owners and an excellent book for new owners (or potential owners) of other computers.

McWilliams, Peter A. *The Word Processing Book: A Short Course in Computer Literacy*. Rev. ed. New York: Quantum Press, 1984. Full of valuable information for the novice. The book is divided into three parts: "What Word Processing Computers Are and What They Do," "The Uses of Word Processing Computers," and "A Brand Name Buying Guide" (for computers, printers, and software).

Zinsser, William. *Writing with a Word Processor*. New York: Harper & Row, 1983. A chatty, first-person narrative of the author's early experiences with a computer, including the troubles he had and the psychological blocks he thinks other people will bring to their first encounter with a word processor. Explains various parts of computers; includes a chapter on his method of writing on one and a chapter on other methods.

Research

Edelhart, Mike, and Owen Davies. *Omni Online Database Directory*. New York: Macmillan, 1983. A valuable tool for doing research by computer. Discusses such topics as choosing an on-line database service, getting hardware and software, estimating costs, and conducting database searches. A directory of on-line services groups them by subject and ranges from advertising and marketing to transportation.

Shafritz, Jay M., and Louise Alexander. *The Reston Directory of Online Databases, Your Computer's Phone Book: A Travel Guide to the World of Information That Can Be Called Up on Any Computer*. Reston, VA: Reston Publishing Co., 1984. An introduction to on-line database research. Describes what information is available on what databases. Takes reader through the steps of planning and running a search and printing the results. A directory lists databases alphabetically.

Todd, Alden. *Finding Facts Fast: How to Find Out What You Want and Need to Know.* Berkeley, CA: Ten Speed Press, 1979. A compact, unpretentious, but fact-filled guide to research for the ordinary person. Based on methods used by reference librarians, scholars, investigative reporters, and detectives.

The Writing Process

Elbow, Peter. *Writing with Power: Techniques for Mastering the Writing Process.* New York: Oxford University Press, 1981. This book and the author's earlier *Writing Without Teachers* are known for their influential analysis of the writing process. Elbow emphasizes creating (articulating feelings and intuitions) and criticizing (thinking critically, judging, revising).

Flower, Linda. *Problem-Solving Strategies for Writing.* 2nd ed. San Diego: Harcourt Brace Jovanovich, 1985. Excellent practical advice on writing in real-world situations. Discusses problem-solving strategies for different stages of the writing process. Particularly good on showing how to transform writer-based prose into prose that meets the needs of readers.

Strunk, William, Jr., and E. B. White. *The Elements of Style.* 3rd ed. New York: Macmillan, 1979. A delightful classic. Written about the time of World War I and privately printed by Professor Strunk as a "little book" for his English classes at Cornell, it was edited some fifty years later by one of his famous students, essayist E. B. White. White's introductory essay and Strunk's pithy advice are deservedly famous.

Revision

Judd, Karen. *Copyediting: A Practical Guide.* Los Altos, CA: William Kaufmann, 1982. A very readable how-to book that takes you step-by-step through the copyediting process. Designed for writers and students as well as professional editors.

Lanham, Richard. *Revising Business Prose.* New York: Scribner's, 1981. A compact book that describes highly effective yet simple ways to revise business prose according to the "Paramedic Method." Written with wit and imagination by someone who understands the enormous changes computers are bringing to the writing process.

Lanham, Richard. *Revising Prose.* 2nd ed. New York: Scribner's, 1987. More general than his *Revising Business Prose,* this book is also highly recommended.

Grammar and Usage

Bernstein, Theodore M. *The Careful Writer: A Modern Guide to English Usage.* New York: Atheneum, 1965. A standard desk reference to good written English that is both charmingly written and highly useful. The more than 2000 alphabetized entries clarify matters large ("Punctuation") and small ("Frankenstein").

Fowler, H. W. *A Dictionary of Modern English Usage.* 2nd ed. Revised by Sir Ernest Gowers. New York: Oxford University Press, 1965. Often known simply as "Fowler," this book is a revered statement of what is right and what is wrong and why. Although it covers British usage rather than American, it is an invaluable reference for any writer in the English language.

Miller, Casey, and Kate Swift. *The Handbook of Nonsexist Writing.* New York: Lippincott and Crowell, 1980. An excellent book that defines sexist language and offers sensible advice on how to avoid it.

Nicholson, Margaret. *A Dictionary of American-English Usage.* New York: New American Library, 1957. This book does for American usage what Fowler did for British usage. Every writer should have a copy of one (or both) of these books.

Handbooks

Branshaw, Bernadine P., and Joel P. Bowman. *The SRA Reference Manual for Office Personnel.* Chicago: Science Research Associates, 1986. Covers standard grammar and writing rules but also includes items of special interest to writers in the business world: how to write and format letters, memos, minutes, reports, and manuscripts; how to create and use visual aids; how to use electronic mail and word processing. Provides a bibliography of reference books useful in business.

Brusaw, Charles T., Gerald J. Alred, and Walter E. Oliu. *Handbook of Technical Writing.* 2nd ed. New York: St. Martin's Press, 1982. Designed for technical writers. In addition to grammar and writing, it also discusses proposals, questionnaires, reports, specifications, technical manuals, and the like. It shows how to display equations and how to use tables, schematic diagrams, flowcharts, and graphs. A bibliography of technical reference books is included.

Hodges, John C., and Mary E. Whitten. *Harbrace College Handbook*. 10th ed. San Diego: Harcourt Brace Jovanovich, 1986. A compact presentation of the correct rules of grammar, writing mechanics, punctuation, spelling, diction, sentence structure, and paragraph construction. This is a longtime favorite, having gone through ten editions, but all the major publishing houses put out handbooks for writers, usually through their college textbook division.

Style Guides

Gibaldi, Joseph, and Walter S. Achtert. *MLA Handbook for Writers of Research Papers*. 2nd ed. New York: Modern Language Association, 1984. A short but comprehensive book on doing research in the humanities and writing up the results; includes chapters on the research process, the mechanics of writing, formatting the formal research paper, and documenting sources. Of special interest to writers outside the humanities is a list of style manuals in other disciplines: biology, chemistry, geology, linguistics, mathematics, medicine, physics, and psychology.

The Chicago Manual of Style. 13th ed. Chicago: University of Chicago Press, 1982. The standard reference work on bookmaking, style, and production and printing. The style section covers topics such as punctuation, spelling, names and numbers, illustrations and tables, mathematics in type, abbreviations, documentation, bibliographies, and indexes. A bibliography at the end lists specialized style guides and other useful reference works for writers.

Publication Manual of American Psychological Association. 3rd ed. Washington, DC: American Psychological Association, 1983. These guidelines were developed for APA journals but are followed by other journals as well. Covers all aspects of preparing and submitting manuscripts for publication: writing style, grammar, punctuation, nonsexist language, statistical and mathematical copy, tables, figures, footnotes, citations in the text, reference lists, and more.

Style Manual. Washington, DC: U.S. Government Printing Office, 1984. Contains style rules for government documents and a guide to the typography of nineteen foreign languages.

A Uniform System of Citation. 13th ed. Cambridge: Harvard Law Review Association, 1981. A standard reference book for those doing legal writing.

Document Design and Graphics

Lambert, Steve. *Presentation Graphics on the Apple Macintosh.* Redmond, WA: Microsoft Press, 1984. Takes the reader step-by-step through the process of creating charts and graphs on the Macintosh using Microsoft's Chart program. Gives a good introduction to effective graphing techniques, from identifying the message to ensuring contrast, unity, and balance.

Lambert, Steve. *Presentation Graphics on the IBM PC and Compatibles.* Redmond, WA: Microsoft Press, 1986. For users of Microsoft Chart on the IBM PC and compatibles; covers the same ground as the author's book on Macintosh graphics.

Guidelines for Document Designers. Product of the Document Design Project, funded by the National Institute of Education, American Institutes for Research, 1055 Thomas Jefferson Street, NW, Washington, DC 20007. Provides basic guidelines for writing and organizing text and designing the typography, layout, and graphics of a document. Also cites the research supporting these guidelines. Concise and easy to understand.

Desktop Publishing

Bove, Tony, Cheryl Rhodes, and Wes Thomas. *The Art of Desktop Publishing.* New York: Bantam Books, 1986. Thoroughly covers the tools and processes of desktop publishing using either an Apple Macintosh or an IBM PC (or compatibles). Refers throughout to specific software programs, describing what they do and evaluating how well they perform. Chapters cover such topics as using printers and typesetters, working with graphics and images, designing page layouts, and carrying out the actual production of documents.

Traditional Publishing

Skillin, Marjorie E. *Words into Type.* 3rd ed. Englewood Cliffs, NJ: Prentice-Hall, 1974. A guide for writers, editors, proofreaders, and printers who are preparing manuscripts for publication. Excellent sections on grammar, usage, typography, and illustration.

Chicago Guide to Preparing Electronic Manuscripts. Chicago: University of Chicago Press, 1987. A guide for both authors and publishers who need to prepare electronic manuscripts on disks or tapes for typesetting. Part 1 gives practical instructions to authors, Part 2 describes the generic coding, and Part 3 guides publishers through the electronic publishing process.

Literary Market Place. New York: R. R. Bowker Co., published annually. A directory of American book publishing. Lists names, addresses, and key personnel of publishing houses. Also gives many other book-trade addresses, from book clubs and book review journals to writers' conferences and book manufacturers.

Writer's Market: Where and How to Sell What You Write. Cincinnati, OH: Writer's Digest Books, published annually. Lists 4000 places to sell articles, books, fillers, gags, greeting cards, novels, plays, scripts, short stories, and so on. Gives names and addresses of editors; describes precisely what each publisher is looking for and how manuscripts are to be submitted. Also gives each publisher's royalty payments, numbers of titles published per year, and the percentage of first-time authors. Other sections list detailed guidelines for preparing manuscripts, names of authors' agents, and titles of books on how to write for highly specialized markets.

Index

An italic page number indicates an illustration.

Joan P. Mitchell

Joan P. Mitchell is a lecturer in the Department of English at the University of California at Santa Barbara, where she has pioneered in the use of computers as a new writing tool. She has taught computer writing classes at all levels and has given workshops in word processing and computer graphics to faculty, graduate students, and teaching assistants. She has also advised faculty from other schools on setting up computer writing programs. A writer as well as a teacher, Mitchell is the author of two mystery novels.

The manuscript for this book was prepared and submitted to Microsoft Press in electronic form. Text files were processed and formatted using Microsoft Word.

Cover design by Becky Geisler-Johnson
Interior text design by Darcie S. Furlan
Principal typography by Lisa G. Iversen

Text composition by Microsoft Press in Century Old Style, using the Magna composition system and the Mergenthaler Linotron 202 digital phototypesetter.